Getting to

Getting to Nimble

*How to Transform Your Company
into a Digital Leader*

Peter A. High

KoganPage

First published in Great Britain and the United States in 2021 by Kogan Page Limited

2nd Floor, 45 Gee Street	122 W 27th St, 10th Floor	4737/23 Ansari Road
London	New York, NY 10001	Daryaganj
EC1V 3RS	USA	New Delhi 110002
United Kingdom		India
www.koganpage.com		

Kogan Page books are printed on paper from sustainable forests.

ISBNs

Hardback	978 1 78966 757 8
Paperback	978 1 78966 755 4
Ebook	978 1 78966 756 1

British Library Cataloguing-in-Publication Data

A CIP record for this book is available from the British Library.

Library of Congress Control Number

2021930463

Typeset by Integra
Print production managed by Jellyfish
Printed and bound by CPI Group (UK) Ltd, Croydon CR0 4YY

For Alex and David, who keep me nimble

CONTENTS

FOREWORD

by General Stanley McChrystal

At West Point many years ago, my comrades and I studied the concept of inertia— the reality that, unless subjected to outside forces, an object at risk remains at rest. Also, an object in motion remains in motion— in the same direction. At the time, little did I realize how important that concept would prove through my career.

The world has evolved significantly in recent years such that whether you are talking about business, geopolitics, or war, an ability to adapt is key. The old ways of working will no longer suffice, and there are tremendous risks in believing that the factors that have led to your successes to date will sustain you going forward. But adapting requires us to act.

I saw this firsthand through my military experience. When my soldier grandfather served, his expertise remained largely applicable throughout his long career. Warfare evolved, but not so significantly that it rendered his hard-earned experience irrelevant. There were many innovations between World War I and World War II, but many key elements of strategy were similar in those two wars despite the passing of decades between them.

I first met Peter High when each of us spoke at a conference in California. My remarks provided lessons from my book *Team of Teams*, and Peter's were from his book, *Implementing World Class IT Strategy*. We would meet several times more at conferences where we were invited to speak and got to know each other well enough that I invited him to meet me in my office in Arlington, Virginia. By then, I had started the McChrystal Group, bringing the lessons from my military career to corporate clients, as I believe that what I saw on the theater of war was happening in companies around the world.

Peter's theme of nimbleness is an effective description. He defines it, in this book, as setting one's organization up such that one can seize opportunities more readily or stave off issues more readily. Just as I learned through my military experience, the skills you learn at university provide a foundation to learn, but the specifics of what you learn may quickly be rendered irrelevant given the pace of change and the wiliness of the competition.

When I led the Joint Special Operations Command (JSOC) in the mid-2000s, warfare was going through a significant shift. Al-Qaeda was highly networked and highly adaptable, driving them to victory in many cases despite our having advantages in almost every conceivable traditional metric used in warfare. It led my team and me to evaluate why organizations tend not to be adaptable or nimble. We determined that there are often the advantages of smaller organizations rather than behemoths. We determined that factors such as a common purpose, trust, and the empowerment of individuals to act were among the hallmarks of these smaller teams. We would change the way in which we worked, creating a team of teams, each with the feel of the smaller teams that had the advantages and reaped the rewards noted above. The theme that emerged is one that you will find throughout this book: the breaking down of traditional silos.

As Peter correctly notes in these pages, military hierarchy like large corporate hierarchy has traditionally been a top-down exercise with generals or CEOs setting strategy and leaders of different silos doing their part, from their vantage point, to deliver against that. Today, those leaders and the teams in those silos must collaborate to a greater degree. There is value in mixing the disciplines, and there is a need for people to develop skills that cross the traditional silos.

Peter organizes this book into the buckets of people, processes, technology, ecosystems, and strategy. In my experience, I believe each must, indeed, be rethought. Our people must strive to learn new skills and upgrade their capabilities. Our processes must be more agile in nature, and they should facilitate greater levels of experimentation and collaboration across silos. Technology facilitates better gathering of and dissemination of information, fostering better and faster insights. Likewise, building a coalition or ecosystem around your organization, drawing inspiration and insights from them becomes crucial in the current environment. Finally, strategy has and will always be important, but it now requires a willingness to reevaluate and change course more readily when the inputs prove that is necessary. It cannot just be a top-down exercise. Rather, it must also draw in greater insights from the field, often meaning from the most junior members of your team.

By following the lessons Peter offers herein, you will set your organization on a path to sustained success. The stories he offers, and the leaders he profiles should offer you the confidence to emulate the practices highlighted throughout this book.

Introduction

Only the nimble survive

> The future rhymes with the past. The pace of change is faster than it has ever been, and it will never be this slow again.

Imagine a consumer packaged goods company that largely worked with traditional players in the retail space to sell its goods. One day, a fast-growing, disruptive retail player emerged that could dictate prices and practices from those who sold goods through them. The retailer had so much power and gained so many customers so fast that it was feared that it would put small retailers out of business. Amid the disruption, the CIO of the consumer packaged goods company saw an opportunity to work with this major retailer. He also saw a chance to work better with the traditional, smaller, and regional players and mom-and-pop operations through the use of mobile technology, which provided salespeople with the tools to note feedback and place orders upon delivery of goods. That technology also enabled data analytics, which evaluated the profitability of different customer relationships and allowed salespeople to act accordingly. The technology, together with the team that brought it to life, provided information for better decision-making and helped the company remain competitive. Using financial return as the guide and making a strong case to the CEO, the technology leader helped set up an organization and a culture that was nimble. By "nimble," I mean the organization was able to pivot rapidly toward opportunities and away from threats as they presented themselves.

I bet that you had a guess about who the major retailer is that has been cast as the disruptor, leading traditional and regional players to shutter their businesses: Amazon. That guess would be incorrect. The story that I've begun to tell is not a modern story, but rather a story from the 1970s and 1980s. The major retailer was Walmart, and the consumer packaged goods company with the forward-thinking CIO was Frito-Lay, the maker of iconic snacks like Doritos and Lay's potato chips that is now a division of PepsiCo.

I begin with the story because a part of the broader message in this book is that the disruptive change that is coming is not new. History repeats itself, and it is useful to understand the lessons of history and apply them to the present. As you will see, through Frito-Lay's and others' stories, disruptive change is not always easy to recognize, nor is it easy to get the broad support to drive significant transformation initiatives forward. I hope these stories will provide you with lessons that can help you seize new opportunities in your own companies, as well as avoid repeating mistakes of the past.

Change is coming. Will your organization be nimble enough to pivot away from the issues that arise? The product or service that provides the lion's share of your revenue and profit today may go away or at least be altered to the point that you will need to figure out other revenue streams and profit centers. In addition to your direct competitors, your product or service will also face challenges from new products or services that are currently in adjacent spaces.

The good news is that new methods, processes, technologies, and skills are being developed as we speak to make your operation better. Will your organization be nimble enough to seize the new opportunities? Will you be able to seize these opportunities, even if it means cannibalizing your current offering?

In this book, I share stories, both cautionary and inspiring, about companies whose decision to take advantage of those opportunities—or not—has made all the difference. I will also introduce a model that your team can follow to evaluate how nimble you are now relative to your people, processes, technology, ecosystem, and strategy. After reading this book, you will be able to evaluate where you are on the continuum from immature to mature, from unprepared to prepared, and use the tools and insights I provide to implement changes immediately with your team.

The history that is repeating

After Frito-Lay expanded to 32 separate divisions that spanned the United States between the 1930s and 1960s, the expansion of the interstate highway system and the size and speed of trucking and rail created the backbone of cross-country commerce and made it feasible to create a national company. During the 1960s and 1970s, Frito-Lay had done some centralization to get leverage in purchasing, manufacturing, and back-office functions. However, Frito-Lay sales remained decentralized and regional during that era. The model worked, the incentive structure and broader infrastructure were in place to ensure that each of the regional operations ran like clockwork, and customers were happy. Remember, however, that a consumer packaged goods company like Frito-Lay, then as now, has two layers of customers that they serve. First are you and I—people who actually consume the potato and corn chips. Second, however, are the retailers whose shelves the product is stocked on.

Up until this period, grocery stores were mostly regional. Kroger was based in and served the Midwest, Safeway was based in and served the West Coast, A&P was based in and served the East Coast, and so on. The regional model that Frito-Lay had maintained for customer-facing functions served these regional players well. Promotions and some level of product assortment were generally the only factors that varied based on the region.

In addition to the new interstate highway system, there was another significant innovation that made a big impact on Frito-Lay. The mainframe computer, which allowed data that was entered by someone at one location to be accessed at all other locations, became much more commonly and expansively used in business. The last, and perhaps the biggest, catalyst for change came in the form of that large retailer, who made great use of the mainframe computer: Walmart.

By leveraging the power of the mainframe technology, networks, and databases, Walmart changed the business model for all retailers and producers of consumer packaged goods, like Frito-Lay. Walmart was not willing to do business with 32 Frito-Lay regional sales teams or with Coca-Cola's 86 franchises. By creating national supply chain power, Walmart required companies to accommodate them with a national "Everyday Low Price," and clear inventory visibility at all times. As a result, Kroger, Safeway, and all the other regional groceries had to increase their supply chain power.

Frito-Lay laid some groundwork that would aid their transformation in the face of growing and pervasive demands from Walmart. It leveraged the IBM mainframe technology and began to change its model to a national snack food company. In addition to the previously centralized accounting, finance, purchasing, manufacturing, distribution, and human resources, Frito-Lay created seven major zones for sales and national marketing to capture the emerging TV advertising phenomenon. The combination of these efforts helped build products such as Fritos, Lay's Potato Chips, Doritos, and Cheetos into billion-dollar national brands. But in the 1970s, the distribution model began to clash with customers' models. By the time the 1980s rolled around, the complexity and scale of Frito-Lay had grown and its primary customers (the retailers) had become more sophisticated and powerful, making it nearly impossible for Frito-Lay to continue down its current path.

Enter Charlie Feld, an important individual in the history of technology who has been present for and even a driver of several of the key changes in the business and technology landscape. He is a good friend of mine who is in his 70s today, but despite his age, he is still actively engaged in the CIO profession and is remarkably progressive in his thinking about the business landscape. He has been an invaluable resource to me throughout my career.

Feld first engaged with Frito-Lay in 1970 as a systems engineer, working for IBM. At the time, Frito-Lay was trying to consolidate its 32 divisions. In 1962, Frito-Lay had become Ross Perot's and EDS's first outsourcing customer, under a 10-year contract. By 1972, the contract with EDS was up and Wayne Calloway, the CFO of Frito-Lay at the time, wanted to bring IT back in-house.

Over the course of the rest of the decade of the 1970s, Frito-Lay was going through CIOs (they were called heads of management information systems at the time) every two years. A new leader was introduced in 1972, 1974, 1976, and 1978, and Feld worked with all of them. The issues with these CIOs were varied. Some had deep technical know-how but no executive presence. Some others had the executive presence but were not technical enough for the role. Still another one had great technical know-how and good executive presence but was unable to build a great team.

With the rotating door of CIOs, Calloway and Mike Jordan, by that time the CEO and Head of Operations at Frito-Lay, respectively, asked Feld if he would be interested in taking on the role. He hesitated at first, but when the role came open yet again in 1980, he elected to jump over from IBM. Feld noted, "I had the leadership skills, the business skills, and the technical skills because IBM had trained me so well. I was able to bridge the blind spots and talk to both groups. I was technically strong enough to lead the IT organization."

Since he had worked and lived in the Frito-Lay environment for a decade, by the time he took the CIO role, Feld knew where the problems in the organization were, and he already had a plan to solve them.

However, the first thing he did was reach out to two Harvard professors—Richard Nolan and David Norton—and their firm Nolan Norton to have an assessment of his IT function done to establish a baseline of performance and to help identify how far the organization would have to go and how quickly. Even though he had a clear point of view himself, he wanted to bring in Nolan Norton for their brand credibility and for their framework and scorecards to structure the conversation and measure progress. Together, Feld and Nolan Norton evaluated the IT organization, the processes and technologies that they used, the technical architecture, and IT partnerships inside and outside the enterprise.

A major change was potentially afoot due to Walmart's power, but Frito-Lay still needed to serve the company's customers the way they wanted to be served. Given a possible change to the business model and the strategy to support it, Feld needed a starting point for IT backed by the executive team. "We couldn't just be national, since most of the large retailers (other than Walmart) were still regional, and the preponderance of our customers were still local. However, we needed to maintain our national leverage," Feld noted. That national leverage came in the form of 40 manufacturing plants, 200 distribution centers, 10,000 route salesmen, along with national brands and national purchasing.

After Feld's first 100 days, Nolan Norton and he presented his findings to Calloway, Jordan, and a few other executives. The IT organization was in turmoil; turnover was 30 to 35 percent at the time. Processes were strong, but the team was not in a good place. The takeaways were that the company needed to bring in a technology team that was able to communicate with the rest of the business and execute complex technology solutions. He successfully made the case that the transformation ahead would take multiple years and would require investment and talent.

Feld understood that the first step was to change the culture of IT. He began by building an organization that understood the business better than it had historically. IT had suffered from being an after thought as part of a support organization historically, as most IT organizations were at the time. As such, the team was insular, and did not have an appropriate degree of business acumen. To begin to find new talent, Feld rethought college recruiting, focusing on people who were like he was when he joined IBM: smart, curious, trained in business and technical disciplines, but hungry to learn more. As a side note, it turns out, 30–40 years later, that several people who were college hires of Feld and Frito-Lay in the 1980s went on to become enterprise or global CIOs later in their careers. Feld was hiring a dream team of young talent for the present and big potential upside for the future.

Architecting a business solution

Next, Feld had to solve a dilemma. Frito-Lay needed to engage and serve unique customers while evolving to a leveraged model through purchasing, manufacturing, and distribution. The company could remain centralized for leverage, quality, and cost, or the executives could decentralize again for greater customer centricity, innovative product solutioning, pricing, and speed of decision-making. Either direction was flawed for obvious reasons. To help him make his decision, Feld elected to speak with the founder of the business, Herman Lay, who was retired and in his 80s, but was still accessible.

According to Feld, Herman Lay shared with him what I think of his "founder's pearls of wisdom."

According to Feld, Lay's advice was to keep things simple. "Frito-Lay is a simple business," Lay said. "All we do is buy potatoes, cook them, put them in bags, and take them to the stores. If the consumer likes the product, they buy them. We collect the money and buy more potatoes. Everything else is about size, speed, and scale."

Next, Lay expressed that "Nothing good ever happens in a warehouse. Things get lost, broken, stolen and in our case, they go stale. Constrain the warehouse to no more than three days [worth of product] and make everything else build around it." With the advent of digital commerce, this has come back in style!

Finally, Lay said, "The front line people are all that matter. Everyone else has to have a really good reason for being on the payroll."

Where he had been seeing a morass of challenges that needed individual solutions, he began to imagine what needed to be done in its simplest form rather than in its most complex. He recognized the execution to come would still be complex, but the plan did not need to be. He thought about how some capabilities could be standardized to create leverage while others could be unique to a specific customer, route, or promotion. In a way, Herman Lay was not only the founder of Frito-Lay, but he was also Frito-Lay's first "business architect." Feld and his team built their first capability model and focused heavily on data that was required, noting where it was required and when.

Architecting a technology solution

Remember that in the early 1980s, technology solutions were limited. That was both a blessing and a curse relative to today. On the one hand, there were fewer options to choose from, which helped narrow down the options, but it also meant that there would be a need to push the envelope further than it had been previously in the company or in the industry. Feld's simple solution would lead to radical technology innovation.

The personal computer (PC) had been broadly released in 1981, but it had not gained much traction in corporate America beyond technology departments. From his days at IBM and through the deep training he received, he understood the power of this technology, but he did not know exactly where it would take Frito-Lay. Rather than block it or try to control it, he wanted the entire executive team to learn together. So, instead of simply making the case to the executive team about specific solutions right away, he purchased personal computers for every business executive in Frito-Lay. Moreover, he did not just put them on his colleagues' desks; he implemented them in their homes. That meant training was accessible to the executives as well as their families. He wanted his colleagues to hear about the usefulness of the PC from spouses and from children so that he would be aided on multiple fronts if he had to address any misgivings that the executives might have. It cannot be underscored enough how unusual and innovative this thought process was. Remember, it came a generation before smartphones would "consumerize" technology and become a staple of modern business.

Feld's plan worked, and he created advocates of most of the executive team. That same team learned to trust Feld and his IT team because he conveyed the value the rest of the company would garner in terms they understood. Since he was able to effectively make the case with the PC, he primed his fellow executives to take a leap of faith with him when he soon introduced something much more radical.

By 1983, the Frito-Lay executive team understood the power of the PC and distributed computing. The challenge was, how do you take that same power and make it accessible to the 10,000 salespeople? Salespeople were among the front line employees that Herman Lay indicated were important. They not only delivered products to the stores where they were sold, but they also spoke with the owners of the businesses; they understood what was selling well and what was not; they had insights that would lead to price changes or suggested sales. Arming them with a tool necessary to capture data more readily and make it accessible to all salespeople became important. With these tools in the hands of the route salespeople and the innovative data and infrastructure behind those tools, Frito-Lay would be able to get the national operational leverage they needed *and* serve national, powerful retailers like

Walmart *and* be flexible and precise in tailoring pricing, promotions, product mix, and service to a variety of regional and local retailers.

Feld and his colleagues leading the sales organization concluded that salespeople needed technology that would have the benefits of the PC but could go with them wherever they went. The device needed to be small and durable enough to work in hot or cold climates while getting bumped around in the trucks. Feld and his IT team looked for tools that were being used by other companies and by the military for inspiration. Nothing quite stacked up to their vision, however.

They elected to partner with Fujitsu to spec out the handheld computer, which came to be referred to as the HHC, and a hardened printer. Once a working prototype was developed, two strategic locations were chosen to pilot the prototype: Mesquite, Texas, and Minneapolis, Minnesota. These were strategic inasmuch as they offered dramatic contrasts in temperatures, the former with 100-degree heat in the summer, and the latter with below-zero-degree cold in the winter. If the HHC and printers could make it through a Texas summer and a Minnesota winter, Feld and his team could proceed with greater confidence that they were durable enough for all 10,000 routes.

The team, along with several technology partners, also created different styles and stacks for different purposes from central mainframes to distributed servers, store and forward devices, and a new satellite telecommunications network. The need to "invent" this new architecture was required because, at the time, generally available technology could not handle the data volumes or carry real-time data transfer loads to and from 10,000 routes in the field.

Feld and his team created an early version of a data warehouse. He used software from a company called Comshare for back-end analytics and production of route-level performance reporting and profit and loss statements through every part of the business, including channels, products, customers, geographies, and routes—at every level of granularity and for all of the cross-tabs. Feld and his team had to externalize the business rules, including data for pricing, promotions, sales, and marketing. This was managed through spreadsheets on the front end. As Feld recalls, "We had to get the developers out of the middle of these changes and empower the sales and marketing teams." This was all enabled by an early version of what we, today, would call a layered, loosely coupled (not monolithic) technology architecture.

Lessons from Frito-Lay

Frito-Lay's modernization started with people. Charlie Feld's first step was to assess the IT function to create a performance baseline and determine the most appropriate path to improvement.

Feld recognized that in order to drive change he would need to change the culture of IT. To do so, he brought in a new technology leadership team that was able to communicate more effectively with the rest of the business. He also took proactive steps to involve IT more closely in everyday business activities, blended longtime employees with newer hires, rethought recruiting processes to bolster the talent pipeline, and used job rotation programs to boost retention and build leadership across IT. We see some themes emerging related to people, including the importance of modernizing one's culture as well as the importance of training and learning agility.

Feld understood the need to modernize the company with new technology, as well as the importance of retiring old systems to make room for the new. He helped shift the company's mindset, driving home the importance of defining a clear strategy and determining which capabilities can be standardized versus those that need to be specialized. We see the importance of strategic alignment across the company, of setting a sound IT strategy, and of retiring antiquated technology.

To help realize his vision, Feld tapped many members of the ecosystem for help. He spoke directly with Frito-Lay's founder to gain necessary context into the company's past and its potential future. He also engaged the academic community and strategic vendor partners to gain deeper insights into what was possible. The importance of building and leveraging a broader ecosystem is noted. Feld benefitted from his network of peers and other external partners.

He also solicited feedback directly from customers and business owners to gain insights that would inform future decisions. He also worked with external technology partners to develop and scale new technologies that put capabilities into the hands of front line workers and customers. He would not have framed it that way in the 1980s, but his practices were agile in nature, iterating on ideas, and engaging the intended users of products in their creation. Agility is an important theme to bear in mind, as well as creatively engaging customers and external partners, as previously noted.

On the technology side, Feld's team was ahead of the curve. His team layered loosely coupled architecture, introduced a mobile device that digitized paper-based processes, and developed tools to help staff in the field. Feld also understood the importance of bringing others along for the journey, buying personal computers for his colleagues and their families to create built-in technology advocates. He clearly communicated the transformative potential of technology and gained trust in IT in the process. Here we again see the theme of strategy and culture, but also change management and communications.

With all of these changes, IT saw itself and others saw it as a thought leader and source of ideas. This, in turn, made it more magnetic for others to join. The topics of culture, recruiting, agile processes, tech modernization, and developing and fostering better ecosystems, among others, will be covered in depth in this book.

As you will see throughout this book, many technology leaders have found themselves—and continue to find themselves—in situations similar to Feld's. The task of transforming a company so that it is nimble enough to respond to potential disruptions is a daunting one, but one that can be done by focusing on people, process, technology, partnerships, ecosystem, and strategy. I'd like to share three more stories to offer examples both cautionary and hopeful for you to consider.

From customer focus to customer out-of-focus

If I asked you the industry from which the company with the best stock performance among Standard & Poor's 500 stocks in the 1980s hailed, what would you guess? The 1980s was a decade in which the financial services companies thrived due to increased merger and acquisition activity and increasingly complex financial investment vehicles. It was also a time of great innovation among industrial companies like General Electric. It was a decade of great advances among consumer packaged goods companies like Coca-Cola and Procter & Gamble, as these companies gained both in the United States and abroad.

However, the best performer was actually a retailer. The best-performing US stock in the 1980s among S&P 500 stocks was Circuit City. If you had participated in its initial public offering in 1984, in less than six years to the end of the decade, you would have gotten an 8,252 percent return on your investment.[1]

Why was Circuit City so successful in an industry that was so difficult? It rethought customer experience. The company, which was founded in 1949 in Richmond, Virginia, by Samuel Wurtzel, pioneered the consumer electronics superstore format in the 1970s. The late 1970s and early 1980s were times of growing demand and complexity in consumer electronics. Televisions were growing in size; VCRs allowed people to watch movies in their own homes to a greater extent while recording television programming; stereos and the peripherals around them led to better music listening experiences. Circuit City had a new format to its store: large open spaces where people could see the vast merchandise in action along with talented salespeople who were good at explaining how the different electronics fit together. The company was legendary for having customers come through the doors with the intent to purchase a television and going back through the doors with two or three other items to enhance the use of that television.

The company's success continued in the 1990s. In fact, the company's stock ran up another nearly 700 percent in the '90s. In that decade, the company used its growing financial war chest to start other companies, including a financial institution developed to operate the company's private-label credit card, First North American National Bank, in 1990; a used car auto superstore concept, CarMax, in 1991; and a technology company launched as an alternative to DVD, DIVX Video, in 1997. In 2001 in the bestselling business book, *Good to Great*, Jim Collins included Circuit City among 11 companies that had made the leap from merely good performance to something extraordinary.

Of course, many readers are likely aware of the denouement of this story: Circuit City was liquidated in 2009. Sam Wurtzel's son, Alan, who was CEO of Circuit City between 1972 and 1986, chairman of the board from 1984 to 1994, and then vice-chairman from 1994 to 2001, would go on to write a book entitled *Good to Great to Gone: The 60 Year Rise and Fall of Circuit City* (Diversion Books, October 9, 2012). He, among others, detailed the many missteps that led to this dramatic fall after the rocket-like rise. Perhaps chief among these was that the company forgot what had made it special: a laser-like focus on customer experience.

As noted above, the 1990s were a period of investment in many side projects for the company. One of these, CarMax, would go on to be a tremendous success. In fact, we will cover some of that company's best practices in this book. During this period of focus on extracurricular activities for the company, a major competitor in the electronics retail space, Best Buy, focused on the development of the Geek Squad. In the 1990s and 2000s, as consumer electronics became even more compelling and more complex, Best Buy offered to install customers' new technology for them in their homes, a major differentiator for the company. Circuit City would not develop its salvo in this battle until 2006 with the launch of Firedog, but by then it was too late. By losing focus on providing a cutting-edge experience for its core customers, the company whose stock was the best performing for a decade ceased to exist 25 years after its IPO.

Circuit City had been remarkably innovative until it wasn't. As issues arose, and revenues started to decrease, the company responded by firing its most senior (and knowledgeable) store associates. Of the many missteps by management at the time, some believe this to be one of the worst. All of a sudden, Circuit City stores were largely populated by novices who did not have the knowledge, experience, or confidence to upsell people on products or recommend peripherals to the purchase the customer wished to make. At that point, the death of the company was inevitable.

The company had calcified. It was not nimble enough to stave off issues. Its responses appeared to be made in a vacuum unaware of the downstream and long-term consequences. It was neither culturally nor strategically nimble.

Fast forward, and though Best Buy has performed admirably in the decade since Circuit City's demise, there is a new company that can be viewed as the consumer electronics leader, and, in fact, the leader in all of retail: Amazon. What is remarkable about Amazon is that, until recently, the company did not have any physical stores. Moreover, Amazon makes it difficult to find a phone number to call the company with a question or a complaint—those are typically submitted digitally. And yet, Amazon is a company that knows us so well. They know what we buy, how long it takes us to pull the trigger on a purchase, what we browse for but then let die on the vine. Amazon understands where we are most apt to purchase an add-on to our purchase (taking a digital page out of Circuit City's analog playbook). The mechanism that Amazon uses, data analytics coupled with artificial intelligence, allows the company to collect such a vast amount of data that it is not just historical but predictive: they know enough people who have something in common with you based on your patterns to make suggestions that are relevant to you.

Amazon has the advantage of being a digital native. It was set up that way, but importantly, the company is built to be nimble. It does not wait for the change to be brought to it. The company has set been set up to scale, to pivot toward opportunity, and away from problems. Even though it is among the largest companies in the world, it is as innovative as ever.

Lessons from Circuit City

Circuit City experienced a meteoric rise in part due to its relentless focus on delivering a great customer experience. The electronics retailer created large, open stores where customers could see products in action and learn from knowledgeable salespeople about how the different electronics fit together, which often resulted in customers buying more. Here we see the importance of the theme of strategy, innovation, and the need to collaborate with one's ecosystem, especially customers.

As it experienced tremendous growth, Circuit City used its financial war chest to expand into other sectors, launching companies including First North American National Bank and CarMax. Unfortunately, this focus on extracurricular activities took Circuit City's eyes off the ball and made it less prepared to respond to the rise of the firm that would soon become its primary competitor: Best Buy. Best Buy took the customer experience a step further with Geek Squad, which managed the installation of customers' new technology purchases in their homes. Ultimately, Circuit City wasn't strategically or culturally nimble enough to respond to the strategic threat posed by its competitor. We see the theme of strategy here, and Circuit City's getting away from the strategy that had been their source of differentiation.

Circuit City also faltered in its focus on people. As revenues began to decline, the company fired many of its most senior and knowledgeable staff, and showroom floors became populated by novice salespeople without the know-how to upsell customers or suggest complementary products. In its effort to save itself, it had lost part of the magic that made it so successful in the first place. This underscores the critical themes of people and culture, more specifically, as a force multiplier for change or a boat anchor working against the change that is necessary, in this case.

Today, the Best Buys and other major retailers are under threat from Amazon, which has leveraged technology to develop a top-notch digital shopping experience, driven by data. Its advanced analytics and artificial intelligence capabilities allow the company to predict buying trends and make suggestions based on the products you are likely to buy, and it all happens mostly without physical stores.

Out of focus

Many companies resist the change needed to become nimble because of a flourishing traditional business. Like Frito-Lay in the early days of Walmart's rise, there was little incentive to change the business model.

Kodak is one firm that highlights this trend. The company pioneered the world's first consumer camera, and built a business model around processing film for customers. It formed the foundation of Kodak's business model, which was similar to that for razors and razor blades. Customers would buy a camera once, and then spend much more money replenishing and developing film. It is similar to buying printers today: the hardware is relatively inexpensive, but we spend a lot on ink, toner, and other supplies.

By all accounts, the company was a massive success. By 1976, 85 percent of cameras and 90 percent of film bought in the US came from Kodak.[2] It employed 60,000 people in Rochester and was one of the city's largest economic engines. Fast forward to 1992, and Kodak was number 18 on the list of Fortune 500 companies, with revenues of more than $19 billion.[3]

When the company realized early on that digital photography was growing, it made investments to address the shift. It created a digital business unit that was completely separate from the traditional film business. The traditional side of the house "had really developed ways of doing things that were great for the film business but might not be so appropriate for the digital business," noted Willy Shih, who ran the digital group. "They wanted to get us away from all the practices and also the burdens of the traditional business, which had been very, very successful for a hundred years." This is not entirely unlike an established company building an innovation lab or digital center today. We will cover this concept in some detail in Chapter 6, but innovation labs have a tendency to be irrelevant labs, as they create shiny new things that do not scale, and leverage processes and technologies that do not make their way back into the broader organization.

By the mid-2000s, Kodak was the leading producer of digital cameras in the world. But the digital business was nowhere near as profitable as the traditional film business. Kodak began to realize it was in trouble. Kodak had to rethink its business model, but doing so would prove difficult, particularly given the success of the established business model.

The transformation also required a massive cultural shift. For many years, those in the traditional film business felt that their profits were being used to subsidize a money-losing venture. After 100 years, it was difficult for Kodak to change its ways. The culture had hardened.

As digital photography took off, Kodak tried a number of initiatives to cut costs and bring in cash, including making inkjet printers, developing an online photo sharing site, and going after patent violators, but those initiatives ultimately failed to launch at sufficient scale. In 2012, the 131-year-old film giant filed for bankruptcy. The company emerged from bankruptcy the following year, but the company was a shadow of itself, and it was bleeding talent. Today, the company makes 35mm film for the movie industry, which is also going digital. It also makes 3D printers and fabric coating for drapery and awnings, among other things. Kodak licenses its name for headphones, baby monitors, and some clothing.

At its peak, Kodak posted tens of billions in annual revenue and employed more than 145,000 globally.[4] In 2018, revenues were $1.3 billion[5] and its headcount around 5,400.[6]

Kodak's story highlights how a company can actually own the technology of the future and either not entirely realize the value in their possession or the extent to which it should be exploited. Of course, to do so would have meant cannibalizing a major source of profit for the company, so we need to understand that in retrospect, all of this may seem obvious in a way that it clearly was not when lived in real time. The nimble part of Kodak was its tail—the digital division. But the brain and the heart of the company would not allow the insights wagging away to impact the body.

Lessons from Kodak

Kodak serves as an example of an innovative and successful company that was slow to adapt to digital change, despite being a pioneer in the field of digital camera technology. As is often the case, many firms culturally resist transformational change, particularly when the traditional business is flourishing.

Anticipating the digital shift, Kodak developed a digital business unit that was separate from the traditional film business. The company saw this as an opportunity to bring in fresh ideas and begin to think about the trends that would be relevant years in the future, not unlike many innovation units that companies build today. But as we will see later in the book, innovation units can serve little purpose if they do not create products that scale, or leverage tools and processes that make their way back to the rest of the organization. There were also cultural issues, as many in the traditional film business felt their profits were subsidizing a money-losing venture. Indeed, it is not just about changing the business model. The culture must transform as well. Again, we see the importance of a clear strategy, of fostering innovation, but innovation that scales, even if it cannibalizes traditional revenue streams. Ultimately, we see the importance of culture, and the need to foster a comfort with and an ability to change.

Kodak's story highlights how a company can own the technology of the future and not entirely realize its value or the extent to which it should be exploited. Doing so would have meant cannibalizing a major profit center, which creates its own layer of business and cultural challenges. The nimble part of the firm was the digital division, but the heart of the company prevented it from creating the broader change necessary. Later in the book we will explore how to create strategic alignment when developing digital strategy and how to overcome some of the cultural issues that often accompany it.

What was old becomes news

We have seen how failing to act quickly in the face of changing trends can lead to trouble for once iconic companies. But for those who recognize major shifts and act accordingly to address them, the payoff can be immense. Let me cover another remarkable transformation in an industry that has been a poster child for disruption and decline: the media business. The *Washington Post* has long been a legendary paper in the United States capital. It played a leading role in unearthing the misdeeds of the Richard Nixon administration at the Watergate complex in the 1970s, holding President Nixon to account. In August 1974, he left office as a result. The *Post* won Pulitzer prizes for the coverage, launching the careers of Bob Woodward and Carl Bernstein in the process.

In 1973, legendary investor and Berkshire Hathaway Chief Executive Officer Warren Buffett invested in the company, paying $11 million for a stake that would grow to $1.1 billion by the time he sold it.[7] The company continued to grow throughout the 1990s, investing in new initiatives such as the paper's website.

This Washington Post Company began a performance decline in the following decade. In fact, in the period between 2004 and 2014, US paid daily circulation of the *Post* was down 33 percent, and between 2005 and 2014, advertising revenue was down 60 percent. During that period, the Washington Post Company faced seven straight years of declining revenue and decimated its news staff along the way. If you were to state a belief that the Washington Post Company would go out of business, it would not have been a controversial point of view at the time.

The companies that impacted the Washington Post Company's business model most were the stalwarts of the digital economy. Google became a much more efficient and accurate means of advertising, and thus the money that used to go to newspaper advertising was making a bee-line to Google. Facebook became an aggregator of news, and there was an increasing expectation that news should be free, despite the great cost required to assemble a team around the world to provide in-depth reporting on important stories of the day. Facebook provided a means to draw from many sources to the point that the source became less recognizable. Brand strength in the media field eroded in the process.

In response, CEO Donald Graham made several key moves. In 2009, he integrated the print and digital operations of the company. This small change created a seamless bridge between the old world and the new world. It also started the process of changing the culture from an antiquated, analog culture to an active digital culture.

One of Graham's key hires during this period was Shailesh Prakash as chief information officer (CIO) in 2011. Prakash was hardly a household name. In fact, his most recent experience was with another struggling brand: Sears, where he was vice president of engineering. Prior to that, Prakash held engineering leadership roles at Microsoft, Netscape Communications, Sun Microsystems, and Motorola. Prakash, however, came with a different orientation than most CIOs. His engineering and product background led him to weave himself into the product of the company—the news—to a greater extent than the typical CIO.

Prior to Prakash's arrival, outsourcing attempts coupled with the need to find cost savings wherever possible led to the decimation of the *Post*'s IT staff. Prakash built enough credibility with Graham to make the case for reversing this trend and reinvesting in staff and technology. He suggested that these investments would pay off in the form of some cost savings, but ultimately, broader value creation. If the *Post* might be able to control its own destiny to a greater extent, Prakash reasoned, it would be able to pull back from a period where the company was operating at the whims of negative external forces.

Ultimately, Prakash strived to move the *Post* from a traditional IT mindset to a product-focused engineering mindset.

Within product-centric companies, there are often engineering teams that are separated from IT. They do some of the most strategic work in the company, developing and enhancing the products that are its lifeblood. It is for that reason that in many product-centric companies in Silicon Valley, the cofounder or number two person in a company is often the chief technology officer. This is in stark contrast to the chief information officers of old, whose abilities to innovate with their own resources were dwindling.

This was the mentality that Prakash brought to the *Post*. He sought to build a team that would think like a product company. First, that product mentality would be focused on the newspaper's traditional business. As the integration of print and digital operations had been undertaken two years prior to his arrival, Prakash now seized the opportunity to further mature the organization toward where consumers were heading rather than where they had been.

As the *Post* hoped to grow readers of all relevant ages, they needed to face the reality that the younger the reader, the less likely they would be to purchase a physical newspaper. One option that many newspapers have chosen (in many cases to their own detriment) was to provide the content from the physical paper for free online. This drove more people to digital channels, as the content in the physical paper was literally cheapened. Prakash hoped to counter this trend by creating such a compelling digital experience that it would justify payment for reading online content.

He hired innovative team members with backgrounds in design and data analytics. He also provided reporters with an arsenal of data to determine what was popular and what was not.

During this time, as he worked with his colleagues to understand what improvements would make their lives easier, he received complaints about the digital platform. One issue was when someone would publish an article, not all publishers could see that it had been published due to cache coherence issues in the platform. It was not user-friendly. Prakash was told that an improvement in user experience would make employees' experience better while adding value to readers. He set the wheels in motion to develop a solution to this problem.

At first, the team started out by trying to rebuild some systems on their own. Prakash emphasized the importance of internal development because of accountability. If CIOs rely on myriad external solutions, it becomes easy to hide behind problems of incompatibility. However, if these solutions are produced in-house, the CIO has full responsibility and it creates a proactive environment where the CIO becomes a first-class citizen in business discussions.

To aid the creation of these internal solutions, Prakash emphasized the importance of training as an investment in the future. Without having a sense of return on investment (ROI), Prakash encouraged willing team members to take tech courses, and get certificates and degrees that the company would pay for, no questions asked. This offer was available to anyone who had been working for the *Washington Post* five years or more. After six months, many people signed up for these courses and gained skills that were essential to propelling the *Washington Post*'s digital transformation. Prakash's engineering-centered approach also transformed the internship program from targeting MBA interns to engineering interns and providing real work and competitive pay that kept talent at the company from flocking to Silicon Valley giants.

The result of these changes was a product called Arc, which streamlined the process and created a much more compelling user interface both in the background where stories are published, and, importantly, for readers.

Prakash also understood that if he and his team further capitalized on this platform, it could have much more potential for the company beyond its internal applications. He took inspiration for what came next from Amazon. (Jeff Bezos purchased the paper in 2013 for $250 million. It is important to note that this was a personal investment of Bezos'. The paper is not a division of Amazon.)

Amazon's growth has been so significant that planning for the technology needs of the company itself has been a challenge. The promise of cloud computing provided a way for the company to address this challenge. What eventually became Amazon Web Services (AWS) started out as an internal solution for Amazon itself. Once the need was addressed, company executives, Bezos prime among them, of course, noted that Amazon's needs were about as complex as any other company's would be, since it was growing more dramatically than most. In solving Amazon's needs, it had the most complex use case for the solution that had been developed. The quintessential business-to-consumer company now had an opportunity to become a business-to-business company as well.

Knowing this story, and now having access to its author, Prakash recognized the same thing in Arc. He raised the idea of selling Arc to other periodicals, and he gained support to do so with a controlled group. He first approached college newspapers, offering for them to use it for free. These periodicals were hardly competitors, but they were sophisticated enough to be relevant use cases for the company. The feedback was overwhelmingly positive. Prakash and the executive team were confident enough to launch with more traditional, professional periodicals. Today, Arc Publishing has become a platform-as-a-service (PaaS) and gained enormous traction around the world, managing complex multi-site publishing and audience needs across video, web, apps, subscriptions, and ad monetization, providing a competitive advantage enhanced by a set of sophisticated machine learning and AI-powered tools. Now, the company has hundreds of customers, over 1.5 billion unique visitors to the platform per month, tens of billions of page views per month, and is on its way to producing over $100 million in revenue.

The broader successful digital transformation at the *Post* has moved the company back to profitability. The company has hired scores of new reporters, and monthly unique visitors were up 194 percent over the period between 2013 and 2019. Prakash is widely credited with architecting this business-reviving digital strategy and turning the *Post* into one of DC's top tech employers. He was named a Top Tech Titan by the *Washingtonian* magazine in 2017. He was named one of the Most Creative People in Business by *Fast Company* in 2017. And he was named a Top 50 Indispensable Tech Player by *Adweek* in 2018.

Prakash's own career trajectory has also been a rocket ship upward. He was hired initially as CIO, as noted above, in 2011. His profound impact on the company's product led the company to name Prakash the Vice President of Product in addition to his CIO responsibilities in 2012. Bezos himself asked Prakash to join the board of his space company Blue Origin in 2017. Prakash would be more firmly in the figurative orbit of the world's wealthiest man.

Lessons from the Washington Post

A number of changes helped the *Washington Post* avoid the fate of some of its peers in the media industry. First, then-CEO Donald Graham integrated the company's print and digital operations, a move that began to bridge the legacy and digital worlds and set the stage for a larger cultural shift to digital. Here we see the importance of the theme of strategy and the translation of it at the enterprise level into the digital strategy of the company.

Graham also hired Shailesh Prakash as the company's chief information officer. Prakash's engineering and product background allowed him to quickly weave himself into the product of the company—the news—to a greater extent than the typical CIO. During the initial stages of his tenure, Prakash brought more staff and technology in-house and shifted the company from a traditional IT mindset to a *product-focused* mindset that could accelerate the company's transformation. He also invested in training initiatives to ensure his teams had knowledge of the latest business trends. Like Feld, Prakash also revamped the recruiting process to find more engineering talent and created incentive structures that made them more likely to stay at the company. Here we see the theme of modernizing culture, and doing so through both the training of people and the hiring of new people with the skills of tomorrow. We also see the theme of the move from a project to a product orientation fostered by the CIO and the technology team.

Prakash invested in improving the user experience for customers and employees, a move that ultimately delivered significant value to both groups. He also took a lesson from Amazon's cloud computing business, Amazon Web Services, when considering new product development. Under Prakash's leadership, the *Post* created Arc, a publishing platform that the company sold to other publishers in addition to using the tool internally. The platform-as-a-service has gained enormous traction around the world and continues to drive value for the company. He also improved the user experience with data, arming the company's reporters and editors with an arsenal of data to better understand how stories performed. The theme of the broader ecosystem comes up again, especially around engaging with customers and external partners. The broader enterprise architecture and the need to modernize technology also emerges as a theme through this vignette.

We will discuss the shift to a data-driven, product-focused organization, the move to bring more technology talent in-house, and the technology leader's role in product development later in the book.

Delivering innovation

Let's cover one of the best-performing digital companies of the 2010s: Domino's Pizza. "Domino's Pizza?" you may ask. Remarkably, it is a company that has become a talent magnet for engineers, and its stock was one of best performing of the decade. How did Domino's Pizza become a digital leader? Part of it was out of necessity.

Domino's was born in 1960 when two brothers, Tom and James Monaghan, bought a small pizza chain in Ypsilanti, Michigan, for $500 and changed the name from DomiNick's Pizza to Domino's Pizza. It became famous nationally in the 1970s for its pizza delivery back when food delivery was novel, offering to get a pizza to your door within 30 minutes, eventually adding "or it's free!" This fueled extraordinary growth for the company. But it eventually ran into issues. The company grew to the point where those who wanted pizza delivered quickly were already customers. Would-be customers wanted better pizza than Domino's provided. By the mid-2000s, same-store sales were negative. Unfortunately for Domino's, this coincided with the growth of social media where one person's bad experience could quickly become known by everyone in that person's network through Facebook or Twitter. The company was clearly in a downward spiral.

Domino's CEO at the time, Patrick Doyle, took an unusual step as he plotted a turnaround: he broadcast a national advertising campaign in which he acknowledged shortcomings in the product. The Domino's documentary *Pizza Turnaround* shows the company's comeback journey, starting with facing the brutal customer feedback head-on. Feedback such as "Dominos tastes like cardboard," "the sauce tastes like ketchup," and "boring, artificial imitation of what pizza can be" makes up the first half of the ad. Doyle hoped that a mea culpa would be an indication for customers that the company heard customer complaints and was willing to do something about it. He was committed to improving the company from the crust up.

Once the product was on a more solid footing, Doyle and the leadership team recognized that the dire situation for the company presented an opportunity for a fuller reinvention. Just as they had been bitten by advances in digital media through poor word of mouth which spread like a forest fire over social media, the team determined to become more digitally savvy themselves.

This was easier said than done. After all, the company was headquartered in Michigan rather than in, say, Silicon Valley. Though there are many great universities in the state, it is not a hotbed for technology talent on the same scale as cities like San Francisco, Seattle, Austin, New York, or Boston. Moreover, the product was pizza. That might be America's favorite food, but it is not America's favorite industry to work in for those with engineering or computer science backgrounds. Domino's had another major issue in attracting technology talent: it had outsourced major portions of the company's IT department. Like many companies in the 2000s, there had been a debate as to how strategic IT was, and the logic of outsourcing major parts of it seemed compelling: put the burden of building and maintaining major parts of the technology stack on those who are experts in technology and do so at a lower cost than was possible in-house. This was the decision many companies made, and in recent years, the logic has proven hollow, and many of those companies have walked it back. Domino's would do the same.

The company made the decision to insource IT talent to rebuild infrastructure and bring tech in-house. The company was serious about digital transformation and recognized that to overcome some of its relative shortcomings on the technology front, leadership needed to be steadfast in its commitment to transform. Just as the product would be rebuilt from the crust up, the technology had to be rebuilt from people to processes to the technology itself.

An imperative for Domino's leadership was to adopt a data-driven, agile way of working and close alignment between the broader business and IT. The company also converted all franchisees to a proprietary point of sale system called PULSE. Domino's view of itself shifted from a pizza company that sold online to an e-commerce company that sells pizza, and it made the changes that would make that a reality.

Hiring new people was an essential first ingredient. Domino's Chief Innovation Officer Dennis Maloney has been with the company since January 2010, and he has been a significant driver of the transformation. He recognized that there was a concentration of technology talent on the coasts of the United States, so he and the company, generally, focused on identifying people who had a connection to Michigan—those who went to university there, those who had been raised there and wished to return, and so forth. Some of the key early hires were in this mold.

New people came with important experiences and a mandate for change. Moreover, with the imperative to modernize, the new staff could focus on modernizing processes, beginning with a focus on agility. Agility focused on better partnerships inside of the company with those who developed solutions and those who would use the solutions collaborating through development. Importantly, investments were made to retire older systems, eliminating redundancy and complexity while reducing both costs and risk in the process. This step has layers of value, as I note, and yet it is a step that eludes many technology and digital departments due to the natural tendency to focus on creating and implementing the new rather than retiring the old.

Over time, convenience and personalization became important themes for Domino's, impacting customer experience in a profound way. No idea embodied these themes like Domino's *Anywhere* suite of ordering technology. The success of expanding from desktop to mobile ordering offered insights into the advantages of providing flexibility to customers. Domino's worked with Twitter, Slack, and Amazon (and its Echo) to leverage these technologies for ordering and tracking. Customers could text the company and establish that medium as the point of contact. As customers realized the multiplicity of options at their disposal, curiosity led to broader use, which led to greater mindshare for Domino's. Greater mindshare led to revenue growth such that by 2017 the company surpassed Pizza Hut to become the largest pizza chain in the United States for the first time in history.

Maloney had experience at world-leading brands prior to Domino's, including Coca-Cola and P&G. From those experiences he brought to Domino's a need to listen to customers, and to meet them where they wished to be met. "Within the digital space, customers have the power," Maloney told me. "They dictate how and when they will interact with your brand. As a result, we need to create the best and most memorable experience for them."

Consumerization of information technology has led to greater power in the hands (literally, in the form of smartphones) for customers. Their expectations have changed, and they have become more fickle as a result. Gone are the times in which companies could dictate to customers as to the medium they must use. Businesses need to take the necessary steps in order to handle the back-end implications in order to interact with customers and fulfill their orders of products and services through the mechanisms that they believe to be best.

The company has also experimented with a number of new concepts, some of which will become platforms of the future, such as autonomous car delivery, drone delivery, and cars outfitted with ovens that keep the pizza hot en route. With each trial at the art of the possible, Domino's reputation for innovation has grown. The company has even gained press attention (and I am writing about it here) for building a website, pavingforpizza.com, where customers can nominate their towns for a small grant to fix potholes. Maloney indicated to me that the team had anecdotes of drivers and customers driving home, hitting a pothole, and having pizza dropped and be ruined. "We want to be known as a company that will go to great lengths to improve customer experience. We have done paving projects in all 50 states in the U.S." It is doubtful that Domino's will replace the United States Federal Highway Administration and its mandate to maintain highways across the country, but they are playing a surprising role. What might appear to be a strange foray beyond the company's knitting has been a means of communicating with talented would-be employees that, by joining a pizza company, you can work on some of the coolest projects around. The strategy worked. Maloney wants customers and employees alike saying, "Did a pizza company really just do that?"

As a result of this, for the decade just passed, Domino's stock appreciated roughly 2,500 percent. That is more than 2,000 percent greater than Google and Facebook, greater than 1,500 percent over Apple, and more than 1,000 percent greater than Amazon.[8]

During the COVID-19 pandemic, the restaurant industry was one of the hardest hit due to the prolonged quarantine that had people in their houses rather than eating out. The steps that Maloney and his colleagues had put in place proved remarkable in fostering resilience in the company. "The technology modernization that we had undertaken made us more flexible and able to respond even faster than we would have if we had not been stretching those muscles," said Maloney. "It did not take much for us to tweak our offerings to be able to deliver to parking lots, to deliver without any contact between driver and customer. It proved to be the best contactless experience possible."

When I asked him what aspects of this experience are most likely to remain once we achieve a new normal, he highlighted the fact that when people have amazing digital experiences, they tend to reset habits. "Digital ordering accounts for 65 percent of revenue, and we see that growing."

In summarizing his extraordinary 11-plus years with the company, Maloney told me, "We have transformed from a pizza company that sold online to an e-commerce company that sells pizza."

The wonderful thing about this story is that if I told you a story of the ascent of leading native companies over the past decade, some great yarns could have been spun, but how accessible are these stories? How much does your business look like Amazon's or Apple's? Do you have a multi-billion-dollar war-chest available to you for innovation? My guess is the answer is no. But surely you can emulate the steps a pizza company undertook to become a digital leader, right?

Lessons from Domino's

Domino's focus on meeting customers wherever they happened to be, and its willingness to openly acknowledge the need for transformational change, have helped it regain a position of leadership in its sector.

Necessity drove the company to become a digital leader. When customers noted dissatisfaction with the product, the company launched a "Pizza Turnaround" that put the core product back on solid footing. The experience also helped Domino's recognize the need for a broader reinvention. We see the theme of strategy and its continued importance during times of great change and dynamism.

As with previous examples, people were core to the company's change efforts. Facing challenges to attracting great talent to Michigan, much of the company's IT department had been outsourced. Part of the transformation included insourcing much of the company's IT talent to rebuild technical infrastructure and bring more capabilities in-house. We will discuss this trend at length later on. The importance of monitoring the skills you have and the skills you need for the future, which I refer to as the supply and demand for people and skills, is highlighted.

Domino's also revamped a number of its technology systems. The company built a new point-of-sale system to improve operations for franchisees, and it made critical improvements to its e-commerce capabilities. Leaders retired older systems and eliminated redundancies, understanding the need to remove technical debt while bringing in new systems. Here we see the themes of change management, the need to retire antiquated systems, and the sanctity of developing a solid IT and digital strategy.

Domino's also invested heavily in data architecture, which allowed it to create more personalized customer experiences. It also developed mobile ordering features that put the customer in the driver's seat when creating their orders. This allowed Domino's to drive value by meeting customers wherever they preferred, from social media to smart speakers. Here we see the importance of a strong ecosystem, of better enterprise architecture practices, and of customer engagement.

The company has also placed a focus on innovation, testing concepts ranging from autonomous vehicle delivery to drones and oven-equipped cars. These experiments have helped the company spot potential new trends. It also helped Domino's gain attention among customers and the media, which can further attract curious talent to the company. There is a theme of innovation and recruiting, each of which are about thinking about the future, and new possibilities and opportunities.

Focus on getting to nimble

From across these stories, whether the cautionary tales of Circuit City and Kodak, or the virtuous stories of Frito-Lay, the *Washington Post*, and Domino's, we see the importance of renewal, of modernizing, of accepting change, and of not resting on the laurels of the past. Those who succeeded focused on modernizing people practices, processes, and technologies, in that order. They recognized that each can be boat anchors for their operations. While modernizing these foundational items, it is also important to seek the wisdom of a broader ecosystem, to include customers, peers, strategic vendor partners, venture capitalists, and executive recruiters, among others. Modernizing the approach to people, processes, technologies, and ecosystems contributes to a better path toward creating better strategic plans and, ultimately, a path to sustainable innovation.

Technology and digital teams can be the source of nimbleness, but they can also be a primary hindrance to nimbleness. This book will offer lessons from companies, especially among what I have come to refer to as digital immigrants—those companies born before the digital age, who have reinvented themselves to better compete. As you read through this book, reflect on how your team is doing relative to the themes and sub-themes that are introduced. Where are you mature, where are you maturing, and where are you immature? That which gets measured gets done, after all, and it is important to undertake a "warts and all" assessment of your organization and take corrective action accordingly. I look forward to being your guide for this journey.

Notes

1 Joshua Friedman. Decade's hottest stocks reflect hunger for anything tech, *Los Angeles Times*, December 28, 1999

2 Ibid

3 A database of 50 years of *Fortune*'s list of America's largest corporations, 1992, archive.fortune.com/magazines/fortune/fortune500_archive/full/1992/ (archived at https://perma.cc/NQ2N-3PPM)

4 Antoine Gara. Kodak's bankruptcy: Manufacturing a 21st century rebirth, *The Street*, August 1, 2013

5 Kodak reports full-year 2018 financial results, *Business Wire*, April 1, 2019

6 Form 10-K of the Security and Exchange Commission, April 1, 2019

7 Jia Lynn Yang and Steven Mufson. Warren Buffett in negotiations to relinquish $1.1 billion stake in Graham Holdings, *Washington Post*, February 13, 2014

8 Based on 10-year stock price analysis from *MarketInsider*

01

The path to nimble

In December 2016, I visited Shamim Mohammad, then the senior vice president and chief information officer of CarMax. In November 2018, he would add the chief technology officer role to his CIO role. He gave me a tour of his digital lab at the Shockoe Bottom neighborhood of Richmond, Virginia, within walking distance of the city's downtown area and about 20 miles away from the company's headquarters. We sat for our interview, and I concluded it with a question I ask most of my interviewees. It is some version of, "What trends excite you as you look to the future?" Mohammad offered thoughts on cloud computing, machine learning, and blockchain. Then he said something that stuck with me:

> I do not know how the world is going to be in three or four years. It is hard
> to predict. What I am trying to do as CIO is position [CarMax] so that we are
> ready to take those changes and be nimble, agile, and responsive: an organization
> that can move quickly. That is what I do because I cannot predict what is going
> to happen. I have to position [CarMax] to be that nimble company.[1]

This was poignant, and it struck me immediately. Having asked a version of that question to more than 500 people (as of this writing), he is the only one to speak so directly about the need to reorient the technology and digital function to be a source of nimbleness. That word stuck with me, and I thought about that answer for much of the drive back from Richmond to my home in the Washington, DC area.

Nimbleness is, in many ways, the greatest value a technology or digital organization can offer to a company. The ability to pivot quickly to seize opportunities or to stave off issues is important now more than ever during a time when the pace of change has never been faster, and yet it will never be this slow again.

Measuring your nimbleness

Both the cautionary tales and the stories of rebirth are enlightening, providing a guide for digital immigrant companies (those born before the digital age) to compete. In the case of the *Washington Post* and Domino's, each company had to rethink five factors in order to better compete:

- people
- processes
- technologies
- ecosystem
- strategy and innovation

People

It is a truism to say that people are a company's most important asset, and yet many companies do not think enough about how to attract, retain, and grow the best talent. Moreover, many team members are not given or do not seize opportunities that are presented to grow their skills to reflect where the business and technology landscape is going rather than where it has been. The concept of nimbleness begins with teams that are nimble in their approach to training, nimble in their approach to recruiting, and nimble in their approach to understanding where new skill needs are emerging and determining how to grow those skills or buy those skills.

In Chapter 2 we will highlight **culture** and its importance. Though it seems like a squishy topic to some, a company or a department's culture is always there; it is just a question of if you define it or not and how you should use it. We will talk about the need for **clear titles, roles, and responsibilities,** while highlighting job families and room for growth inside and outside of one's department. We will cover the process of inventorying skills you have today and the method to understand the skills necessary for the future through workforce planning. Consider this **supply and demand of people**. We will cover the best methods for **evaluating people**, and the ongoing debate of whether annual or semiannual reviews are helpful or not, and how they should impact compensation, as well as how else to recognize good work. As aforementioned, we will also cover the topic of **growing existing people**, which I believe to be the key ingredient to ensuring that companies remain current. Training is an important lever (besides meaningful work, which, itself, offers training of a sort) in keeping the best people within your company. We will talk about retention, and the various levers that are in place. We will also cover scenarios where companies have attrition rates that are too low. Finally, we will cover **recruiting**. How do you compel people to join your company, and what criteria do you use? In fact, you should strive to hire the kind of colleagues who you would be delighted to have leave their fingerprints on the company.

Your company's people will be the biggest determination of your ongoing success or not. Identifying the best people and giving them reason to stay in your company should be the primary task of every leader.

Processes

Processes are critical in guiding actions of teams. They guide behaviors, they determine the methods and the efficiency of delivering products or services to market, and they also highlight how to recover when issues arise. It is important to note that each section of this book will have processes associated with them. There is a process that guides each of the topics that I noted above regarding people, for example. Therefore, I will focus on the processes that are critical in the digital age.

In Chapter 3 we will cover how nimble companies have rethought processes more generally. **Agile** processes are a cornerstone to a nimble organization. In fact, the concept of agility is akin to nimbleness, albeit a bit narrower, but you should strive to develop ideas in an agile fashion, iterating along the way, engaging with the intended users of each idea in the process. Traditional waterfall methods, where one team takes orders from another team and then develops a project in a vacuum, waiting until the project is near completion to have it tested and validated only to find that major corrections are necessary, wastes time, and, inevitably, wastes money. This method works against the experimentation required to innovate.

We will cover an important shift that nimble companies are making from a **project** orientation to a **product** orientation. This is more than words and requires a reset of a technology and digital division's operating model, including how companies structure teams and work. We will cover project/ product development processes to highlight how one generates ideas, as a starting point. Ideas are the lifeblood of an enterprise, and they should be sought from junior as well as senior members of the team. One should engage customers, external (vendor) partners, and one's peer group as well.

In this chapter we will also cover **DevOps** and its broad implementation across the technology landscape. DevOps is a portmanteau combining the terms (and more importantly the practices) of software development (Dev) and information technology operations (Ops). The combination of these practices highlights the opportunity to shorten the systems development life-cycle while providing continuous delivery with high software quality.

Another process we will cover will be **change management**. The only constant in business is the constant state of change. Without an acceptance that change will not cease, expectations will be set not only incorrectly but in a way that will work against progress.

The **service desk** is, in many cases, the front door to the technology and digital division of the company. Though many companies have elected to outsource some or all of the aspects associated with the service desk, it is also an area of great differentiation for many companies. We will cover some examples of this.

The last process that I'll cover herein is **knowledge management**. Ideas will be founded on knowledge, and companies that develop ideas that leverage existing knowledge rather than reinventing knowledge will have the fastest path to success. I will highlight how best to undertake this and measure progress or lack thereof.

As in Chapter 2, a theme that will run through this chapter will be the removal of silos, or at least the creation of more permeable membranes at the edge of traditional silos of the company to ensure that greater collaboration takes place between those who are developing the products and services of the company and those who are the intended users of the products and services of a company.

Technology

No matter the industry that you play in, technology is central to your success. What began as automation of manual processes as a means of eliminating wasted effort and errors has grown to the point that technology, using algorithms, machine learning, and artificial intelligence, now ensures that data collection, synthesis, and analysis, which used to require hours if not days of work by an army of people, can be done through technology, and can ensure that the point at which a human interacts with data to make decisions is at a higher plane. This means that a greater percentage of human time will be spent on the highest-value activities for a company.

None of this can be accomplished with antiquated technology. The sad reality is that today, most digital immigrant companies are weighed down by technical debt, and key data resides in systems that may be older than some of the companies' employees. Part of the issue is one of change: again, it is not in our nature to want to change. Part of the issue is that people find it easier and more interesting to pursue the development of the new rather than contemplating the retiring or shutting off of the old. Therefore, companies are often mired with a Baskin Robbins 31 flavors of technologies. Lastly, part of the issue is one of cost: there is a perception that the medicine will cost more and cause more pain than the ailment itself.

We begin with the mapping of all technology. This includes both software and hardware. An important process to leverage is **enterprise architecture** (EA). According to one of the definitive works on EA, the *Enterprise Architecture Book of Knowledge* (EABOK), "The framework successfully combines people, data, and technology to show a comprehensive view of the inter-relationships within an information technology organization."[2] Enterprise architecture provides a comprehensive framework to highlight architecture, data architecture, and technology architecture, and as a company sets strategy and pursues initiatives to bring that strategy to life; contemplating how those initiatives will be woven into the fabric of what is already in place is critical. This ensures that as the new is introduced, the context in which it is introduced is well thought out. It should also provide context into what is rendered redundant and should be retired. I have worked with a vast array of technology leaders and their teams in the past 25 years, and this is perhaps the most immature topic of all within the technology and digital organizations that I have advised. It is human nature to want to move from one task to the next, from one project or product to the next. It is critical that we stop to contemplate what the new items that have been introduced are meant to replace.

Next, it is important to gauge **cloud penetration**. Many companies have critical data flowing through older systems. Oftentimes, these were created before modern, more stable, and more flexible technology was introduced. Cloud technology is the modern, more stable, and more flexible option. Digital native companies are built using cloud technology. Your technology should reflect this. Leveraging cloud technology is the best method of making sure that your technology footprint grows or shrinks as your business does the same.

Next, I will highlight the topic of **microservices and application programming interfaces (APIs)**. Microservices offer the ability to grow by remaining small and nimble with one's technology. Rather than relying on the monolithic technology of yesteryear, breaking technology into logical bites makes more sense. APIs provide the basis for data sharing inside your enterprise and outside with partners and customers. The combination of these practices enhances the ability to move faster to seize opportunities, while ensuring that movement happens in a secure fashion.

Security is the last topic covered in Chapter 4. One of the keys to the nimble organization is to be in a position to stave off issues as they arise. Unfortunately, cyber threats are increasing, and the creativity of the approaches hackers are using is growing as well. It is unrealistic to think that your company can outsmart all hackers all the time. Rather, it is important to have plans in place knowing that eventually you will be caught in the crosshairs of a smart, well-funded bad guy (or gal). The key is to have a framework that facilitates playing an effective offense and defense simultaneously.

Ecosystem

It is said that company-to-company competition should no longer be the focus for executives. Rather, ecosystem-to-ecosystem competition should be. Thus, executives should focus on growing and better leveraging their ecosystems. The most important part of the ecosystem is one's **customers**. Being nimble means having the channels in place to rapidly get customer feedback and being able to process that feedback. It also means having channels open with customers as you test ideas for new or enhanced products or services. Getting customer feedback is the best way to be nimble in addressing their needs and being first to market with new ideas that will delight them.

The next level of the ecosystem is one's **peers** at other companies. If you are a CIO, CDO, or CTO, you should develop a network of your peers, and you should find opportunities to get together with them, virtually or in person. You should find peers who you trust enough to test hypotheses with or to poll for advice when you reach a crossroads of one sort or another. Thankfully, there are so many tools available to develop, engage, and collaborate with your network.

The next member of the broader ecosystem is the **venture capital** community. It is important to understand where smart money is being spent and why. It is also important to understand which companies are emerging that might be worth investing in, either literally or figuratively. The venture capital community is also quite keen to gather the insights from buyers of enterprise technology, so this truly is a symbiotic relationship.

The next layer of the ecosystem is **executive recruiters**. They are important to get to know to help fill roles that are open, but they can also offer invaluable counsel on skills on the rise, those that are falling in demand, and what sorts of organizational models are emerging.

The final members of the ecosystem are **external partners** or vendors. I have mentioned that many companies outsourced technology talent to too great a degree, and many companies are rethinking those relationships and insourcing a lot of talent as a result. That said, most if not all companies need to establish external partnerships with key vendor partners. These may be for staff augmentation or for more strategic assistance. These may be longer-term relationships or short-term ones. No matter the size and duration of the relationship, these partners should be offered as sources of inspiration and innovation. Too often, they are viewed as fulfillers of work rather than as sources of strategic insight. That needs to change.

Strategy and innovation

Value no longer resides in silos of the corporation; value is created at the intersection of disciplines across the company. Therefore, **communications** are paramount for the nimble organization. There must be easy means of sharing information, and these should include traditional pathways such as via phone, email, or in-person meetings, but they should also include more modern methods such as video and podcast communications.

Solid communications channels are essential after **strategic creation and alignment** occurs. Creation must happen at the enterprise, business unit, and functional areas, and alignment between each is paramount. I cover this topic in great depth in my book, *Implementing World Class IT Strategy: How IT Can Drive Organizational Innovation*. I'll provide some abridged lessons from that book here. A clear strategy provides direction to the company to ensure that everyone pushes in the same direction.

Next is the development of an **IT/digital strategy**. It may seem logical for a single strategy to be created, but I believe that the enterprise-level strategy needs to be translated into the different divisions of the company. Every for-profit company has some version of "grow revenue" as an objective. If it is left at that, what is marketing's role in growing the revenue versus sales versus product or service divisions of the company? Each must translate what they will do. Likewise, if new technical capabilities are needed in order to help grow revenue, let's say, artificial intelligence, but there are insufficient AI skills or technologies in-house, this will likely translate into an IT or digital strategy.

A key facet to incorporate into the strategic planning exercises once the enterprise, business unit and divisional, and IT and digital strategies have been developed is a **data strategy**. Data is sitting in your company like crude oil in the ground. It needs to be gathered, processed, and refined in order to be of value. The data strategy ensures that the data goes from information to knowledge to wisdom. It is the wisdom that will drive new innovative ideas for the company.

As the technology and digital division of the company becomes more woven into all that the company and its customers do, it has an unusually vast and relevant perspective on how the company works. IT and digital leaders should play an important role in defining the **business capabilities** across the company. These capabilities are then areas that the technology and digital division can work in concert with the relevant leaders and teams across the company to drive improvements and innovations.

Once the strategies across the company are well defined and articulated, and the ecosystem is awakened to develop ideas, as well, the company can focus on **innovation**. Innovation works best when it is pointed in a specific direction. Strategy provides that direction. It also works best when the broadest set of constituents focus on how to bring it to life. Thus, the role of the ecosystem in innovation.

The five themes form a virtuous cycle. Without great people, the other four topic areas will be suboptimal to say the least. Next, one needs to define and refine processes to ensure that the right actions are taken, efficiently and effectively. Next automation (technology) should be in place to ensure that repeatable processes are automated, and that the point in which humans work is at a higher plane of value for the company. Once those three are in place and effective, fostering better partnerships inside the company is critical. This should lead to better collaboration and insight at the intersection between disciplines. Once the strategy has been crafted, you must engage the broader ecosystem for insights. This is where innovation will be brought to life.

The five themes that are noted and the 27 sub-themes beneath them form a set of continua that are reinforcing, each a virtuous cycle.

I hope that this book encourages you to measure your team's performance along these lines. When I evaluate teams on these topics, I use the dashboard in Figure 1.1 to do so.

As Figure 1.1 highlights, it is important to have each of the five themes (at the head of the columns) and the 28 sub-themes organized on a page.

FIGURE 1.1 The getting to nimble dashboard

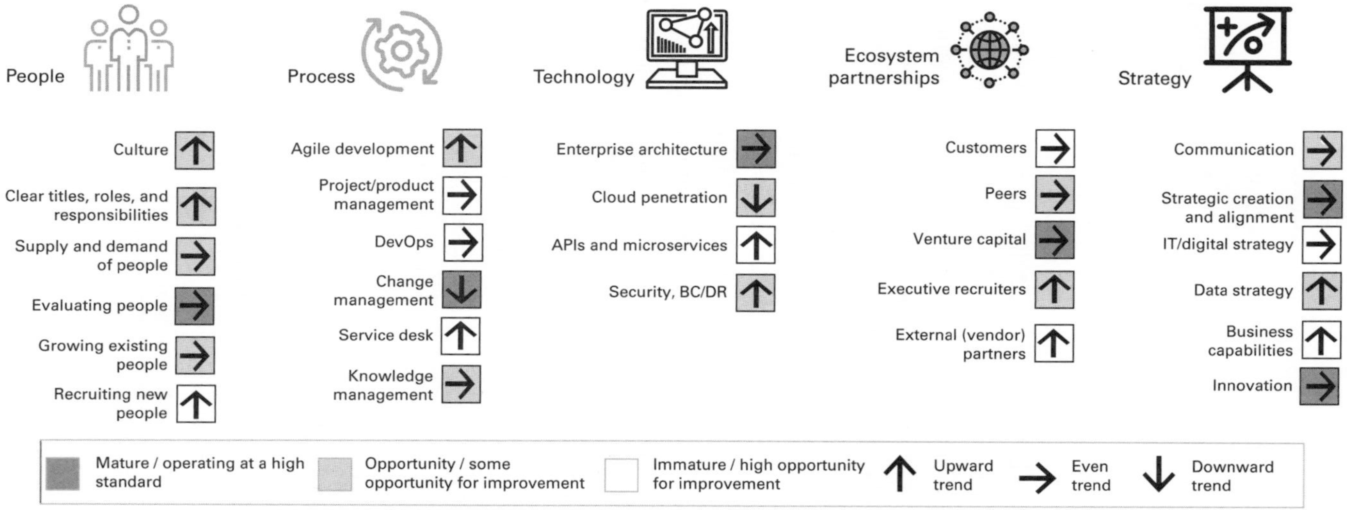

People

- Culture ←
- Clear titles, roles, and responsibilities ←
- Supply and demand of people ↑
- Evaluating people ↑
- Growing existing people ↑
- Recruiting new people ←

Process

- Agile development ←
- Project/product management ↑
- DevOps ↑
- Change management →
- Service desk ←
- Knowledge management ↑

Technology

- Enterprise architecture ↑
- Cloud penetration →
- APIs and microservices ←
- Security, BC/DR ←

Ecosystem partnerships

- Customers ↑
- Peers ↑
- Venture capital ↑
- Executive recruiters ←
- External (vendor) partners ←

Strategy

- Communication ↑
- Strategic creation and alignment ↑
- IT/digital strategy ↑
- Data strategy ←
- Business capabilities ←
- Innovation ↑

Legend:
- ■ Mature / operating at a high standard
- ▨ Opportunity / some opportunity for improvement
- □ Immature / high opportunity for improvement

- ← Upward trend
- ↑ Even trend
- → Downward trend

FIGURE 1.2   Roles responsible, tools, and metrics to be weighed for each sub-theme

Role(s) responsible   Tool(s)   Metrics

The shading highlights levels of maturity from immature to mature. The arrows highlight the trends. For example, if there is an initiative afoot in one of these areas, but it has not concluded, and the value of that initiative has not been realized, then the trend would suggest that improvement is on the way, but it cannot be marked as a higher level of maturity just yet.

The means of evaluating maturity will be covered through the methods noted throughout this book. In the chapters, I will highlight some practices to bear in mind relative to the role or roles that I would recommend leading each, the tool or tools to use to automate the methods covered in the chapter, and some sample metrics to use to gauge progress or lack thereof. The images in Figure 1.2 will be used to demarcate them.

These are meant to be guideposts. You may have reasons to have others than the roles I have noted responsible. You may have a different toolset to automate the methods described herein. You may choose different metrics, perhaps including those that are specific to your company or industry. But consider these a starting point.

Maturity should be assessed initially by whether there is a current role responsible for the topics raised, whether the methods noted related to the sub-themes are being enacted, whether there is automation, where appropriate, related to each area, and whether there are metrics that are monitored and actions taken based upon them. If the answer is no to each, the grade on the scorecard will certainly highlight immaturity. If each are in place and working well, there is a better chance to be gauged as mature, but improvements may be necessary upon further contemplation. Of course, if there are some in place and working well, and others that are not, "some opportunity for improvement" will be noted.

With all of that in mind, let's dive in!

Notes

1 Peter High. Shamim Mohammad, SVP and CIO of CarMax, *Technovation with Peter High* podcast, December 16, 2016

2 MITRE Center for Innovative Computing and Informatics. *Enterprise Architecture Body of Knowledge*, MITRE Center for Innovative Computing and Informatics

02

The foundation: people

At the end of the 2010s, Capital One thought of technology like a lot of companies did. It had outsourced a lot of it, and though the department was important, it was not truly strategic. In 2011, the company acquired ING Direct, which accelerated the company's deepening appreciation for the changing landscape in financial services toward digital offerings. Rob Alexander, the CIO then and now, recognized a sea change. He recognized that he needed much stronger engineering talent, and he needed to introduce processes and technologies that would compel them to stay and thrive at Capital One.

The company depended on outsourced labor and commercial, off-the-shelf technology, neither of which were differentiating. Alexander wanted the bank to create its own differentiating technology. He posed a tricky question to himself and to his leadership team: "How do you become a great technology organization if you do not start as one?"

He began with a core group of engineers who would form a center of excellence in building software. He recruited people who had a pioneer's mentality and who thrived on change. This small center of excellence inspired a certain segment of the existing staff to want in on the new ways of doing things and this new vision. They acted as proselytizers of a kind. The people and skill modernization would lead to process and technology modernization, with a major commitment to agile, to DevOps, and to cloud technology, to name three of many changes that were ushered in by the members of the emerging center of excellence. Once those changes were on the way, Capital One turned a corner, and talented engineers began to notice a cultural change afoot at the company.

Capital One developed a reputation as a leading technology company that was going somewhere. The IT department, which Alexander rebranded as the technology organization as part of the transformation, reflected the company's values more generally, which are openness, collaboration, teamwork, and truth-seeking.

This is the kind of change that most companies need to recognize. Of course, the process and technology changes are critical, but they take a back seat in this transformation to the people and cultural changes necessary for this to gel. The software and hardware that IT and digital divisions implement create value for the company and the company's customers, and the scale of that advantage increases as all businesses become increasingly digital. However, no technology is as important as the people who build and implement it. The best technology in the world cannot overcome a mediocre team. A motivated, gritty team can move mountains and create innovative products that will substantially improve the performance of the company.

The way in which teams are organized borrows heavily from the military. The larger the company, the more complex it is to manage, the greater the need to organize functionally across the enterprise, it has been assumed. Just as an army has a general at the top of the organization with a number of colonels reporting to them to ensure that the strategy is enacted, the CEO has a number of business unit and functional heads across the organization, from the chiefs, such as the chief financial officer or the chief operating officer, to executive or senior vice presidents who lead business units. Like the general, the CEO traditionally sets the strategy, and they work with these reports to enact the plan.

The greatest value is derived at the intersection of these functions, and I would argue that no other function is as key to these partnerships as the digital or information technology area. Not long ago, the other leaders of the business could be blissfully ignorant about the role technology played in the company and the importance of the IT department. It has never been more crucial, then, to ensure your department understands what the IT department does on a day-to-day basis, and it is crucial that all departments successfully interact with technology. Technology is the central nervous system of the company. Imagine if it were unavailable for a period of time. Operations would cease and revenue would drop as a result.

Under the **people** theme, there are six sub-themes that contribute to organizational nimbleness:

- culture
- clear titles, roles, and responsibilities
- supply and demand of people

- evaluating people
- growing existing people
- recruiting new people

It is important that each of these reaches a solid standard of maturity in order to be nimble. If any are immature, the company will be operating at a suboptimal level to say the least. Since people are the most important resource of any company, whether a product or service company, progress relative to each must be measured frequently. Let's delve into each topic.

Culture

Culture is an amorphous term, applying to nations and yogurt alike. Within a company, a culture takes a shape whether planned or not. Typically, it spawns from the personal attributes of the founders of the company. If they are friendly or collegial, they are likely to hire people who are the same, and that is a cultural attribute that is likely to flourish. If they are confrontational and argumentative, the desire for intellectual tennis may dictate that others who are so inclined will be sought out.

The Society for Human Resources Management (SHRM) notes that culture defines:

> the proper way to behave within the organization. This culture consists of
> shared beliefs and values established by leaders and then communicated and
> reinforced through various methods, ultimately shaping employee perceptions,
> behaviors and understanding. Organizational culture sets the context
> for everything an enterprise does. Because industries and situations vary
> significantly, there is not a one-size-fits-all culture template that meets the needs
> of all organizations.[1]

Rick King, the former CIO of Thomson Reuters and, until his recent retirement, the company's executive vice president of operations, noted when I asked him to define culture:

> Culture is not only the words that you write down to describe your company
> or your department; it is the actions you take. You may say you put your
> employees first, but do your actions say as much? If you do not live your
> culture, there is risk because it will lead people to question the most
> fundamental aspects of your business.[2]

Atticus Tysen, Chief Information Security Officer, Chief Fraud Prevention Officer, and Chief Information Officer of Intuit, shared his thoughts on culture in a conversation I had with him:

> Culture is something that you have to actively cultivate, and you absolutely have to nurture it. You have to shape it. It's a real thing you have to talk about because if you don't, it exists, but you're blind to it. Culture should be defined, but it is realized through the actions of the company.

Defining culture

Assuming that you will define culture for a going concern, it is critical to acknowledge the past, present, and future of culture. Where many new executives get things wrong is in defining culture as though it begins with their arrival. Even in situations where a new executive has arrived to replace a leader who was fired and believed to be ineffective, there are surely some attributes of the culture from the prior administration that should continue. To not take these into account would be tantamount to indicating that the many people on the team who remain and who will be crucial to the new leader's success have been operating in the wrong manner for years or decades, depending on their tenure. No one wants to be told that their career to date has been wrong or a waste of time.

Therefore, you must understand what was good about the past culture. The process to draw these out requires a lot of interviews of four existing groups: existing employees inside and outside of the technology and digital division, strategic partners, and, where applicable, customers. $5.4 billion revenue Novant Health's Chief Transformation and Digital Officer Angela Yochem said to me when reflecting on her arrival at the company in January 2018 and learning its culture: "Culture change needs to start by listening and understanding the way things are done." The executive needs to be flexible and not arrogant enough to believe that it is everyone else that needs to change. You should also get an unbiased view into how each of these four constituent groups would define the IT department. The questions should begin with, "What words would you use to describe the IT department?" By asking the question without pushing for positive or constructive feedback, the speaker can push in any direction they wish, which is helpful before pushing for specific feedback.

For example, if the feedback were to come back that the team were hard working and dedicated, but lacked a means of prioritizing, this is important feedback about how the team strives to be a good partner and will work hard to do so. The lack of prioritization may lead to issues of pursuing the wrong initiatives, or it may lead to initiatives being delivered slower than they should be. The positive attributes should be underscored. Additionally, if you are a digital or technology leader, the culture you define for your team needs to marry with any cultural attributes that are more broadly defined within the company. If they are misaligned, the team could be working against the rest of the company, creating an "us versus them" culture in the process.

By definition a digital transformation of a business requires a culture change of sorts, as it requires that enough of the practices of the business change while also requiring significant additional resources in the form of new employees who possess the skills that reflect where the digital team is going.

Another key to pulling positive threads from the past culture is to think about the company at its founding. Are there unique attributes of the company that should be highlighted? Meg Whitman spoke about the attraction to her in joining HP as chief executive officer on September 22, 2011: Despite the many challenges that the company had, the founders Bill Hewlett and David Packard had built the DNA of the company in a way that she believed it could be accessed again. She noted that the DNA of one of the first true Silicon Valley companies was predominately innovation-centric. She needed to find ways to draw upon its illustrious history and collaborate across the company and with customers in a way it had not before.

It is also important to define the aspirational attributes of the future. How does the cultural DNA translate and support the future of the company? What behaviors, actions, and attributes do you and the team aspire to? For this, it is good to incorporate more voices, from the leadership team and from some select people across the company. This should not be a "boil the ocean" exercise with an attempt to incorporate everyone, but instead the people you choose to engage should be the ones who you wish to have the rest of the company emulate.

In defining culture, develop a cultural statement and supporting cultural attributes. A cultural statement should be short and easy to memorize for your people. If one of your staff is at a cocktail party, speaking about their job, you would want them to be able to easily quote the cultural statement. The cultural attributes should be the long-form version of cultural definition.

Words that often appear in cultural statements include:

- collaborative
- innovative
- creative
- collegial
- flexible
- inclusive
- passionate
- risk-taking

Of course, this list is nowhere near exhaustive, but it should offer ideas to draw from. Here is an example of a cultural statement from Etsy, the e-commerce website focused on handmade or vintage items and craft supplies:

> As an Etsy employee, you can do the work you love, be yourself, and make an impact in the lives of millions. Our commitments to diversity and inclusion, team culture and the spaces where we work all reflect our mission to keep commerce human.[3]

By the way, this cultural statement appears on the company's careers section of its website. The company hopes that those who apply to work at the company share these attributes.

An example of a long-form cultural statement is Johnson & Johnson's credo. Robert Wood Johnson, who was chairman of the company from 1932 to 1963, crafted the credo himself in 1943 just prior to the company going public. The company believes it is both a moral compass, but also "a recipe for business success."[4]

> We believe our first responsibility is to the patients, doctors and nurses, to mothers and fathers and all others who use our products and services. In meeting their needs everything we do must be of high quality. We must constantly strive to provide value, reduce our costs and maintain reasonable prices. Customers' orders must be serviced promptly and accurately. Our business partners must have an opportunity to make a fair profit.[5]

Jim Swanson joined Johnson & Johnson as the executive vice president and enterprise chief information officer in October 2019. It was his second stint with the company, as he also spent nine years with the company spanning from the mid-1990s through the mid-2000s. Swanson was already familiar with the credo when he took his current post, and reflected in a conversation with me on its importance during times of opportunity and trial:

> Our key decisions are anchored in the credo at all times. As an example, we are in the process of developing a vaccine for the virus that has caused COVID-19. Our credo states, "We are responsible to the communities in which we live and work and to the world community as well. We must help people be healthier by supporting better access and care in more places around the world." Those words were meaningful to our company as we pursued a vaccine, creating a "supply chain at risk."

He noted that the typical processes to develop vaccines include serial steps that the company has done in parallel. The credo gives leaders license to do the right thing, even if it means doing it in an unconventional way. The company's website notes, "Our credo challenges us to put the needs and well-being of the people we serve first."

He also highlighted that the credo is noted throughout employee surveys. These "Credo Surveys" have a 92 percent participation rate, highlighting the passion employees have for the ideas included therein. "We connect the dots on the messages from the credo to the survey," said Swanson. He offered as an example the section related to employees:

> We are responsible to our employees who work with us throughout the world. We must provide an inclusive work environment where each person must be considered as an individual. We must respect their diversity and dignity and recognize their merit. They must have a sense of security, fulfillment and purpose in their jobs. Compensation must be fair and adequate and working conditions clean, orderly and safe. We must support the health and well-being of our employees and help them fulfill their family and other personal responsibilities. Employees must feel free to make suggestions and complaints. There must be equal opportunity for employment, development and advancement for those qualified. We must provide highly capable leaders and their actions must be just and ethical.

Swanson noted that the company asks employees through frequent surveys whether it is living up to this message. The company's website sums up the value of the credo in noting:

> Our credo is more than just a moral compass. We believe it's a recipe for business success. The fact that Johnson & Johnson is one of only a handful of companies that have flourished through more than a century of change is proof of that.

Lastly, we focus on integrity. That applies to our systems and to us as individuals. If we hire people with integrity, and we do not do anything to spoil that integrity, then special things can happen.[6]

In your division of the company, your cultural statement and cultural attributes should support those of the company more generally. That said, there is no reason why you should not set a more ambitious standard than is set globally within your company. Technology and digital functions should be ambitious, and the culture should reflect this. Where divisional cultural statements and attributes fall flat is that they are framed less ambitiously than the corporate standard, where one exists.

The other mistake that many technology functions make is that they believe it to be presumptuous to define technology or digital divisional culture when a corporate cultural statement is nonexistent. By setting a standard, your division can be the inspiration for others to follow.

At the end of the day, the cultural attributes that you highlight may be unique to you, but there are three factors that I would recommend you highlight and encourage: change, a productive way to disagree, and team collaboration. Let's focus on change menagement for a moment. The topic of change management will be addressed in the next chapter, but change is not a naturally comfortable state of being for people. Many organizations have gone bankrupt because the company was not able to make changes necessary to evolve with customers' preference. Therefore, encouraging comfort with change becomes important.

Google: making change a core competence

Google Chief Information Officer Ben Fried has been with the company in that role for more than a dozen years. The growth he has seen in his tenure has been breathtaking. However, as the company has grown into one of the largest companies on earth, it has maintained an entrepreneurial spirit that seems paradoxical. When I asked him how it has maintained that edge, he noted in a conversation with me, "We have focused on making change a core competence." In essence, the need for change is enmeshed in all that the company does.

By making change a cultural attribute, you are more likely to recruit people who are growth-minded and will make change happen for themselves, their teams, and the company more generally. It will also help in evaluating your team. Who on the team is resting on the laurels of their past accomplishments versus getting training on new business and technology disciplines? Who is challenging the status quo? Who is developing ideas for new products, even if there is the possibility that they are cannibalizing the existing offering?

Part of what fosters change is a culture that is open to people calling out when something that has worked for years is no longer doing so. That person, no matter their seniority, should be able to voice that opinion and provide the data to back up that point of view. Of course, in most cultures, voicing disagreement or dissent respectfully is necessary so that the points raised are not lost in a statement that appears to be inflammatory or derogatory to someone in the room.

The third factor to foster is team collaboration. Many companies make the mistake of inadvertently fostering a hero culture. In that scenario, it is best for any individual to shine individually, as that is the path up in the company, the misinterpreted logic goes. Today, more than ever, with advances in agile practices, product orientation of the IT team, DevOps, and innovation driven at the intersection of disciplines—to name four topics that we will cover in detail later in this book—it is the evaluation of team performance even more than individual performance that matters.

Other steps to take as culture matures

After your cultural statement and attributes are defined, develop a communications path for each. These will only be as successful as your organization's knowledge of them. In the early stages of the rollout, you, as a leader of your function, should hold brownbag lunch sessions and all-hands meetings with your team to explain the attributes. It is even more powerful if each member of the leadership team in your group provides their own explanation, so it is apparent that leadership is singing from the same hymnal, so to speak.

Additional points of communication might be to have posters made and strategically placed around the department, say, near elevators or staircases, restrooms, and the cafeteria, as appropriate, to reinforce the message. The more people have reason to interact with the cultural attributes, the more they will understand them and live them.

It is also important to explain these cultural attributes to the leadership team of the company as a whole. This will help the other executives understand what your team believes to be sacred. Depending on your company, you may wish to get their buy-in as well as constructive feedback on a mostly baked version of the cultural attributes.

FIGURE 2.1   Culture

Role(s) responsible	Tool(s)	Metrics

- CIO/CDO
- IT/digital executive team

- Technology and digital division-specific websites
- Signage in appropriate places around the office
- Lead pages in technology and digital division presentations
- Onboarding materials

- Increase in positive survey results on team members' understanding and adherence to cultural attributes
- Increase in positive survey results on colleagues outside of technology and digital division regarding technology and digital living the cultural attributes
- Increase in positive survey results on vendor partner understanding of cultural attributes

Additional ways to ensure that culture becomes lived by your team include making it a part of the recruiting process. I mentioned that Etsy includes the company cultural statement on the careers page of their website so that recruits have reason to see it early in the recruiting process. Wharton Professor Adam Grant notes about culture, "It's never too early to think about the culture that you're shaping. And it's a lot easier to shape culture through who you let in the door than through trying to radically change people's behaviors."[7]

The same can be said for the engagement of external partners. We will cover this topic in greater detail in Chapter 5 of this book, but why not use your cultural attributes as a screen in determining other firms to engage? You should make your cultural attributes known to these parties and ask for evidence of the support of them.

Use the cultural attributes when evaluating your team. Those who exemplify the attributes best should be called out, with a description of the rationale in order to provide the motivation for others to emulate these behaviors. This might be extended to the point of giving out awards or even a monetary bonus to those who are models of the team's culture. These people can then become cultural ambassadors in the process.

Lastly, the rest of the company and the company's customers, where appropriate, should also see the value of the digital or technology organization's culture. You should evaluate this with some frequency as well. Monitoring this not only reemphasizes the importance of the cultural attributes to the rest of the company and the customers of the company, but it is a chance to course-correct and to identify people who live the culture best.

Cultural nimbleness

A nimble culture is not one that changes its cultural values with frequency. In fact, if culture is important, it ought to have a longer shelf life. The nimbleness in one's culture is demonstrated when everyone understands the cultural values and lives them, day in and day out. Define culture with the effectiveness of your department, high value contribution from it, and the fulfillment of your team in mind. If you do, and your team embodies these attributes, your organization will be a force multiplier for the company more generally.

Interdependencies of culture

The first dependency on your culture as a digital or technology leader is the culture of the company, more generally. As noted above, it is essential that these are aligned. Therefore, consider this exercise a translation of the corporate culture into your organization with a description of the touchpoints and means of supporting the broader culture. That said, if a corporate culture has not been defined, do not use this as an excuse not to define the culture of your team.

Culture is dependent on people and, therefore, it should be included in surveys to the team to ensure that they understand it, agree with it, and believe in living the attributes encompassed in the cultural definition for your company. Thus, communications are a key dependency for the success of this sub-theme.

The broader ecosystem can impact how you evolve your culture. It is an important topic to cover with your peer technology leaders, as well as with the startup community that you can tap through a network of venture capitalists. Granted, you will not be able to quickly adopt the best practices you learn about, and nor should you, given the fact that every company is different. That said, it is useful to tune your culture with some of what you learn, or at a minimum, you may learn of ways to continue to validate the culture.

Clear titles, roles, and responsibilities

Almost every company has titles, roles, and responsibilities. The issue usually is that they are not updated as time passes, and the pathway from one role to another and from one title to the next can be unclear. This can be a source of frustration, particularly for more ambitious employees who cannot see a path forward for themselves at the company. Leave them guessing too long, and the journey will be up and out of your company.

The other question that arises is the appropriate number of titles or roles in a company. The answer is the less than satisfying, "It depends." The tendency is to have too many rather than too few. As with processes and technologies, people like to dream up the new, but are hesitant to retire the old and redundant. This adds considerable confusion. It is important to have titles, roles, and responsibilities that are descriptive and clear. They should be defined in a way that suggests a pathway to rise through the organization. Where roles become less relevant, bite the bullet and eliminate them, while providing training and other opportunities wherever possible for those who have those roles to transition to new, more relevant positions for the future.

Having advised leaders of perhaps a hundred companies around the world, the other variable I have noted as inconsistent is how titles align with seniority. I worked with a financial services company a dozen years ago where everyone seemed to be a vice president at least. There are other companies where the reports to the chief executive officer have the vice president title. Some companies have senior vice presidents, and executive vice presidents, and even senior executive vice presidents. Other companies give their business unit heads the title of president. While there are no hard and fast rules that fit all environments, there are a few general factors to consider.

Clarity

Clarity makes a tremendous difference. As with strategic plans, the clearer the title, role, and responsibility is, the better the team can enact their various duties. The dynamism of digital operations and information technology departments are such that roles that were in abundance yesterday (e.g., manual software testers, computer hardware engineers, and email administrators) can be less relevant tomorrow, and new sets of responsibilities (e.g., SCRUM master, or a DevOps manager) may appear almost out of nowhere, reflecting roles required to shepherd in new practices. So, where does one begin in maturing clarity of titles, roles, and responsibilities?

First, tabulate all current titles, roles, and responsibilities. You cannot either adhere to or modify what you don't know exists. You should conduct job evaluation through observation, while offering questionnaires to clearly identify the jobs people are actually doing. This fills in gaps to the existing portfolio of titles, roles, and responsibilities. Next, though titles are likely to be the best understood of the three topics here, the differences between them may require some articulation. This ensures that people better understand what the path of advancement entails. Likewise, any roles and responsibilities that are not defined should be defined. It is important that these roles and responsibilities be standardized as much as possible across the company. This may be challenging in multinationals or companies that have grown through acquisition, but it is best to do this work to ensure that you have a single team that is operating optimally. It is also best for instances when an employee in one geography, say, is transferred to another one. Lastly, during the foundational phase of establishing clear titles, roles, and responsibilities, you must modernize and right-size the structure of the team, as noted above.

As this principle area matures, you should be sure that an organizational structure and chart is developed and communicated. On rare occasions, this is something that is kept close to the vest, understood only by the senior members of the team. If you wish to motivate the most ambitious people on your team to rise in your organization, you will be aided in this by showing them the pathway up.

It is also important to educate the rest of the organization and your external partners on your organizational structure. Having worked with dozens of digital and technology departments of companies, the vast majority of non-IT employees of those companies and external partners to the departments do not fully understand who does what. While your finance department may not need to understand the job of hundreds of members of your team, they should know the basic breakdown of the department, the areas of responsibility, and who to interact with about what.

It is also important to develop responsible, accountable, consulted, and informed (RACI) matrices to help define who is responsible for what in different settings. These designations will not be the same for each title or role no matter the initiative, mind you, but having a mechanism to define this will help determine who has ultimate authority to make decisions, and who else needs to be involved along the way.

Clear titles, roles, and responsibilities: nimbleness

The idea of being nimble relative to clear titles, roles, and responsibilities requires that the organization be mindful of how strategy translates into demand, and how demand translates into skill needs. Ultimately, this will help the organization understand what roles and responsibilities will be needed. Titles are likely to change as an organization grows. Silicon Valley startups tend to have very few chiefs, and often the functional heads carry vice president titles such as vice president of human resources, vice president of marketing, and so on. These are often people who have never carried a "chief" title, and therefore it does not feel like a diminution of responsibilities.

As a company grows, it becomes increasingly important to hire people who have led similar functions at companies similar in size to what your company aspires to. That is often the point when the chiefs are hired, or if the VP has grown in value, they may be promoted into that role.

The smaller the organization, the more nebulous job titles tend to be since individuals are usually working across a variety of functions. The company may need to have some generalists as a result of the company's size and growth. This is the period when the CEO may answer customer calls, make coffee, and book reservations for him or herself out of necessity.

Larger and older organizations can learn a lot about the productivity of teams by visiting with startups. I recently took a group of Fortune 500 CIOs to visit with an augmented reality technology company in Los Angeles. Among other uses, the company's product was used by companies that had complex and, at times, dangerous processes in which having instructions in your field of vision made the process easier, faster, and safer. Though the company was funded by one of the best venture capital firms and had garnered a great list of customers in the United States and abroad, it did all of this with 15 people. As we left our tour, a friend of mine who was the CIO of a major cargo company said, "I wish I could take my team here to see how much can be accomplished with just 15 people." As teams proliferate, there is a tendency for the scope of work to expand to keep everyone busy. Although it is not always the case, of course, more work can sometimes be done by fewer people.

Employees crave role clarity, but as the team leader, it's important to keep a certain amount of flexibility built into each role. While you don't want employees working completely out of alignment with a role definition, if someone wishes to be promoted, I believe that they should already have demonstrated their ability to meet the responsibilities of the position above them. It need not be 100 percent, but they should have experience with at least 50 percent of the role's responsibilities.

FIGURE 2.2   Clear titles, roles and responsibilities

Role(s) responsible	Tool(s)	Metrics
• CIO/CDO, HR representative for IT/digital	• Human resource information system (HRIS)	• Increase in positive survey results related to technology and digital division employees regarding title, role, and responsibility clarity from technology and digital division employees
		• Increase in positive survey results related to technology and digital division employees regarding title, role, and responsibility clarity from non-technology and digital division employees of your company
		• Increase in positive survey results related to technology and digital division employees regarding title, role, and responsibility clarity from external partners to the division

Supply and demand of people

After the culture has been defined, and the titles, roles, and responsibilities have been defined, take stock of who is in your organization and what skills they possess. What skills does your organization need? What skills are not as critical? This is essentially a supply and demand issue. There will be ebbs and flows of demand for each skill.

Likewise, assess how skills are changing. Consider your enterprise, divisional, and IT or digital strategy. As the enterprise architecture of the company is plotted and as the strategy impacts the roadmaps, this is another important input in evaluating supply versus demand. Let's walk through some steps in order to get this process correct.

Supply of people

Let's begin with the supply side of the equation. First, develop a common taxonomy of skillsets to evaluate technical skills and nontechnical skills.

This is typically best done with your senior team in a brainstorming session. Note which skills are currently critical. Technical skills may be related to topics such as:

- application development
- programming
- analytics
- data management
- cloud computing
- virtualization
- cybersecurity
- networking and wireless
- enterprise architecture
- AI and machine learning
- help desk and tech support

Examples of non-technical skills might include:

- project management
- product management
- vendor management
- writing
- research
- verbal communications/storytelling
- multilingual skills

Once the taxonomy is in place, check it against the skills of a cross-section of members of your team. Are there important skills missing? If so, add those to your list.

Once you feel confident in the taxonomy, create a portal or repository into which the data will flow. This portal should include a mechanism for employees to self-assess, for managers to be able to review, and for the human resources department and the digital or technology organization to conduct trend assessments. The questionnaire or other means of drawing the data from employees should be finalized.

Next, select a function within the organization to undertake a self-assessment. Choose a group that is representative of the broader organization. In addition to completing the self-assessment, ask employees to provide feedback on the taxonomy itself so you can find out if there are key skillsets that are not noted. You may opt to have one more subset of the overall team respond to get final feedback on potential changes to the skills noted. Once you have done that, you are ready to introduce this to the entire team.

Managers should review the self-assessments to ensure that employees are reporting skills accurately. Employees may list a skill that is not there, or a particularly modest member of your team may possess a skill that they do not list. In either case, managers should validate what is noted. The goal is to get 100 percent of your team into the system with their skills noted. This will represent full supply.

Keeping the skill supply up to date

As your employees embark on new initiatives and take training courses, their skills will grow and change. You can keep your skills inventory current in a few ways.

Particularly mature companies dictate that there be a formal step at the conclusion of any training and at the conclusion of every project that employees note new skills learned. This helps keep your skill inventory up to date almost on a daily basis. Absent this step, or perhaps on your pathway to that step, you should have three triggers for skills updates:

- when an employee is hired
- during employee mid-year or end-of-year performance evaluations, if you do them at that cadence
- when an employee leaves the company (either voluntarily or involuntarily)

When a person is hired, noting their skills is crucial to understand how and where they might fit into the team. Optimally, this would be a step in the process before an offer is made, as these skills are relevant to where, how, and at what level they will work.

The performance evaluation process is also a good time to check in on employees and their skillsets. If your firm has a formal process to evaluate performance, be sure it includes a review of new skills. If your company has abandoned semiannual or annual reviews, set aside a session once or twice per year in order to more formally gather this information.

It is also important to note competency levels for each role. There should be certain skills that are necessary to fill a role or to advance beyond that role. The prior sub-theme covers the definition of these roles and responsibilities, and it is likely that the competency framework may be defined then. If not, do so at this stage of your evolution. This will force a discipline, and push people to take advantage of training to gain the necessary skills to advance.

Strategic partners can also be a source of valuable information for your skills inventory. This may not be necessary at the individual level, since a strategic partner's resources may move on more rapidly, but at least assessing what skills you have hired partners for is appropriate. It provides a more comprehensive view of the supply of talent serving your division and your company. It can also lead to interesting insights about the kinds of skills you source from strategic partners versus the kinds of skills you rely on employees to fill. For instance, if there is a skill that is deemed strategic but in short supply in your department, you may seek partners to fill in these gaps for a time. Evaluating when to cut the tie with the partner should be based on data around how many employees on your team have grown those skills, or how many people you have hired with the skills necessary to do so. We will cover other aspects of how best to contemplate this mix in Chapter 5.

Another ancillary benefit of accumulating the team's collective skills is to understand who might be in a position to train others on a skillset. Ultimately, this process should be set up in order to encourage people to acquire new skills, especially those that are growing in importance. Should a key person leave the organization, understanding who has the skills to take over for them will determine whether a successor is available internally or if the firm needs to consider external options.

Without an understanding of the supply of skills that you have, it will be impossible to be nimble, as you will not understand how spikes in demand for certain skills may be detrimental. Likewise, if you have a number of key lieutenants who are on the cusp of retirement, you may not understand fully how this will impact your division's ability to deliver all it needs to. This is a key strategic ingredient to ensure that the digital or technology department can deliver all it needs to for the company and its customers.

The nimbleness of the supply of people is also impacted by regular monitoring of people and their skills, updating them when someone is hired, trained, or after a period of time such that work experience can be reflected in their skills assessment.

Demand for people

Demand for your people and their skills should be thought of both as a present state and a future state assessment. Given the load of projects and initiatives that your team has currently, you need to understand which skill-sets are rising in demand and which ones are falling.

It is necessary to contemplate strategic plans and enterprise architecture to understand how demand will be shaped in the future. Your team needs to establish close relationships with the rest of the company and with customers in order to understand the nature of demand as early as possible.

This will help you determine which skills are strategic and therefore ought to be built internally, and which skills are not strategic and could be handled by strategic partners.

Where demand for some skills outpaces supply, a stopgap before hiring and training that can fill that void is to engage external partners that possess the skills necessary, as noted above. For this reason, it is important to have among your strategic partners a firm that is able to provide this coverage. Where there are emerging skills needed that are in short supply—like those associated with machine learning and artificial intelligence in recent years—finding firms that can provide those skills while you build yours is of the utmost importance.

Workforce planning should be aligned with the budgeting process to ensure that funds are available to hire new people or train existing people, as necessary. Keep in mind that digitization and automation will have an impact on future skills that will be necessary for the future. Monitoring how technologies like robotic process automation, machine learning, and artificial intelligence will impact the workforce of tomorrow is paramount.

There are other sub-themes that impact the nimbleness of the demand side of people and skills:

- enterprise architecture, which highlights how demand will be shaped and the skills that will increase or decrease in importance as a result
- strategic planning, which provides insights into where the company or your division is going, and should also highlight the rise and fall in demand for certain skills
- customer feedback, which should underscore where new opportunities might arise to meet their needs
- peers, who can validate hypotheses about shifts in the technology landscape

- venture capitalists, who can offer thoughts about rising technology trends that you may choose to take advantage of, which may require new skills on your team
- executive recruiters, who can offer insights into the skills other companies like yours are growing and why
- external (vendor) partners, who can offer insights from across their client list as to areas of growing or fading importance for you to be cognizant of

Evaluating people

In recent years, the methods of evaluating people have changed considerably. One-third of United States-based companies are replacing annual reviews with frequent, informal check-ins between managers and employees, according to a study documented in *Harvard Business Review*.[8] The authors note that performance declines when people are rated relative to others. There are also issues of the time and cost of annual or semiannual reviews, as it takes many of the highest cost and value team members out of commission to fill out their assessments and to meet with members of their teams. The authors cite the fact that annual reviews restrict creativity, create paperwork, and create a transactional view of performance.[9]

A separate article in *Gallup* notes that annual reviews cost an estimated $2.4 million to $35.0 million per year in lost working hours for an organization of 10,000 people with little return on investment to show for it.

FIGURE 2.3 Supply and demand of people

Role(s) responsible	Tool(s)	Metrics

- Technology/digital leadership team
- HR representative for IT/digital

- Human resources information system (HRIS)

- Decrease in time to fill open position
- Decrease in time to commence high-priority projects
- Decrease in reliance on external partners for skills deemed strategic

Moreover, only 14 percent of employees strongly agree their performance reviews inspire them to improve, and almost half of those surveyed say they receive feedback from a manager "a few times per year or less."[10] The implication is that due to an annual review process, managers feel less compelled to offer regular touchpoints where improvements can be made.

The same Gallup poll notes that if the cadence of feedback increases to weekly, employees are more than five times more likely to strongly agree they receive meaningful feedback, more than three times more likely to strongly agree they are motivated to do outstanding work, and just under three times more likely to be engaged at work.[11]

While this feedback is compelling, it doesn't necessarily mean you should scrap your annual or semiannual process. Having a more formal process helps when the company wishes to reward performance, since that is not likely to be the topic of the week-to-week or month-to-month conversations. The more formal annual or semiannual process also tends to be better if yours is an organization that wishes to have cascading goals from the chief information officer, say, through to their direct reports and on throughout the team. The formal reviews ensure that everyone is aligned and pushing toward the same objective. And finally, a more formal process is better for documentation of performance issues, which are necessary if an employee is terminated. If you use the less formal but regular cadence reviews, capturing this information becomes that much more important to avoid legal issues.

If you are going to make a change to your review process, make sure you provide the necessary training in order to help managers adapt to the new cadence. Ensure that feedback and measurement methods are consistent across the team in order to prevent fast paths to promotion for people who do not deserve them. You should also communicate why you are making the change and to what end or value.

If you currently have an annual or semiannual process, you might want to try a hybrid approach, which incorporates more frequent touchpoints with staff along with a less-intensive annual or semiannual process. The more detailed annual or semiannual process can be used to gather updates on skills and to solicit more comprehensive feedback on career planning. No matter the cadence, it is important to standardize your process. Make sure that cultural attributes and the descriptions of titles, roles, and responsibilities are tied to your review process so that performance evaluations reinforce company values.

Performance feedback needs to be constructive and specific so that employees are clear on what they need to do to improve. Employees should be given specific steps for improvement with detailed recommendations on specific training courses to take. Employees should also be encouraged to self-assess their performance in order to develop their own awareness of job requirements.

Incorporating 360-degree reviews can also be helpful as it allows managers to hear from those who they manage. This ensures that they are kept honest in their own assessments, knowing that their team will have a chance to highlight strengths and areas to improve as well. Naturally, the best consequence of this is an acknowledgement that we all have room to grow and improve, and we should get that feedback from those who know us best. It is important to communicate the desire for constructive feedback so that everyone feels safe to offer it. If you still have a sense that people are shy, creating channels through which people can offer anonymous feedback can build the necessary trust. This must be followed up with an acknowledgement of the feedback and the plan of action to improve the areas noted.

Measuring the team

Another big change in evaluations is measuring the performance of teams as much as if not more than individuals. With the establishment of Agile teams, DevOps teams, and product teams, collaboration across the team becomes more important. If a project or product is delivered on time and it contributes the value intended, the entire group deserves credit. If there are bugs or issues, everyone contributes to fixing it. Of course, just as pay and bonuses are still individualized, there is still a need to evaluate the individual, and it is not as though promotions will happen at the team level. That said, the effectiveness of the team needs to be contemplated and evaluated.

In the evaluation of individuals and teams, you should ensure that there are written goals and supporting metrics at the beginning of the year or performance cycle. These should be written first by the individual and then shared with the manager. Teams that work together should be encouraged to share goals so that each knows what the other is shooting for and can help contribute to their mutual success. As the review cycle comes, these written goals and metrics should be reevaluated to determine whether the individual accomplished what was intended. If not, hopefully the data will bear that out and there will not be a disagreement. If there is one, there should be an appeal process in place, perhaps engaging a member of the HR team, or someone else who is outside of the reporting chain.

The role of compensation and recognition

While there are many studies that suggest that meaningful work and earning the respect of one's colleagues are primary performance motivators, compensation still matters.

When designing a compensation plan, it is important to benchmark your firm against firms of like size and like geography. Bands of pay should be established within the titles and roles. These may differ depending on whether someone works in a high cost-of-living city like San Francisco compared with a low cost-of-living city like Des Moines, Iowa, but within those offices, the pay grades should be banded.

BONUSES

Of the many companies that I have advised, I would estimate that more than half of the companies did not have bonuses for all employees. Exemplary performance should be rewarded, and the bonus is the best instrument for that. Many companies also use "spot bonuses," which might come in the form of small payments of cash or a gift as a way of thanking someone for a job well done. If presented correctly, this is often the sort of reward that can be more meaningful than you would expect.

NONMONETARY RECOGNITION

It is important to get to know your team well enough to understand how people wish to be recognized. For some people, being recognized in front of their peers is a blessing. For others, it is a source of anxiety or embarrassment. Finding the right way to recognize good work is important so that the reward actually feels like one. As you mature in this area, developing a repository to determine who has been recognized most is helpful to establish who your best performers are. Instituting a way for peers to highlight MVPs in their midst is also a way to determine who the strongest team players are.

Nimbleness in evaluating people comes through more frequent evaluations so that people get feedback in a more timely fashion. It also comes through regular benchmarking of compensation levels to ensure that great work is compensated fairly. Lastly, recognizing good work—whether through a simple thank you, a written note, or through an out-of-cycle bonus based on remarkable work—can be an important way of making great team members feel special.

Nurturing existing people

Professional development comes in two broad categories—career guidance and professional training. Offering career guidance signals that you care about your employees. Career conversations should be bidirectional, drawing out insights, hopes, and dreams of the employee while providing feedback on what is possible and the steps to take in order to accomplish those dreams. Professional training encourages employees to grow within their role and to develop skills that they do not employ in their day-to-day work life.

CAREER PLANNING

Career planning is as much about managers offering advice to their team members as it is about eliciting from them who is most ambitious. Those who exhibit ambition together with the skill and grit to back it up should be encouraged. The path upward should be made clear to them. If a talented person is in the path of another talented person beneath them, the latter should be given opportunities to join other parts of the company. Better to lose an employee to another division of the company than to another company entirely.

An aid to career planning is the institutionalization of onboarding coaches and access to mentors throughout an employee's tenure. Optimally, these will be in addition to the employee's manager. The mentor should be someone with whom the employee can confide, ask questions, perhaps be a bit more vulnerable. This adds a different dimension to the career planning process.

It is in your company's interest to provide career guidance to everyone, with particular attention paid to your emerging leaders and most valuable contributors. These are the people upon whom your company's future depends, and they should be given reason to see themselves as part of that future for the long haul.

CASE STUDY
T-shaped careers at Ford

There are some companies that have been talent factories, with an unusual number of chief information officers coming from them. For example, Ford Motor Company has produced the following CIOs:

- Ted Colbert (Boeing)
- Sanjeev Addala (AES)

- Sangy Vatsa (FIS)

- Vijay Sankaran (T.D. Ameritrade)

- Jim Scholefield (Marriott International)

- Adriana Karaboutis (National Grid)

- Kim Hammonds (Deutsche Bank)

- Keith Rohland (US Foods)

- Matt Fahnestock (Dana Corporation)

This highlights what a fertile breeding ground this has been, and it is not an exhaustive list. Nor does it include great CIOs who have retired from Ford, like Marcy Klevorn (who advanced to the role of President of Mobility and Chief Transformation Officer) and Jeff Lemmer, who has spent more than 30 years at the company leading IT. In order to advance to executive ranks within Ford, it is necessary to have what some refer to as a "T-shaped" career. This indicates someone who has both depth in a business discipline, but also breadth of experience across the business. For example, Lemmer was an executive vice president of Ford Credit before becoming CIO. Klevorn was the CIO of Ford in Europe.

In a traditional setting, one joins a division of a company as a junior member of that division. If they work hard and well, there may be an opportunity to reach the senior ranks of that division. At a company like Ford, to gain access to the C-suite of the company, one must first do a "year abroad" of sorts, literally or figuratively, either working in an operation in another country, or working in another division or functional unit of the company. The logic of this is that when one gets the c-level job, they have a much greater appreciation and knowledge base about how value is created across the company. There are a number of other companies who have this mentality that have become talent factories. General Electric, Procter & Gamble, and Vanguard are three that come to mind.

CASE STUDY
Union Pacific's distinguished technologist

Union Pacific Corporation has a storied history. The company was incorporated on July 1, 1862, under an act of Congress entitled Pacific Railroad Act of 1862. The act was approved by President Abraham Lincoln. The company is based in Omaha, Nebraska, which is not exactly Silicon Valley when it comes to technology talent. Lynden Tennison was the company's chief information officer from 1992 until 2019, and spent most of his last year with the company carrying the chief strategy officer role for the company, as well.

He had a number of deeply talented technologists in his organization. They were hard to find and hard to replace. Often the only route to keep them was to promote them to a management career track, which was not always the best fit, as they were great technologists, but were not always great managers, and by having them rise to management, the expectation was that they would be doing less of the work that they enjoyed and conducted best. This became a risk in multiple ways and led in several cases to losing great people.

Tennison developed a technical career track within the information technology division. He worked with human resources on the titles, roles, and responsibilities. He even went through a difficult negotiation with HR to be able to make "in-band" promotions.

Ultimately, this led to the creation of the Union Pacific Distinguished Technologist program. It was modeled after AT&T Labs and IBM, which, historically, had had similar designations for their best technologists. The role came with a name plate on their office, highlighting this distinction, and the honor appeared on one's business card. The role even came with new responsibilities, like being more involved in enterprise architecture, mentoring other rising stars, and ultimately being on the committee that could pick new members to the group. It became an aspirational role for people within IT.

By the time Tennison left the company, there were 24 or 25 distinguished technologists. The attrition among this group was remarkably low, as the thought of losing the honor and the better work that goes along with it was incentive enough (among others) to remain. In so doing, Tennison was able to nurture his best people and keep them in the fold longer than he otherwise might.

FIGURE 2.4   Evaluating people

Role(s) responsible	Tool(s)	Metrics

- Technology and digital division managers
- HR representative to the technology and digital division

- Human resources information system (HRIS)

- Improvements in the median and mean evaluations scores
- Improvements in NPS scores of technology and digital division regarding team and work quality
- Increasingly positive survey results from technology and digital division employees regarding quality of team and output

Growing existing people

When I spoke to Capital One Chief Information Officer Rob Alexander about what he looks for in a great employee, he said, "We look for great athletes." In other words, if they have learning agility, and the grit and ambition to succeed, they will do well at Capital One.

I spoke with the head of the largest executive recruiting firm, Korn Ferry's CIO practice, Gerry McNamara, and he reminded me of the firm's definition of learning agility as "not necessarily an academic skill, rather it encapsulates an individual's ability and passion to quickly study a new problem and use their own learning process to gain deep understanding before making a decision."[12] If you graduated from university, think about your major. How much of the information that you studied do you retain? Especially if you majored in a technical discipline, how much of what you studied is relevant? The pace of change means that the answer is likely that it is minimal. Hopefully what you learned at university was the love of learning, and the desire to continue to do it the rest of your life.

Learning agility needs to be a cultural attribute to foster in your organization. Following the lead of companies like Google, which has made change a core competency, you need to staff your team with people who are excited by the unknown, humble enough to admit that they don't know everything, curious enough to seek knowledge, and ambitious and gritty enough to do so even if it means doing so on their own time.

Making training available is key. The good news is that there has never been so much high-quality training material available at such a low cost. The massive open online courses (MOOCs) such as Coursera, Udacity, edX, Alison, and LinkedIn Learning each have great materials from professors and practitioners alike. It is important to make these available to your team, and to have them rank those courses that are best for others to take as well.

A prominent example of a major company partnering with a MOOC is AT&T's partnership with Udacity. As AT&T expanded into new areas such as home automation and connected vehicles, the skillset of their 160,000-plus employees needed to evolve. AT&T partnered with Udacity to develop nanodegrees with a curriculum tailored to their needs. Employees use the digital platform to learn through a combination of bite-sized online videos, interactive exercises, real-world projects, and support from coaches and peers. AT&T has reskilled thousands of employees in areas such as data science, mobile development, and web development.[13]

It is also important to make traditional training such as conferences on specific topics available, though it is also good, where possible, for those who take the training to then teach others back at the office what they have learned. This ensures that the person taking the training actively participates, learns the material in order to train others, makes it stick in their own mind through the training process, and then others have the benefit of the same training in the process.

Among the dozens of companies that I advise, often employees report that they do not take advantage of the training that has been made available to them. Reasons cited most often include busyness at work, lack of understanding of the materials that are available, a perception that training is not a priority, and a belief that funds are not available for training. Thinking of a lack of training as money saved can have deleterious consequences in the long term in opportunity lost and possibly colleagues lost. Technology and digital professionals tend to be an ambitious bunch. They want to learn the latest technologies. They want to understand new processes that are becoming the new state of the art. If you do not provide the support to allow the best employees to keep learning, they will be right to feel that their skills are becoming stale, and they will go elsewhere to freshen up.

It is important to make the priority of training clear. Judge managers based upon the training of their teams, and the percentage of staff who have been trained. Whenever possible, reemphasize the criticality of learning agility for the team, and the critical role training plays in establishing that agility.

It is also important for senior executives to model the behavior. I recently spoke with the founder and CEO of the MOOC edX. He mentioned that among the best ways to encourage people to take advantage of training is for the leaders of the firm to take training, and to share the learnings from that training back with the team. If someone as busy as the boss takes time for training, the logic goes, then everyone should be able to carve off time for it.

Business school for your company

For an advanced practice, think about developing a curriculum made up of the different disciplines across the functions of your company. Encourage your finance team to develop a 101 and 201 version of finance as it applies in your business. Have your marketing and human resources teams do the same. As a digital and technology leader, you should do the same for the rest of the company. There should also be training on the company's products and services that is updated as the products and services are introduced or upgraded.

This idea occurred to me when I learned Bruce Hoffmeister's story. For nine years until mid-2020, Bruce served as CIO of Marriott International. Interestingly enough, he did not study engineering or computer science as an undergraduate. In fact, the majority of his time at Marriott was in the finance function. When he first collaborated with the IT function as a finance leader, he recognized that key members of the IT team did not understand the makeup of the key metrics that drove the business, chief among them revenue per available room. He drew up a training curriculum for IT so that the team would more readily draw a connection between their work and value for the company. In so doing, he created a bridge that he eventually crossed on his path to becoming CIO.

If you could create a business school-like curriculum, though, with your business as the centerpiece, this would arguably be the most valuable training that could be provided.

To take this a step further, some companies have established universities within their walls. Capital One has established a tech college focused on training cutting-edge technology skills. CIO Rob Alexander conceived of Capital One's Tech College as a way to keep the IT department up to date

FIGURE 2.5   Growing existing people

Role(s) responsible	Tool(s)	Metrics

- Technology and digital division leadership team
- Head of technology and digital training

- Human resources information system (HRIS)
- Learning management system (LMS)
- Massive open online courses (MOOCs)

- Increased percentage of technology and digital division employees who develop, fulfill, and demonstrate knowledge grown based on training
- Increased quantity of training materials produced by the technology and digital team for the technology and digital team garnering high ratings by users

given the pace of change in IT. Tech College is available to thousands of engineers as both online courses and in-person training sessions. Capital One offers more than 250 courses in six disciplines. A key goal of Tech College is to make Capital One a preeminent machine learning company, for instance. There are plans to add seven additional disciplines and open Tech College to all employees, including engineers, product managers and designers.[14]

Recruiting new people

Recruiting new people is always a challenge, especially during periods of economic expansion and low unemployment. While it may be tempting to simply fill open positions with available talent, the best long-term strategy is to develop a strong talent pool from which you can source employees as needed.

Offering a strong internship program can be an effective means of attracting talent to your organization. In order to create a better pool of talented people in Omaha, Lynden Tennison, the former CIO and chief strategy officer of Union Pacific, established a 10-week summer intern program. Tennison noted, "It's the best thing we ever did to improve our staff." Union Pacific targeted eight to twelve schools and focused on building long-term relationships with them. The majority of these schools are Midwestern universities with excellent engineering programs. The company typically accepts 40–50 summer interns each year. The company offers competitive pay along with free housing through nice dormitory rooms at a local university. The company also pays for transportation from the dorms to the office and meals. Therefore, almost all of the money the interns earn goes directly into their bank accounts.

The interns live together. There is an IT welcoming committee that helps create a community among the interns and organizes regular outings such as bowling, movies, and music events. Each intern has a mentor to help guide them through the summer. Perhaps most importantly, the company gives interns meaty projects. This is interesting work indicative of the work they will do if they join the company full-time. Some interns continue to work with Union Pacific on a part-time and remote basis after they return to university. Union Pacific gives offers to roughly 75 percent of its interns, and 80–85 percent of them accept the offers. This creates an incredible pipeline of talent for the company, and it is a great way to lure talented undergrads to a city that has a lot to offer, even if it is not as well known as other tech hubs.

Rob Alexander, the CIO of Capital One, echoes this sentiment. He notes that it is hard to hire away from other companies. "If someone is a star at their company, they receive adulation, promotions, raises," he said in a recent conversation with me. "They are less likely to look around and to leave. It's more difficult to pry them loose." He also believes an important way to attract talent is through university recruiting.

"Our campus program has been a centerpiece of our tech recruiting," said Alexander. Where many companies fall short is they do not realize that it is something that is built over years. One must think about it like building a brand. Once enough people from a given school have been hired, those alumni go back to campus and generate energy for the company. The key is to have a top-flight intern program, where interns do interesting work. "Vault.com rates intern programs, and we are almost always at the top of the heap," noted Alexander. That was not done in a single year; it took years of investment to develop. Now the company hires hundreds of interns each year, and a majority of them return to the company as full-time employees.

Recruiting efforts must blend tried and true methods with modern techniques. Traditional methods such as on-campus recruiting and engaging executive recruiters should be blended with modern tools that use artificial intelligence to find new candidates as well as search your applicant tracking system for candidates who have applied for other positions at your company. These tools can also scour social networks such as LinkedIn for candidates who have certain characteristics that you deem important. The applicant tracking system is an important means of tracking candidates that your team identifies, but it can also be a great place for candidates to identify themselves as options for open roles. New technology can also help nullify unconscious bias that can emerge in divisions of the company that have traditionally had problems appealing to diverse candidates.

One of the most important ways of determining if a candidate is a fit is to have them do a "job audition." By this, I mean they should spend a day working through a case or project that is realistic to provide real-world scenarios to test fit and capabilities. Another job audition of sorts is hackathons. These can be helpful means of getting a number of candidates into a room at the same time working on actual opportunities or projects for the company for a period of time. Again, this is a great test to determine if a candidate has the know-how to fit on the team.

FIGURE 2.6   Recruiting new people

Role(s) responsible	Tool(s)	Metrics

- Technology and digital division leadership team
- HR representative to the technology and digital division

- Human resources information system (HRIS)
- Recruiting database, if separate from HRIS

- Decreased time to fill open positions
- Increased ratings of new hires six months after hiring

Glassdoor has become the front door to your firm for candidates. It is now often the first place a candidate goes to get information about the firm and the interview process. Pay attention to what you read through your Glassdoor reviews to continue to improve while accentuating the positive.

It is also important to note how important your human resources department is throughout this process. Establishing a strong relationship with HR can ensure that they are as helpful as possible and as knowledgeable about the specific needs of the digital or technology department.

Nimbleness in the recruiting process should yield a faster path from an identified need to filling that need with a great new colleague. In many ways it is all of the steps operating at a high standard that ensures that recruiting is optimized.

Chapter takeaways

I end this chapter where I began: People are the essential ingredient in your organization. You must find the best people, give them reason to stay with your organization for the long term, and provide them with the tools to create value for the company.

This begins with defining your culture. This will be a reflection of the culture of the past and present, but it should include aspirational attributes that the entire team can buy into. The cultural attributes should be used for the hiring of people and to gauge the success of current staff and the engagement of external partners.

Next, you must understand the skills of your team compared with the skills that are most in demand. Continuous monitoring of this will foster confidence that the technology and digital division of the company can deliver all that is asked of it.

Next, you must evaluate people to understand who your best people are and then let them know through the compensation you offer them and through broader recognition of their good work.

You must offer career planning and training for your entire team with special emphasis on your best people to help them reach their goals as quickly as possible.

Finally, you must have a solid means of recruiting new blood into your organization. By following these sub-themes, you will be far along the path to nimbleness.

Notes

1 SHRM. *Understanding and Developing Organizational Culture*, SHRM Toolkits, 2017–present, www.shrm.org/resourcesandtools/tools-and-samples/toolkits/pages/understandinganddevelopingorganizationalculture.aspx (archived at https://perma.cc/2TNN-S2HR)
2 Conversation with Rick King
3 *Life and Culture at Etsy*, Etsy.com/careers (archived at https://perma.cc/2322-F997)
4 Johnson & Johnson website: jnj.com/credo (archived at https://perma.cc/J9Z3-QMTZ)
5 Ibid
6 Peter High. Johnson & Johnson's CIO leverages a proven blueprint for success in the first 100 days, Forbes.com (archived at https://perma.cc/T9BV-K9DQ), February 25, 2014
7 Reid Hoffman. Culture shock, *Masters of Scale* podcast, February 6, 2020
8 Peter Cappelli and Anna Travis. The performance management revolution, *Harvard Business Review*, October 2016
9 Ibid
10 Robert Sutton and Ben Wigert. More harm than good: The truth about performance reviews, *Gallup*, May 6, 2019
11 Ibid
12 May Knight and Natalie Wong. The organisational X-factor: Learning agility, Focus.KornFerry.com (archived at https://perma.cc/6WHM-9A7L), 2018

13 Stuart Frye. Future focused: Udacity and AT&T join forces to train workers for the jobs of tomorrow, Blog, Udacity.com (archived at https://perma.cc/8ZTN-KDR7), September 13, 2018

14 Sara Castellanos. Capital One wants to train all employees in technology, *Wall Street Journal*, October 2, 2017

03

Processes
The path to successful execution

A retired four-star general, Stanley McChrystal is the former commander of US and International Security Assistance Forces (ISAF) Afghanistan and the former commander of the nation's premier military counterterrorism force, Joint Special Operations Command (JSOC). He is best known for developing and implementing a comprehensive counterinsurgency strategy in Afghanistan, and for creating a cohesive counterterrorism organization that revolutionized the interagency operating culture. When I first met him—weighing his remarkable experience, the fact that he apparently eats a single meal per day, and the shape he keeps himself in—I felt like he was a different species from me.

In 2015, he published *Team of Teams: New Rules of Engagement for a Complex World*, describing how the lessons of his military experience apply more broadly. In a conversation I had with him in 2017, he noted the American Civil War led to the invention of the telegraph, the development of American railroads, and the rifled musket. These developments altered the way in which war was waged. The use of aircraft and smokeless powder was a difference maker in World War I, while World War II brought about the blitzkrieg, a new method of warfare. At this point in our conversation, General McChrystal drew a distinction:

> Compared to now, the pace of change was glacial. The reality is, until about the last 20 years, things changed at a pace and at a level of complication that was manageable. This meant that someone could graduate from West Point as a lieutenant and the way they were trained to organize forces and think about war, with some adjustments for the peculiarities of each situation, put them in pretty good shape for their career.[1]

In the last 20 years the pace of change in warfare, like in business, has accelerated. General McChrystal speaks of crossing a line from complicated to complex. By way of example, he says:

> Your car is complicated. You probably do not know how it was built or how to fix it. Nonetheless, when you press the button or turn the key, it does the same thing every time, because it was designed to do that. Complexity is different. With complexity, the number of variables, their interconnectedness, and the speed at which they change makes it impossible to predict what will happen in the future. What I have learned is, when the current environment makes it impossible to predict even the near-term future, or the impact of your actions, you have to approach it differently.[2]

Previously, JSOC would wait until somebody outside the organization got the information, curated it, shaped it, put it in what was called a "target folder," and then gave it to JSOC to execute. General McChrystal likened it to a bullet that is ready to be fired. The decision on the target that the bullet should be fired toward was outside of JSOC's control. JSOC had to move from order-taker to order-maker. Its leaders had to figure out the problem, and then execute. General McChrystal notes:

> Command used to be 80 percent operations and 20 percent intelligence. Our 20 percent intelligence meant that we were basically consumers of intelligence; people would give it to us, we would critique it, and then operate. A year or two after 2003, those percentages flipped. [JSOC] became 80 percent intelligence and 20 percent operations, and a good part of that 20 percent operations were activities conducted entirely to get more intelligence. It became a fight for who could understand the fastest—the foe or us. If we could understand them well enough, we could win. The operational, or kinetic, part of it was not the hard part.[3]

JSOC was becoming nimble. It employed processes to make it more effective. It removed bureaucracy, and gave decision-making authority to more junior people in various theaters of war because they had the best information. It is striking how these same changes apply to the process changes that are necessary within companies.

There are certain process changes that the aspiring nimble company needs to put in place. Like General McChrystal's example, these are designed to increase speed and throughput while increasing the intelligence of each decision.

In this chapter, we will cover the following process sub-themes:

- Agile development
- product management
- DevOps
- change management
- service desk
- knowledge management

Agile development began in earnest in the 1990s as a recognition that traditional development methods were not working as they should. Across many IT teams, projects were frequently delivered past the due date at a much higher cost than anticipated. The IT departments that were judged so harshly had a point when they countered that at least part of the issue was due to fickle colleagues whose minds changed frequently, leading to requirements changes, which almost always meant that more time and money was necessary.

Agile development was iterative. The principles of Agile were defined by a group of 17 leaders who came together to write the *Agile Manifesto* in 2001, and these ideas were adopted at least in part across a great many companies in the decade following its publication. These iterations would bring the developer and the intended user together throughout the development of a project. This helped validate progress and value along the way, while baking quality assurance into the process at an earlier stage. Greater levels of collaboration led to faster development cycles and higher quality.

In addition to encouraging greater levels of cross-functional collaboration, Agile helped to bring a product orientation to technology and digital teams. Product management became a complement to project management. The balance between these disciplines has been a remarkable change in many IT departments. Whereas project management has been appropriate for projects with fixed time horizons with specific deliverables, products, when defined appropriately, evolve incrementally over time. They benefit by having dedicated, cross-functional teams that can modify the product as new customer or user needs are identified. This product orientation, in many ways, brings IT closer to the methods product-centric companies use to release their products to the marketplace, and then evolve them over time.

DevOps is another key ingredient to ensure speed and quality can work in concert. Whereas Agile led to greater levels of communication and collaboration between IT teams and other divisions of the company, DevOps (a portmanteau combining development and operations) created a permeable membrane to the silos that were fixtures within IT teams. The result was the ability to integrate, deliver, and deploy code more frequently, as opposed to waiting for release windows to open on a less frequent basis to accommodate major changes all at once. This method fits the pace of business and the fact that it is ever quickening.

With greater levels of change necessary to meet the expectations of fickle customers and employees, change management remains an important discipline to ensure that the solutions technology and digital teams deliver are used appropriately. It is human nature to be uncomfortable with change. When done well, change management can help make change a core competence and even a strategic weapon.

The service desk is the front door of the company, and it can be a great aid to change management. It remains an invaluable tool to ensure that as issues arise with the technology or digital products the company and its customers use, there is a path to help those users quickly and effectively, as well as identify, diagnose, address, and resolve the root causes of those issues.

Finally, knowledge is a primary differentiating factor between good and great companies. Those with better knowledge more readily accessible and more readily replenished and advanced will win. Too many companies have too much tacit knowledge, which resides in people's memories, and too little explicit knowledge, which is captured, sorted, and readily accessible. The key is to make as much knowledge explicit as is possible, and then to enhance it with processes and technologies to allow that knowledge to be pushed and pulled to the people who need it so that the wheel need not be reinvented.

Agile development

Agile development is one of the key lynchpins for the nimble organization. For most of business history, what has come to be referred to as a waterfall method of project and product development reigned. This was a staged process, often involving different people throughout the different stages of developing the project or product. This was particularly important when initiatives were larger and monolithic in nature. A project that was due to take 12 months and cost millions of dollars required a massive team who specialized in different phases of that project's development.

This is not a nimble way to develop initiatives. For one thing, the pace of change is such that if you begin a 12-month project, by that project's conclusion, the hypotheses that the project was based upon might no longer be valid. Or perhaps 50 percent of the hypotheses will not be, but if the first time the project is used (whether by colleagues for internally directed projects or customers for externally directed projects) is only after the project has concluded, the process of changing 50 percent of the work may mean another six months of work. Again, as time passes, this may prove to be another moving target. No wonder that in the early stages of my career, when I surveyed dozens of Fortune 500 companies' technology or digital departments on the efficacy of their project development practices, more than half of the time the projects were terribly over budget, past time, and ultimately (and most importantly), they did not deliver the anticipated results. This issue was pervasive enough that in February 2001, 17 software development and project development experts met in Utah to develop a better way to develop better projects and products. They would eventually publish *The Agile Manifesto*, which set out the following principles:

- *Our highest priority is to satisfy the customer through early and continuous delivery of valuable software.*

- *Welcome changing requirements, even late in development. Agile processes harness change for the customer's competitive advantage.*

- *Deliver working software frequently, from one week to four weeks, with a preference to the shorter timescale.*

- *Businesspeople and developers must work together daily throughout the project.*

- *Build projects around motivated individuals. Give them the environment and support they need and trust them to get the job done.*

- *The most efficient and effective method of conveying information to and within a development team is face-to-face conversation.*

- *Working software is the primary measure of progress.*

- *Agile processes promote sustainable development. The sponsors, developers, and users should be able to maintain a constant pace indefinitely.*

- *Continuous attention to technical excellence and good design enhances agility.*

- *Simplicity—the art of maximizing the amount of work not done—is essential.*

- *The best architectures, requirements, and designs emerge from self-organizing teams.*

- *At regular intervals, the team reflects on how to become more effective, then tunes and adjusts its behavior accordingly.*[4]

A theme across this book is the pace of change and the need for companies to pick up their pace so they are not left behind. This means that companies need to have a faster path from idea generation through to execution on that idea, to delivering it to the intended audience. Oversimplifying only a little, project management in the past has focused on the people who will build the project drawing requirements from the intended user of what will be produced, going off and building it, and then having users test it once it is near completion. Many of the changes noted through the sub-themes of this book are focused on greater levels of collaboration between builder and user at the earliest stages. This offers the opportunity for greater collaboration early on.

According to the latest *State of the Agile* survey,[5] Agile is the most prevalent software development methodology, with 97 percent of respondents indicating that they have adopted the practice. This signifies a high level of adoption, but it also includes examples of companies that have adopted it across all development done, as well as those who have piloted initiatives using Agile practices. It does not suggest 97 percent of companies can be designated as mature adopters.

Having worked with companies before Agile was broadly implemented, many of them suffered through waterfall practices, which, as noted above, were the opposite of the iterative methods that Agile requires. Ideas were generated by "the business," as business analysts would help define the requirements, scope, and budget for a project, which would then be passed to the project manager, who would oversee the development of the project from start to finish. Testing, including user testing, would happen only after the project was more or less complete. Just as authors of great books are often dissatisfied with the film interpretations of their works, users often were dissatisfied with how their vision was translated into reality. This often led to scope changes, higher budgets, and more friction between IT and "the business." I continue to put "the business" in quotes because this was the terminology that was widely used, even though it was absurd to think that IT was not part of the business. It was a language that highlighted the distance that IT perceived between its activities and the revenue-generating, customer satisfaction earning activities of other parts of the organization. It screamed "order-taker," and waterfall methodology reinforced this idea!

Agile practices are the antidote to many of those issues. It implies much greater levels of collaboration. It drives improvements at the earliest possible stages, reducing the cost and time overruns that waterfall development was infamous for. It also leads to the cancelation of initiatives earlier and more frequently, which is a positive sign. This happens when the hypotheses that the initiative was based upon fall apart or it is determined that taking the project to conclusion will be a pyrrhic victory only. The greater level of funds saved from these earlier decisions means more funds for the next round of initiatives. Most of all, it is a validation point that IT is a key part of the business, worthy of idea generation and deep collaboration throughout the development lifecycle with the intended users of what is being developed, be they customers of the company or the internal operation.

So, what are the hallmarks of a successful Agile implementation? My colleague Özlem Ulusoy is an Agile expert and has identified the following five steps:

1 securing executive buy-in and commitment

2 choosing the right process

3 developing team structures that fit the company's goals and culture

4 committing to continuous learning

5 measuring outcomes and maturity

Let me provide some insights into each.

Securing executive buy-in and commitment

Agile requires a change in approach. As with any change, there are likely to be hiccups along the way. Progress will not be unbroken. It will be of the two steps forward, one step back variety in the early stages. This will provide ammunition to the naysayers who are insecure about whether they can cross the chasm to perform well in this new reality when they are quite certain they can do so in the existing reality. Strong and steadfast leadership is required to take full advantage of this trend.

Moreover, learning loops are essential in effective software and project delivery. Leaders must create safety for those who experiment and fail. The key is to document the failing, learn from it, and incorporate those learnings into future initiatives.

Choosing the right process

Agile does not imply a single method of operation. There are many of them. Among the most prominent are the following:

- Scrum
- Large Scale Scrum
- Scaled Agile Framework
- Extreme Programming
- Lean software development
- Kanban
- Scrumban

When people think of Agile, Scrum is among the most thought of approaches to it, focusing work in sprints, which are iterative and short cycles. Requirements are prioritized based on value to the end consumer or customer (internal or external) of the features to be developed. The team works on them in that order. At the conclusion of each sprint, the consumer or customer can interact with a useable product. The team enhances processes and procedures relative to it based on feedback from the consumer or customer, and then turns to the next sprint.

Large Scale Scrum, sometimes referred to as LeSS, is a method used to coordinate the work of multiple Scrum teams at once in those situations where they are working in concert on a larger-scale project or product. The different teams' actions are coordinated and synchronized to ensure that the broader objectives are reached.

The Scaled Agile Framework, referred to as SAFe, fosters an ability to leverage Agile methods for larger and more complex projects. SAFe leverages systems thinking to coordinate work and results across an organization. The optimal sequence of projects and programs are assessed to determine the order of work.

Extreme Programming, often referred to as XP, is an engineering-based system that minimizes interim work products using automated and focused effort. It integrates results on a daily basis incorporating automated testing that is done by team members in pairs. The pairs review and correct mistakes in each other's work as they continue to work.

Lean software development identifies where value is created for internal consumers or customers and eliminates all steps and processes that do not adequately add value. By eliminating these wasteful steps or activities, the development teams can reduce the time-to-market for products and services while ensuring that focus is on products that the intended users will, in fact, use.

Kanban is a method that offers a "less is more" philosophy of development. It limits the amount of work that is in process at any one time, helping teams gain focus. The team advances to the next stage of an initiative only after existing work has been completed. Kanban is ideal for dynamic scenarios where requirements are added with an irregular cadence and in varying degrees.

Scrumban combines Scrum and Kanban, and, as the name suggests, it includes approaches from each. Short sprints are undertaken, limiting the amount of work undertaken at any one time.

Since each organization and even each initiative is unique, it is important to put more thought into the practices to incorporate. Ulusoy recommends that leaders observe and listen to their teams in order to make the right choices:

> An experienced Agile Transformation lead will look at the existing teams, tools and processes in place to see where the organization is on an Agility scale. They will assess teams in terms of their experience levels and training needs, tools for capabilities and processes for their effectiveness. Based on where the organization currently is, and what their goals are, the right Agile methodology will be selected.

Developing team structures that fit the company's goals and culture

Once a methodology or methodologies have been selected, implementation begins. Ulusoy recommends focusing on roles and responsibilities and team structures.

As mentioned in Chapter 2, titles, roles, and responsibilities are important for people to understand their purview and to execute against it well. If team members are unsure as to who does what, redundant work or incomplete work results. During times of staff reduction, like many experienced during the economic downturn of 2020, roles are often combined. If a resource manager is also acting as a product manager, Ulusoy points out, "Teams then get confused because they are confused about 'who' is talking to them during team meetings. Is it their product owner or is it their boss? Are they receiving mandates or requests?"

Agile methodology and iterative development more generally require frank and frequent feedback. Different aspects of the methodologies under the Agile umbrella noted above require different levels of detail, as well. It is important to assess which approaches will work best for your culture. You may also choose an evolving approach as your capabilities around Agile practices mature. The Scaled Agile Framework and Large Scale Scrum are significant undertakings. Your company may wish to adopt less complex methods before making this broader commitment. The learnings along the way are likely to be instructive.

Getting the team makeup wrong is a common issue in the earlier stages of Agile adoption. Ulusoy highlights the following guidelines to bear in mind:

- Size: Small; 5 +/–2 members, with clear roles and responsibilities
- Skillset: Cross-functional
- Goal orientation: Function/product based
- Focus: Customer/end-user focused
- Quality: Empowered and autonomous team members

Bearing these principles in mind can offer great aid in better Agile adoption and success. By establishing wins through adopting Agile methods, demand for more is likely to result.

Committing to continuous learning

Having worked with a great number of CIOs and CDOs in helping them assess their practices, recommending areas to mature in order to achieve optimal performance, perhaps the area that is missing most is the learning loop associated with the work of technology and digital teams. Often this is due to the fact that teams are in pursuit of the new. They do not want to go back and ask questions regarding what went well, what did not, what hypotheses were validated, and whether value was realized. It can take time to conduct this analysis, and the results may be painful.

Toyota set the standard for high-quality products at affordable prices. In order to achieve that standard, the manufacturing process had to be excellent, and all "fat" from the process had to be trimmed. In fact, they are often cited as leaders in "lean" principles. The former CEO of Canadian Autoparts Toyota, Deryl Sturdevant, noted, "The two pillars of the Toyota way of doing things are kaizen (the philosophy of continuous improvement) and respect and empowerment for people, particularly line workers. Both are absolutely required in order for lean to work."[6] By extension, these concepts are also important for Agile to work effectively.

By combining lean and Agile, teams ensure that not only are they building high-quality products and features, they are also creating what the users actually need or are asking for. Without the feedback loop and learning, you can build the best product that does not solve any problems and is therefore still a waste of time. This is also akin to Toyota putting in quality checks along the assembly line, rather than only at the end of the manufacturing process, allowing them to catch the problems before more resources than necessary are wasted.

Ulusoy highlights this point in writing:

> In Agile, work is broken down into smaller increments, so that learning from each increment can be applied to the following increment. These learnings can be:
>
> - From the customer/user: Is this feature/product meeting their needs, what they wanted/expected, or is it delighting them?
> - From each other: Did the process during the last increment development work? Are there any changes we can make to make it better?

Missing these learning opportunities means achieving less value and developing products at a slower pace. Developing a culture oriented and even hungry for learning is the difference between those who get the most out of Agile practices and those who do not.

Capital One's Agile journey

Capital One has been on an Agile journey that has been particularly dramatic. The company's long-time CIO Rob Alexander pushed the IT organization to adopt Scrum in 2011. First Agile practices were piloted, but as Alexander's team went deeper, there was a recognition that the principles of Agile were universal:

> We found that Agile is broadly applicable as a way of working across technology, and it is not just in some kinds of narrowly confined spaces. Agile is, in many respects, a universal way of working with constant iteration, checking your progress against what the market demands or what your customers demand, and continually iterating on the product until you get to something that is powerful and winning in the market.[7]

Alexander and his team highlight a few key principles that emerged. They wanted more co-location of employees. They wanted an emphasis on employees over vendor partners. There is also a necessity of having IT and non-IT employees working in close collaboration. For every Agile Scrum team, there is a product owner who hails from a line of business product management team. He notes that the product manager role is critical, as they have the vision for what is being built and its place in the market. They should also have a perspective on the order and priority of the backlog of capabilities and features.

In his case, Alexander has chosen the Scaled Agile Framework (SAFe) due to the size and scale of the products and builds. The company has built its working spaces to reflect what works best for SAFe:

> We have technology teams co-located with the business teams so that we can achieve that tight collaboration that we need, and it has worked well. When we create spaces, it is generally open, but we create spaces where those teams can get together and do their Agile ceremonies effectively. Then we also can work across locations.[8]

Alexander believes that Agile practices reflect the way in which people work best. It is human nature to want to collaborate, they like to work efficiently and quickly, and they like to see their work deliver value. It changed the way in which work was done in a fundamental way:

> The teams that were engaged in our Agile pilots early on were energized by this way of working. They liked being together with their team, instead of setting up a meeting or sending emails to get decisions made. Instead, they were sitting around the table and asking each other what is the best way to solve this problem, or what is this requirement and how do I implement it. It did point our way to a new way of working at Capital One.[9]

Agile is a mindset rather than a destination. There is always room for improvement. Shamim Mohammad, the CIO and CTO of CarMax, noted:

> Agile doesn't solve any problems, but empowering teams does. As an example, instead of creating a roadmap, set certain business objectives and create a team for each one. That team will be solely responsible for that objective and key results [OKRs]. Allow lots of experimentation for each team, which leads to more innovation and better outcomes.

One can continue to hone these practices, and we see the addition of new forms of Agile sprouting up to reflect learnings that thought leaders put out into the world. Agile also works best in concert with other practices. DevOps is among those, which is the next topic we will cover.

Measuring outcomes and maturity

Just as the learning loop is a requirement for better adoption of Agile, measuring outcomes and one's maturity with practices is also important. As aforementioned, that which gets measured gets done.

From project management to product management

In most companies, project management has been a critical discipline. Project ideas are assembled either on a rolling basis, or through a solicitation exercise that happens once or multiple times per year. Those projects are prioritized based on criteria that are important to the company. These should include strategic linkage, cost–benefit analysis, risk, the interdependency between projects, and the like. As each new idea is identified, it is added to a queue, and when the project rises to the top of the list, it is kicked off

FIGURE 3.1 Agile development

Role(s) responsible

Tool(s)

Metrics

- Product owner
- Scrum master
- Development team

- Program and portfolio management software
- Road mapping software
- Issue and project tracking software
- User story mapping software

- Increased work delivered by the technology and digital team
- Increased velocity of work by the technology and digital team
- Increased the value of what the technology and digital team produces by the end users of those initiatives (i.e., projects or products)
- Increased quality of product delivered/decreased in number of defects
- Decreased time-to-market
- Improved delivery of value to customers

and carried through to completion. The team that is assigned works on that project until it concludes, and then it is implemented for the intended audience of that project, either inside or outside of the company.

There are aspects of this model that will continue, especially where initiatives have specifically defined targets and well-articulated timeframes (e.g., ERP consolidations to create efficiencies in the organization). Project managers will be judged based on their ability to meet the timeframes. Project managers tend to be aligned with functions of the company, or they might be pooled within the technology or digital organizations. As companies forge ahead with major digital transformations, impacting everything from their operations to the way in which they deliver products and services, a different model needs to complement the project management model.

Project management will continue to be important in activities in which a concrete set of goals are in place and where time, people, and expenses must be tracked in a systematic way. Product expert Mik Kersten, author of the book *Project to Product*, notes that project management is not going away. "Any new product launch; that is a project… Any large new initiative, any new partnership you set up or a region that you move into or expand or move away from; those are all projects," he said.

> [But] no project plan has ever had a technical debt metric on it. Projects are not for measuring that flow of value delivery. Projects are, as an example, for when a car manufacturer sets up a new plant and the car manufacturer plans how to create, evolve their supply chain, and so on.[10]

Kersten notes that this is not the path to measure or plan value delivery, however, because project management assumes a future that resembles today to too dramatic a degree. It does not allow for pivots and the need to adapt that reflect the realities of business. The product orientation allows those pivots to take place as one gains feedback from one's customers, for example.

An issue that arises with the project model is that each project tends to be disconnected from other ones. The learnings from one project may be documented, but the project team is disbanded, and new combinations of teams are brought together for the next project. There is friction in this process that means that the learnings from prior projects must be relearned in many cases, wasting time and dollars. This also inherently limits the incentive to leave the technical estate in better condition than when they found it, because they do not have to "live there forever." An earlier improvement to this was the assembly of projects into programs which are similar. That is an improvement, but in the digital age, it is insufficient.

Though the topic certainly goes further back, I first became aware of the notion of a product orientation within IT departments in 2015. As I spoke with CIOs, this was a topic that first trickled into conversations regarding their plans for transformation, and then it appeared more. Friends like Diana McKenzie (then the CIO of Workday and previously the CIO of Amgen), Trevor Schulze (then the CIO of Micron Technology), and Wayne Shurts (then the CTO of Sysco Corporation and previously the CIO of SUPERVALUE SuperValu and at Cadbury) mentioned this as a change they implemented on their teams. The idea was not presented as a replacement for the traditional project management orientation, but rather was an enhancement to it.

First, what is meant by a product orientation? My colleagues, Michael Bertha and Chris Boyd, define a product as:

> A capability brought to life through technology, business process, and customer experience that creates a continuous value stream. Examples of products are eCommerce, supply chain, or HR. An operating model defines how an organization positions its people, process, and technology to deliver value to both [employees] and customers.[11]

Traditional technology or digital organizations tend to have an orientation toward disciplines like application development, infrastructure, quality assurance, and the like. A product-oriented operating model takes that model and modifies it. Like so many other aspects of this book, it suggests greater collaboration between the technology and digital division and the other divisions of the company. They must develop product strategies, road-maps, and prioritize activities in unison. These should include thoughts on how the product will evolve, how it will be shaped by use of the product (whether inside the company or by the company's customers), and the like.

Although there are project-centric organizations that have gotten past the order-taking conundrum of the IT departments of yore, development of the project list can seem like a to-do list given to IT by the different divisions of the company. The product operating model facilitates a greater degree of collaboration and true partnership. "The fundamental paradigm shift for us was that the level of uncertainty had changed when there was no longer one single imperative," Lenovo's CIO Arthur Hu said, referring to an ERP project. "When we took that away, it was a totally different world and traditional waterfall didn't make sense anymore. Until we as an organization realized that, the business teams and my teams struggled."[12] Product-based organizations rely on continuous customer engagement to remove guess-work from the prioritization process, which often leads to better business outcomes and increased agility.

Bertha and Boyd identify four behavioral changes targeted by a product orientation:

- Work is value driven, not plan driven.
- Teams are dedicated and longstanding, not temporary or part-time.
- Customer feedback is gathered at every sprint, not just at the end of a project.
- Teams are perpetually funded, not on a project-by-project basis.

Let's dive into each of those.

Work is value driven, not plan driven

The traditional way of project planning assumes static deliverables and timeframes that often are grossly over- or (more likely) underestimated. As a result the estimation exercises that the project and portfolio management exercises have traditionally been based on are flawed and do not give an accurate picture of the time and human and financial resources necessary to deliver; and moreover, the historic norm of focusing on on-time and on-budget delivery do not have adequate focus on value contribution.

Former Magellan Health CIO and CTO, Srini Koushik said, "Great companies that have built a product orientation start with desirability and leverage design thinking to have empathy-based conversations to get to the core of problems."[13]

Teams are dedicated and long-standing, not temporary or part-time

The product-centric operating model is based on dedicated teams that own and work on a product, end to end, from inception to retirement of that product. This includes discovery, delivery, testing, maintenance, and support. With fewer changes of resources and deeper expertise in a product area, the team can make a bigger impact in driving value through the product. They develop expertise that project teams would not have the time or the opportunity to develop given the transient nature of traditional projects. Furthermore, project teams require a ramp-up period on most projects, and, in the grand scheme of things, that can mean time wasted. This can get in the way of establishing momentum in the earliest phases of a project.

Customer feedback is gathered at every sprint, not just at the end of a project

Engaging with the user of the product offers a critical feedback loop that can lead to breakthroughs. Validating value and even having stakeholders from across the company participate in standup meetings on a regular if not a daily basis will offer a faster path to ongoing product success.

Atticus Tysen, Chief Information Security Officer, Chief Fraud Prevention Officer, and Chief Information Officer of Intuit, was one of the earliest product proponents in the IT world as he became Intuit's CIO in 2013 after spending time as the director of product management for the QuickBooks team six years prior. He believes in the sanctity of getting to know customers to a degree that most CIOs do not and has led the IT team to organize around delivering for customers. "You have to have customers if you're going to have a product organization," Tysen said. "Product managers in a lot of ways are relationship managers."[14]

Teams are perpetually funded, not on a project-by-project basis

It is necessary to change the traditional budgeting and funding model of IT and digital divisions. Traditionally, the IT department develops a list of projects to undertake into portfolios aligned with the divisions of the company, for instance. These are funded based upon the aggregate budget proposed, and perhaps top-down estimate of funds to allocate to the technology or digital division of the company. Bertha and Boyd point out that:

> Cost estimates often occur before the scope of the project is truly evaluated and understood, and any variations in the plan are subject to an arduous change control process. What's more, funding for these projects usually is locked in for the fiscal year, regardless of shifting enterprise priorities or changing market dynamics.[15]

Product operating models work best with perpetual funding, which is, admittedly, a big change for some companies. Among the advantages of the model, however, is that it provides a stable funding source for products, and where business dynamics change, funds can be reallocated nimbly to other areas.

Another outcome of the product-centric model is that those who are most familiar with products will have an incentive to retire old aspects of the technology, reducing technical debt and risk in the process. The traditional project model often does not provide the right incentive to retire old technology, as it is mostly centered around delivering a discrete project. As a result, many companies are good at delivering the new, but are not as good at retiring the old. If you own a product, however, there is a better chance that evaluating how new functions, features, and technologies render others redundant will lead to actual retirement of the older, redundant technology.

If you are compelled to embark on a product-oriented operating model, how and where should you begin? Again, Bertha and Boyd offer solid steps:

- Identify targeted metrics and establish a baseline.
- Define your products using a value chain approach.
- Define the roles/responsibilities for each product team.
- Define shared services to create scale.[16]

Identify targeted metrics and establish a baseline

It is important to assess business impact to evaluate the effectiveness of the shift to product-centric IT. At the organization level, these should include things such as:

- net promoter score (NPS) to assess business satisfaction with the model and its value
- product team throughput to assess speed to market
- the number of critical defects per product to assess quality

Business impact metrics may also be defined for each product in your organization. A product team responsible for AI-enabled chat bots, for example, may be inclined to track the number of customer inquiries that are resolved without human intervention. If this product team was perpetually funded and granted the autonomy to work on what is perceived to be the highest value within their budget, as opposed to seeking approval for each small enhancement, you might see this metric improve significantly in the product model. Business impact metrics, whether at the organization or product level, should be measured at the beginning of your transformation, and at frequent intervals to assess progress and to provide a means of communicating that progress to the rest of the team. During the transition from project to product, it is also prudent to track metrics that speak to how well your organization is adopting the targeted behavioral changes. One global technology client of mine chose to track the number of products that developed proactive strategic roadmaps to ensure that teams were proactively identifying and prioritizing market trends instead of assuming the role of an order-taker. Another client in the industrial automation sector surveyed product teams quarterly to understand how frequently product owners met with their business counterparts to review and update their product roadmaps.

Defining products

In order to define products, it is best to understand the business capabilities of the company. These include sales, marketing, supply chain, human resources, finance, and product development. These are product groups, sometimes referred to as level one. For most large and complex organizations, it is appropriate to define level two capabilities. For instance, the sales area capabilities might include discovery, lead to cash, and customer success, which includes activation, adoption, expansion, and renewals. These are solid choices for product areas as these processes involve different business stakeholders, targeted key performance indicators, and technology components.

Michael Bertha and Chris Boyd suggest the following guiding principles for product definition:

- Establish clear ownership: The top priority should be to carve out product teams in a way that allows them to truly own and feel empowered to make the changes necessary to mature their product.

- Align with architecture: As much as possible, product teams should be able to own their architectural roadmaps and not have significant dependencies on other teams.

- Build teams around similar process and technology: If work is unique and utilizes different data, processes, and technology, create another team.

- Keep it small: A product team should aim have no more than ten people.

- Be strategic: Ensure your product teams cover the various business stakeholders and strategic goals.

- Continuously evolve: Strategic goals and business priorities shift often, leading to shifts in the product team landscape. Assign someone in your organization to review product team composition on a regular basis to assess the need to develop new products, modify existing products, or sunset products that no longer align with strategic goals.[17]

Clay Johnson, the chief digital and technology officer of Yum! Brands and former CIO at Walmart, suggests looking at things from the customer's perspective. "You look at the customer journey, how they shop, how they

FIGURE 3.2 Examples of product groups and shared services

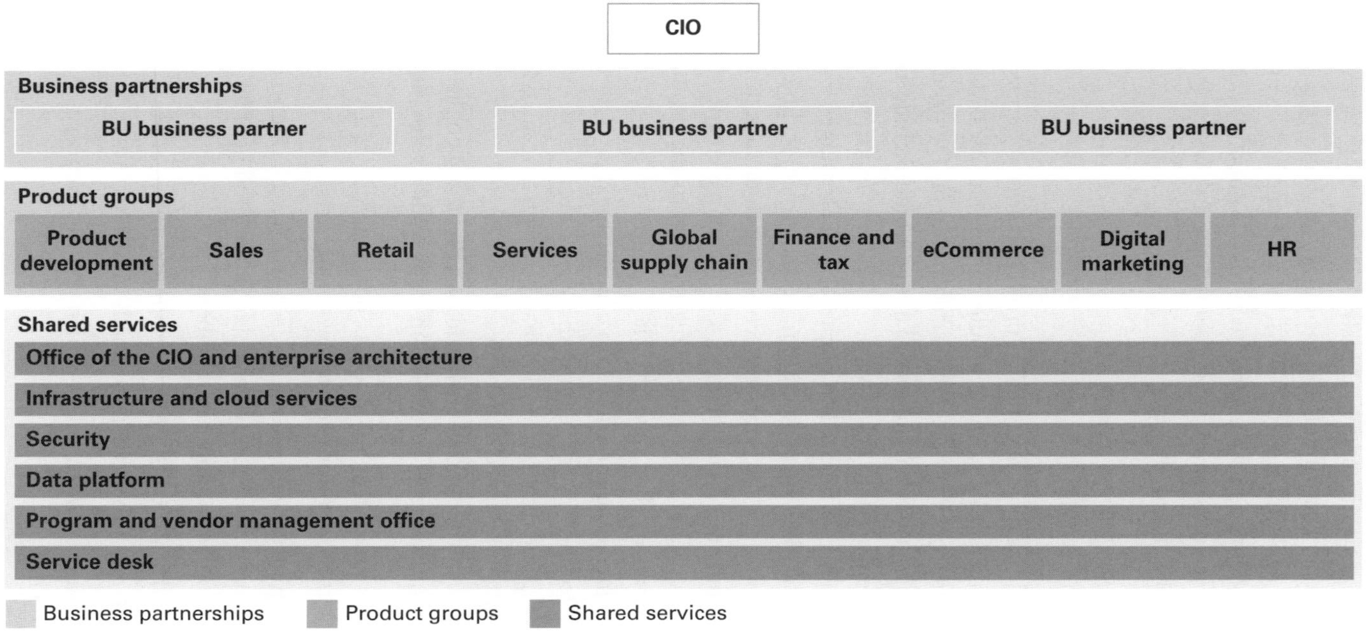

CIO

Business partnerships

BU business partner	BU business partner	BU business partner

Product groups

Product development	Sales	Retail	Services	Global supply chain	Finance and tax	eCommerce	Digital marketing	HR

Shared services

Office of the CIO and enterprise architecture

Infrastructure and cloud services

Security

Data platform

Program and vendor management office

Service desk

Business partnerships � Product groups ▒ Shared services come in and... order a pizza." The customer experience or marketing teams at many organizations have already decomposed the customer journey into succinct steps, each involving various front stage (e.g., websites, portals, apps) and back stage (e.g., CRM, pricing engine) technologies; adopting previously defined business architectures is a good idea to help with change management, but should not be blindly pursued at the expense of the guiding principles noted above.

Product-centric roles

Unlike traditional project teams, product teams are cross-functional, drawing upon diverse skills. These should include technical skills but should also include other business disciplines depending on the product area. The lead to cash product within sales noted above would include sales subject-matter experts to ensure maximum value. The most important role is the product owner, sometimes referred to as the product manager. They should possess business skills like strategy and financial acumen, technical skills that allow them to define the appropriate technical architecture, leadership skills that foster confident decision-making, and the management of a diverse array of stakeholders. They drive the strategy related to the product, and they oversee execution of that strategy. They should be aware of external market dynamics including the competitive landscape. For traditional, operational-oriented technology or digital divisions, these may be new disciplines. Training will be required, or this may be a sign that an external hire with the appropriate experience may be necessary.

Under the product owner should be a blend of people who may be deeper in business, technical, or leadership skills. Other roles include:

- business analyst, who conducts detailed data and process analysis, and who acts as a junior product owner of sorts
- Scrum master, who drives Agile ceremonies, which help to disseminate information on a timely basis, bring common goal and vision, and share team progress to all team members
- technical lead, who creates a solution architecture for the product and orchestrates other technical details and activities
- the engineering/QA team, which ensures delivery of the product with high quality

Define shared services

If you think of the products as vertical bands, there are horizontal bands that cut across the products, which are shared services (Figure 3.1). Bertha and Boyd note, "Just like products, these specialized groups endeavor to mature and develop new capabilities and empower their customers (in this case the product teams themselves)."[18]

These shared services often include:

- enterprise architecture
- infrastructure and cloud
- security
- DevOps
- customer experience/user experience
- data and analytics
- integration (APIs, microservices)
- program management
- vendor management
- IT operations and support
- the office of the CIO

Each of the shared services should publish a service catalog defining processes and offerings. Wherever possible, self-service should be a default. Shared services can become temporary parts of product teams where there is an appropriate demand for a time.

Mik Kersten proposes another methodology he refers to as the flow framework:

1 *Define your product (internal, external, platform?).*

2 *For each product value stream, instead of tracking how many issues were closed, track each of* **the flow metrics:**

   a. Flow velocity

      i. *Why is productivity slowing as more people are hired? One of the most common issues. Software architectures are often not aligned to product value streams (unlike Amazon, BMW, Tech Giants).*

   b. Flow efficiency

      i. *Continuously hiring people can actually create upstream bottle necks. Need to evaluate entire value stream, not just segments of it.*

c. Flow time

    i. *Do you need more workers to be faster? Not necessarily. The work that workers do ends up being a small percentage of the whole process. Instead of optimizing that small percentage, it's better to optimize upstream or downstream processes that create the unresolved bottlenecks that have a bigger impact flow time.*

d. Flow load

    i. *How many projects is your team involved with? Mik suggested that a team should only be assigned to one project at once, as multiple project increases flow load and tanks productivity.*

3 *Correlate these flows to business results:*

a. Value *(revenue, active users) = flow velocity*

b. Cost *(cost per value stream, all the people involved in that value stream, hosting cost, allows you to think about product-lifecycle profitability) = flow efficiency*

c. Quality *= flow time*

d. Happiness *(how happy all of the people in the product value stream are can indicate architectural problem) = flow load*[19]

When to use project management

Not every initiative in the technology or digital division is likely to be a product. Traditional project management may be necessary. A project is a temporary set of activities with a clear definition of what needs to be delivered and by when. This stands in contrast with a product, which tends not to have a clear definition of what must be delivered. A customer or user has needs, and those needs evolve as time passes. Products must evolve with those needs. Customers or users expect needs to be met in the near term not by some far-off date. Product management is a continuous process of delivering new features while improving a product over time. This is the reason why teams are assigned to products and stick with them over time, whereas project teams are connected with a project only until it is delivered and then they are reassigned to a new project, often with a different area of focus. This topic lends itself to other "false starts" that organizations encounter as they begin the shift towards product orientation.

FIGURE 3.3 Project/product management

Role(s) responsible

- Head of IT strategy and/or IT transformation to set strategy for building a product orientation in IT, e.g., analyzing value chain or customer journey to determine how IT's purview will be decomposed into products
- Product owner to drive key product management activities for each product, e.g., define product roadmap and make key decisions around product feature prioritization
- Engineering/QA team to deliver high-quality working products that drive targeted outcomes on the product roadmap

Tool(s)

- Prototyping/road mapping tools
- Task management tools to manage/prioritize backlogs and support Agile execution
- Data analysis tools to aggregate and contextualize user data to drive continuous feedback loops and make data-driven decisions
- Experimentation platform to conduct randomized control studies (e.g., A/B testing)
- DevOps tool chain to automate integration, testing, and infrastructure needed to accelerate delivery, assure quality and security, and scale as needed
- Code management and code quality tools
- API/service catalog tool to promote reusability of code and drive rapid application development

Metrics

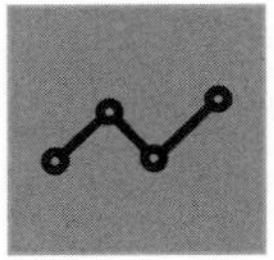

- Increased NPS related to product management inside and outside of technology and digital division
- Increased product team throughput
- Increased deployment frequency
- Decreased number of critical defects per product
- Increased levels of testing and deployment automation
- Increased level of API service reusability
- Product-specific metrics related to key business processes that are improved by operating IT with a product orientation (e.g., opportunity to quote conversation rate in an eCommerce product)
- Increased return on investment for product features

Bertha and Boyd share the following cautionary tales from their experience in the field:

- Assuming everything must be product-based:
  - o There are still examples when traditional, project-based teams and waterfall methods may be appropriate. They mention large-scale ERP implementations as an example.
- Confusing product-based IT with Agile:
  - o Executing two-week sprints does not make your organization product-based. The spirit of the latter is continuous engagement with customers, using Agile to pivot quickly.
- Lacking product management muscles in IT:
  - o It is critical that product managers be cognizant of the competitive landscape and market forces. These are typically new skills for a technology and digital organization, but it is essential to do product management right.
- Not changing the lens on business conversations:
  - o Technology and digital leaders have historically been criticized for speaking an overly technical language. Speaking in terms that the rest of the enterprise understand is key to driving effective product management, gaining the trust and buy-in of the rest of the organization. The focus needs to be on feasibility, viability, and desirability.[20]

DevOps

A problem that early practitioners of Agile development found was that what it offered in speed it sometimes lacked in reliability. Some viewed Agile as an excuse not to document progress appropriately or to take shortcuts. At times, these actions led to reliability, stability, and even security issues. To some it seemed as though you could have speed, or you could have reliability. You could not have both.

Gene Kim is a student of high-performing teams. In 1999, while he was the chief technology officer of TripWire, a software company he cofounded that provided software security and compliance solutions, he began to note his observations of the high-performing teams. One conclusion he drew was that these organizations often had IT operations, security, audit, management, and governance working together to solve common business objectives. This was the beginning of a journey that would lead him to become a big name in the burgeoning field of DevOps.

DevOps is a set of practices that combine software development (the Dev) and information technology operations (the Ops). Says Kim, "What DevOps really represents to me are the cultural norms and the technical practices that enable us to finally get both."[21] DevOps and Agile are opposite sides of the same coin, in many ways. Agile closes a communications gap between users and developers, and DevOps closes a gap between developers and IT operations and infrastructure.

At a time when companies need to be responsive to market dynamics and customer demands, adopting DevOps principles—such as an emphasis on automation, monitoring, and continuous integration/delivery of new code—allows businesses to achieve faster development cycles and more frequent, reliable releases.

Chandra Dhandapani, the chief administrative officer of CBRE, the $24 billion revenue commercial real estate services and investment firm, has led digital transformations at three different organizations. In an interview I did with her, she noted that when she joined CBRE, "This was my third time through this transformation process, so I knew the importance of starting with DevOps. We made certain we had a DevOps center of excellence to train teams."[22] The center of excellence would be a steady resource where teams can get training and serve as a forum to share personal learnings around the transformation. The DevOps center of excellence is a perfect example of building an internal community that increases cross-team learnings and collaborations, while also showing teams that the organization cares and is there to support them through the transformation. Many technology and digital leaders who I have spoken with take a similar view on its importance.

Naresh Shanker, the chief technology officer of Xerox, notes that DevOps requires not just a new set of practices, but also a different mindset:

[DevOps] makes sure that you can deploy the right solutions rapidly; so rapidly, you can push 10, 20, 30, 40, 50 changes into the environment every day, which you cannot do in the monolith environment [with an antiquated mindset].
Because in a monolith environment, it takes weeks and months of planning, and heaven forbid you make a change that brings the whole system down.

Steve Randich is the chief information officer of the Financial Industry Regulatory Authority, Inc. (FINRA), a private corporation that acts as a self-regulatory organization to the financial services industry. He points out that the mindset is difficult for some executives and their teams to incorporate:

> When I talk to people about the cloud journey, they nod their heads [that] they get the DevOps thing, but they don't. It has to be a crusade, an internal crusade towards completely changing the way you look at your IT process. It's easier said than done.

Let's cover a bit about how that crusade can be enabled.

Making the case for DevOps

DevOps has become such a key weapon in the arsenals of technology and digital executives that it is not hyperbolic to say that this is a change you must undertake in order to ensure your company is nimble. This is common practice among digital-native companies, and their nimbleness as a result of tearing down these traditional silos, or more accurately not allowing the silos to be built in the first place, gives them a tremendous advantage. You must emulate this change and make a steadfast commitment to it. Moreover, customer expectations are such that not being able to address their needs, fix issues that occur, and make feature improvements rapidly over time puts your relationship with customers at risk.

The starting point on this journey is to understand what it takes to deploy your products to the market, end-to-end. This requires that you conduct a value-stream mapping exercise to determine what it takes to get from idea to intended value (whether revenue for a customer-facing product, or other value for internally focused initiatives). This should highlight aspects of the process that can be modified to make them more streamlined. This helps identify where value can be created through the application of automation to formerly manual processes.

The steps to DevOps success

The journey to DevOps typically starts as teams get better at Agile software development. Prior to Agile, waterfall development—in which code is written over a period of weeks or months and then is tested at the end of the development cycle—did not force infrastructure or operations teams to work with the same urgency the market demands now. As Agile practices become more mature, continuous integration (CI) becomes paramount. Code is tested iteratively throughout the development cycle, and it is compiled into usable code continuously—further increasing the speed and reliability of software development.

The next step is continuous delivery (CD). The combination of continuous integration and continuous delivery is referred to as CI/CD. Continuous delivery includes additional automation and testing and minimizes human intervention between code creation and code deployment. The code base is always ready to deploy. By introducing automation into the stages of application development, the process becomes more efficient and more effective. Another "CD" is continuous deployment, which refers to automatically releasing a developer's changes from the repository to production, making it useable by the user of the software. Thus, continuous integration encompasses the build, test, and merge steps of development. Continuous delivery automatically releases code to a repository, and continuous deployment automatically deploys code to production.

While it might be easy to cover the general ideas of CI/CD in a paragraph or two, it is important to recognize the hard work required on the ground to make this concept a reality. You will need experts to guide your teams through tasks such as the creation of Jenkins Pipelines (a suite of plugins which supports implementing and integrating continuous delivery pipelines), tying various types of security testing into said pipelines, and determining how your pipelines might vary across different products with different technology stacks. Depending on the breadth of your application ecosystem, this can demand a significant amount of bandwidth.

There are a number of areas that must be considered when adopting DevOps and building momentum, but some of the most important include:

- culture
- roles
- organizational structure
- trust and engagement
- tools

CULTURE

Like the first sub-theme under the people theme, DevOps begins with culture. As with Agile, this represents a rather significant change for a lot of companies. Like the shift to a product mindset, which many believe is intrinsically linked to DevOps, it suggests a deep rethink of organizational silos. In the case of DevOps, the primary silos are within the technology or digital division.

Siloed teams have a tendency to think the same way and resist change due to their common skillsets, purviews, language, and training. By definition, DevOps blurs these lines, and pushes the two worlds to collide. It will likely lead to healthy discussion and disagreement. How healthy will be based upon culture, and whether old norms are able to change. A means of fostering this cultural change is to evaluate teams rather than individuals. If one knows that success will be dependent on others collaborating well, and driving to value together will be an outcome.

It is important to create "a culture of continual learning and experimentation using the notions of high trust culture," says Gene Kim. "The most competitive organizations are ones that can learn, those who can turn local improvement into global solutions."[23]

ROLES

As with any new discipline, training up or acquiring expertise is a requirement. It is typically best to bring in outside experts to consult or train and/ or hire a new experienced leader of the new discipline. The new leader can both hire others who they know (a talent magnet of sorts) and oversee the training of others. That is a broad remit, I recognize, so filling the training needs may be best suited to a consultant for hire. Often what is most successful in jumpstarting DevOps is to do a small end-to-end "tracer bullet" project, where a small team sees what it takes to deploy a lightweight feature all the way into production for a given application. Taking this approach will provide insights into bottlenecks and technology/tool challenges before pursuing changes more broadly. An internal team or a consultant can use the insights from this effort to better target their approach and automation efforts.

Therefore, in the short term, it is likely necessary to take a hybrid approach when building the DevOps talent.

DevOps empowers developers to deliver high-quality code to end-users. It unlocks the ability for engineers to quickly react and solve customer and market problems. The roles necessary to bring DevOps to life include:

- The DevOps evangelist:
  - This is the leader of the DevOps team and the processes that guide DevOps. The DevOps evangelist touts the benefits of DevOps, plots a

path toward transitioning to DevOps, draws in key people from the development and operational teams, and helps set the training necessary to get people where they need to be. Needless to say, if possible, hire someone into this role with experience, as it is best if the evangelist has been to the promised land and can shepherd the converted there.

- The release manager:
  - o This role directs the management and coordination of the product from development through production. They also coordinate the integration of development, testing, and deployment to aid in the conversion to continuous delivery.

- The automation architect:
  - o This role is responsible for analyzing, designing, and implementing strategies for continuous deployment. They must identify the right processes and tools to build an appropriate automated pipeline for DevOps. At its core, DevOps is automation. As more automation is introduced, high-quality code should be easier to introduce more rapidly with each new sprint. This is akin to setting the rails down so that trains can travel smoothly from place to place.

- The software development engineer in test (SDET):
  - o This role combines two roles that some keep separate. This is the builder of the code, but they also are responsible for unit testing, deployment, and ongoing monitoring of the code. Their goal should be to automate as much of the testing process as possible for both quality and efficiency. Manual testing is not nimble enough to achieve the value intended. SDETs replace traditional quality assurance (QA) to a great extent, as QA is drawn out of the development process under the guidance of this role.

- The experience assurance professional:
  - o The XA professional, as they are often known, ensures that user experience is kept in mind and baked into the process as early as possible. They must do that while ensuring that the product has all the planned features in place according to specifications.

- The security and compliance engineer:
  - o Just as quality assurance is drawn earlier into the process with DevOps along with user experience, so too is security. This is increasingly important given the increased risk of security issues. These engineers

must work hand-in-glove with developers, offering recommendations through the process to ensure security and compliance are delivered.

- The utility player:
  - Like a great utility player in sports who can play multiple positions well, this utility player will be asked to be involved in multiple facets of the DevOps process. This will include development platforms, networks, servers, resource management, security, database management, and support.

ORGANIZATIONAL STRUCTURE

Given the changes implied by the roles defined in the prior section, the ability to bring development and operations together effectively can be impeded by the organization structure itself. Natural silos created through reporting structure, co-location, or arbitrarily drawn lines in process make things like accountability and ownership nebulous and hard to manage.

To counter this, technology and digital leaders must define a new topology that drives the change sought through DevOps. A question to ask is how well the development and operations parts of the technology and digital division work together. In organizations where development and operations do not work well together, developing a new center of excellence for DevOps is best. This might draw in forward-thinking members of each team into a separate team together with new recruits experienced with DevOps. In some companies, even without a commitment to DevOps, there has been a recognition of the need for better coordination and collaboration, and it has fostered solid partnership between these traditionally siloed parts of the division. In those cases, the transition may be a bit easier.

TRUST AND ENGAGEMENT

As with the example from General Stanley McChrystal, DevOps will not succeed in a command and control culture. Teams who work on the code must be given autonomy to make changes. The strategy should be set at the top, communicated through the organization, and it must be understood by the teams doing the coding, but they should be trusted to do the right things given the pace of the work that they are undertaking and the need for continuous integration, delivery, and deployment.

FIGURE 3.4 DevOps

Role(s) responsible

- DevOps evangelist
- Development leader(s)

Tool(s)

- Tools that promote automation at each stage of the development and delivery process:
  - development
  - build
  - QA/testing
  - packaging
  - security
  - deployment
  - monitoring
  - analytics
- A source control to track changes
- Tools for configuration management
- Tools that integrate with your Agile development tools

Metrics

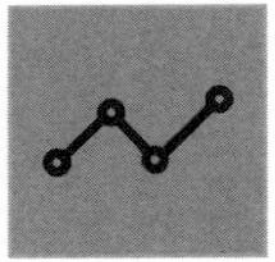

- Decreased time to deploy projects/products/initiatives
- Increased frequency of deployment of projects/products/initiatives
- Decreased lead time
- % test automation
- Decreased code defect rates
- Increased availability
- Improved application performance
- Improved mean time to detection
- Improved mean time to recovery
- Increased percentage of team coding vs. administrative/management activities

Change management

An underlying theme of this entire book is the need to be comfortable with change and transformation. This is contrary to human nature. Many of us may say that we crave the new, but the truth is that most of us seek the comfort of the familiar. Replicate that across a company, and it means that change is often uncomfortable and therefore difficult. In fact, there are often members of the organization who will surreptitiously oppose or even work against the change. They might even say that they will continue to do things the "old way" ("the way we have always done things"), knowing that the person responsible for the change will be let go because the change will be unsuccessful. This is often why companies that are founder-led have the easiest path to change. In this scenario, no one can say that they will wait out a change in leadership in order to avoid the change.

It is critical to institutionalize change management because change will be the only constant in business for the foreseeable future. Every new process, technology, product, or service requires change and the deliberate management of that change. Change management helps ensure that they are adopted effectively and that the value intended is realized. In other words, it is not too much to say that if you are not preparing your company for change, if you are not putting processes in place to foster change, and if you are not hiring and training people to be change agents, the future of your company will be compromised.

I mentioned Ben Fried, Google's long-time CIO, earlier in the book and how that company has kept its innovative edge despite becoming a behemoth. Realizing that technology has never moved as quickly as it does today, Google maintains its competitive edge by making change a core competency. Their concern with outdated practices is the reason for their company-wide "bureaucracy buster days." On these days, employees identify areas where bureaucracy has seeped into the company, note them, and projects are devised to destroy them. Fried said:

> IT sits in middle of some hard realities. On the one hand, people are creatures of habit. On the other hand, computing is arguably the fastest moving discipline in the history of the enterprise. Realizing the advantages that come from computing's rate of innovation means we have to force people out of their technology habits.

He notes that this will not happen without a push because of the strength of inertia. He said, "Plan on making changes every year, and on building an end-to-end technology team that flourishes in change."[24]

Most companies have some aspects of change management in their organizations, but often these efforts start too late or are haphazard in their implementation, which can lead to frustration among colleagues and customers as well as outcomes with higher cost and/or risk. Sometimes, change management may be viewed as a "soft" topic that is difficult to understand and to harness. Effective change management must start as soon as an idea moves to the planning phase. Digital transformation, for example, requires a great deal of change, and 70 percent of digital transformation efforts do not fulfill the promises made.[25] Therefore, now more than ever, effective change practices are required.

Harvard Business School Professor John Kotter is considered by many, including myself, as the leading authority on change. He notes that most major change initiatives do not produce the intended results, often due to a lack of understanding that transformation is a process rather than an event. Kotter notes that most proceed with shortcuts and some declare victory too soon. He insists that shortcuts never lead to the intended success. This, in turn, leads to a loss of momentum that could scupper the transformation. Kotter notes that following the eight steps that he articulates allows the organization to "flex with tectonic shifts in competitors, markets, and technologies—leaving rivals far behind." The following are the eights steps:[26]

1 Create urgency.
2 Form a powerful coalition.
3 Create a vision for change.
4 Communicate the vision.
5 Empower action.
6 Create quick wins.
7 Build on the change.
8 Make change "stick."

One's goal should be to create change management practices and organizational capabilities that not only help ensure the success of an individual change initiative or a portfolio of transformational efforts, but also create the foundation for any future change efforts. As such each change management process should be viewed as helping along and ensuring that change

FIGURE 3.5 Five moments of truth associated with Kotter's eight steps to change management[27]

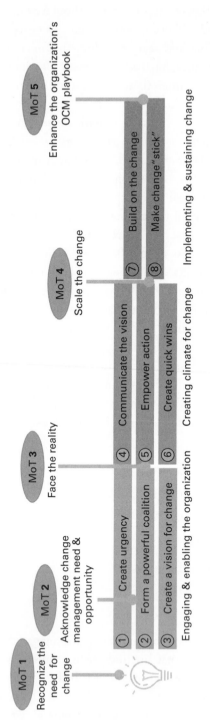

succeeds as much as it is an opportunity to enhance an organization's ability to change, evolve, and continuously improve.

My colleague Alex Kraus has articulated five moments of truth (see Figure 3.5) in change management that work in concert with Kotter's eight steps. These highlight important opportunities—sometimes ignored or missed—that are complements to the framework to further help bring this to life and ultimately ensure the success of whatever the objective and focus of the change efforts may be.

Step 1 (Moment of Truth 1): Recognize change

Not every initiative requires change. First, determine if an initiative qualifies for change management. Those activities that are natural extensions of current practices probably do not qualify. Those that represent something fundamentally new probably do. The criteria used will vary by company, but Kraus notes that organizational culture generally and change-readiness more specifically will be drivers of determining what qualifies. He also notes that it is important to understand the urgency demonstrated through each business case to further qualify when the change should be pushed.[28]

Step 2 (Moment of Truth 2): Determine change management needs/plan for change

Next, it is important to determine the outcomes anticipated for the changes that will be required. Think of this as the risk/return calculus of the changes. There must be an explicit plan in place. Kraus warns against taking short-cuts, which may hide the downstream risks and costs which would have made the change untenable if it had been assessed accurately in the first place.

The change efforts will be more successful if relevant stakeholders understand the change efforts and buy into them. To do so, Kraus recommends:

- Agree on the problem that is being solved.
- Agree on objectives and success measures.
- Agree on a scalable framework and operating model.
- Develop change management plans:
  - Assess scope of change and resources needed to implement effective change management.

   o Include communication plan/strategy.

-    Assemble task force and executive team.[29]

If you are going to use outside experts to facilitate change management efforts, get them in early. If they are brought in too late, you run the risk that they will make appropriate suggestions that will call into question the efforts already undertaken, leading to wasted effort, the need to reboot, and frustrated stakeholders whose steadfast support you need.

Find change agents from across the organization. Charlie Feld notes that even in an organization with thousands of people, it takes tens rather than hundreds of people to make change happen. As a call-back to Chapter 2, as you assess your staff, identify those people who are change agents. Are they charismatic, honest, well networked, and well respected across the organization? These are the sorts of people who can be difference-makers in change efforts.

Kraus's final recommendation relative to this step is for leaders to embrace the role of clearing obstacles in the way of change. These may be bureaucracy, or it may be the anti-change agents hiding in the shadows. Communicating the rationale for change effectively and forcefully helping it along during the hiccups that will inevitably occur is the role of the leader.

Step 3 (Moment of Truth 3): Create a favorable context for change management

In the transition between Kotter's "Create a Vision for Change" step and the "Communicate the Vision" step, Kraus believes it is important to assess not only those who will be your change agents, but also those who you predict will be your critics or blockers. Include representatives from each group in the visioning exercise to understand firsthand the issues to be addressed and to have a collective effort to address any perceived cynicism or pessimism.

He goes on to note that there is a tendency to communicate the full change plan in a town hall meeting, say, and to think of the communications as complete. This is insufficient. The communications plan should include regular updates and progress reports, and they should go through a variety of channels, including in person, through video conferences, via recorded video, and the like. Communicate through the channels that are likely to reach all relevant constituents.

Step 4 (Moment of Truth 4): Scale change

Here is where Agile and change management coincide, according to Kraus. Break down the change into component parts and enact the change using iterative steps. Pursue quick wins to gain momentum, and identify which of the quick wins might be candidates to scale more broadly.

Step 5 (Moment of Truth 5): Constantly improve/enhance the change management playbook

Like all processes, your change management process should not be static. As you learn what works and what doesn't, lean toward the former and away from the latter. Evolve the process so that it becomes more efficient and more successful. This is the way to become nimble in your change management process.

Kraus also notes that it is one thing to enact the change, and it is another to make it stick. The combination of knowledge-sharing, ongoing training, and effective communication will ensure the team understands the change. It is especially important to highlight the success stories of the change. Nothing creates momentum for change efforts like proving the success of them. As always, that which gets measured gets done, so measure progress, and communicate that progress. After the change initiative has been completed, knowledge-sharing and communication should continue. The need for it will fade as the change becomes part of the organizational culture.

While Kotter's change methodology is considered tried and true, it is important to note that there are other models that might be a better fit for your organization. Kotter's eight steps are easy to incorporate and follow because it is a step-by-step model, but it is important to note that no one step can be skipped to reach the next step.

Change management leaders should be involved at the outset to help ensure it is baked into the entire change initiative. Companies will need to adopt more Agile approaches to change. Rather than a waterfall-style, command-and-control model that might view change as a one-off effort, teams will need to embrace rapid iteration, taking a series of smaller steps to implement the change.

It is important not to bite off more than you can chew. Beginning with too ornate a process can defeat the process and lead to the same issues that Kotter noted with transformations not achieving their aims. If your organization is not familiar with or well versed in Agile practices, do not adopt it whole hog and expect things to work. Start small and scale up.

Establishing clear metrics is key to understanding the success of the change effort. New processes may need to be introduced to make this happen (i.e., dashboards, data-driven decision-making, etc.). Change management success measures are really the measures and metrics for whatever the change initiative is supposed to accomplish (business outcomes)—in other words, Agile transformation that has the intended outcome of faster time to market. That metric becomes a measurement for change management as well as the larger change initiative.

What change management success looks like

Successful change management can ultimately be measured by the success of the change effort it supports. This ties change management directly to intended business outcomes or metrics. Successful change management can also be measured by the efficiency with which it is deployed. For instance, you might ask, how much friction did change management introduce into the process? Are there ways to streamline or reduce friction? How does change management help create a runway for change initiatives to move forward?

A mature change management capability does not go away when a particular change effort ends. Rather, teams take lessons from each initiative and build that into their change management playbooks. These learnings allow companies to constantly improve/iterate upon their capabilities.

Service desk

As technology becomes more complex, as it becomes woven more firmly into the fabric of every company, employee, and customer of the company, and as businesses grow and become more geographically distributed, issues with technology are both more likely to arise, and they may have more profound issues when they do. Having a solid method of addressing those issues in a timely fashion becomes that much more important. A well-thought-out service desk function becomes that much more important.

The service desk should provide a single point of contact for issues to be brought to light and to be addressed. The mechanism for addressing these may be quite different. There should be self-help tools, optimally aided with

FIGURE 3.6 Change management

Role(s) responsible

- CIO/CDO, technology and digital leadership team, and (where applicable) change management lead
- Anyone with people, team, or organizational responsibilities
- Team members (affected by change and/or executing change)
- Stakeholders (anyone with a direct or indirect stake/interest in the change)
- Change agents or change facilitators (most likely certain team members, possibly supported by change leaders or external facilitators)

Tool(s)

- Change management flowchart, workflow, and process, mapping tools
- Project and product management tools
- Agile and general collaboration tools

Metrics

- Improved change-readiness assessment results
- Increased adoption of new products, features, projects, and initiatives
- Improved employee/customer satisfaction scores (e.g., net promoter score)
- Improved customer/employee engagement scores (e.g., frequency of usage, views, clicks, downloads)
- Improved communication effectiveness
- Increased training and learning participation and take-rates
- Increased positive survey results regarding technology and digital team's comfort with change initiatives

advanced search capabilities leveraging artificial intelligence to tie requests and questions to a bank of knowledge on the topic with points of resolution that are voted up or down based upon the efficacy of the suggestions provided.

There should also be multiple means of logging issues to be addressed by people who staff the service desk. These should include digital (email, web portal, etc.), phone, and in person. The issues that are raised should be logged into a service management tool. This aids tracking, ties the issue with points of resolution, and can help determine trend information. For instance, if there is a spike in issues related to a certain software product, this is an indication that there is a bigger issue that needs to be addressed.

When a bigger issue is identified such as a security issue, an escalation process needs to be in place to ensure that communications can go broad rapidly to alert others, potentially the entire company, to the issue along with remediation steps.

The service desk is also invaluable when implementing a new service or product for employee use. Any new product is bound to lead to a variety of questions. Training and change management activities should anticipate some of these, of course, but it will not fully resolve things.

Service desk objectives

Information Technology Infrastructure Library (ITIL) is a set of detailed practices for IT service management that focuses on aligning IT services with the needs of business. ITIL v3 sets out the following objectives for a service desk:

- Service is focused on customers and users
- Information is held centrally
- Information is used for auditing and reporting
- Generating statistics to assist reporting and planning
- Reducing the number of calls through analysis and training
- Service seen as being cost-effective
- Faster incident resolution
- Improved skill levels supporting IT services
- Improved IT services and better resilience
- Information available to allow preventive measures to be developed[30]

Responsibilities of the service desk

ITIL v3 also articulates the following responsibilities for the service desk:

- Managing and owning incidents throughout their lifecycle
- Providing a professional interface between customers/users and the IT service provider
- Providing first level IT service support
- Providing management information on IT service provision and producing associated reports[31]

In-person service desk

Many companies have created an in-person service desk, using the model of the Apple Genius Bar as the model. The idea is to have members of your IT team at a high-traffic location, perhaps near the front entrance of your offices or near the cafeteria. It can be a place for employees to bring their laptops to show a service desk person what the issue is and either to have it resolved on the spot or receive a loaner machine while the issue is resolved. This can be a good assignment for a talented service desk employee, who might have more contact with a broad set of people across the business landscape. It often can be a high-value way for the technology or digital team to interact with the broader population of the company.

Outsourced versus in-house service desk

While many companies have at least some portions of the escalation chain of a service desk in-house, many also have outsourced partners to handle some—and in some cases most or all—of their service desk needs. The reasons given for doing so include:

- Scalability: an external partner can scale resources up or down depending on the needs of the company.
- Cost: many external partners in the service desk space pitch their services as more cost-effective, and in some (though not all) cases that may be true.
- Quality: depending on the areas covered by the service desk, and some companies have multiple service desks covering multiple domains, a

service desk partner may have deeper areas of expertise than your company may wish to acquire in a discipline. There is also a feeling in some companies that the service desk staff are the low men and women on the totem pole of the technology and digital organization. By outsourcing this to a company for whom this is strategic, you may have better resources at your disposal.

- Business continuity and disaster recovery: where there are risks imposed on your operation, they are less likely to also be an issue to the strategic partner you have. During a period of some disaster (natural or otherwise), having a partner that is in a steadier state can aid you when contact with the service desk spikes.

There is merit to each of these points, but there are some counterpoints, as well. Chief among them is that if you have employees who run your service desk and man the digital, telephonic, and in-person channels, they have a different set of incentives than an external partner ever can. Their success is your company's success. Their compensation, including bonuses and raises, will be tied most directly to the outcomes they drive for their own company.

Google CIO Ben Fried has some nuanced views on this topic. When asked about the sanctity of the service or help desk, he noted, "If you think of the help desk as being about reading FAQs and recipes, that's a cognitive dissonance—you're approaching it as if change is bad." He said that although many companies have outsourced the help desk, by so doing, they are not equipping the enterprise with the ability to change, as the help desk is a fundamental element in any change management program.[32]

In each of Google's offices, they have a service desk called Techstop. It includes an accessory rack where employees can go if they need a loaner PC or a charger or headphones. In fact, some employees travel light when they travel to another office, and simply borrow the hardware they need to be productive, and then return it to the Techstop before heading back to their home offices.

Whereas most companies think of the service desk as a commodity, Google thinks of it in the context of a Googler's journey from their first day through the life of their time with the company. By looking at it through the lens of a journey, the service desk is educated and improves each interaction along the stages of a Googler's experience.

When Googlers transitioned to working from home on a massive scale in March 2020 due to the COVID-19 pandemic, Google's Techstop talent was prepared to handle the spike in volume of questions and issues related to the move, because of their ability to pivot and solve problems as opposed to reading scripts. The Google team also created Work from Home kits so that staff could get the technology they needed to be as productive at home as they would have been in the office, since offices and the physical accessory racks were no longer accessible.

Fried also thinks of the service desk as a fantastic training ground for new Googlers. The company hires nontraditional employees to the service desk, including people without college degrees. This is a great opportunity for some to gain a foothold in Google and to expand their responsibilities and to move to other roles should they wish. It is a great place to learn about the company, to develop a reputation as a problem-solver, and to start a career at one of the premier technology companies in the world.

Self-service at Comcast

Rick Rioboli is the CIO of Comcast Cable, the cable unit of the $110 billion revenue entertainment colossus. In an interview I did with him, he mentioned the company's investments in augmenting self-service capabilities so that customers need not always wait for a person in order to get the help they need. By way of example, he mentioned an instance when a customer scheduled an appointment for an installation in the home:

> We have made it easy for the customer to request a different time if the time they wanted was not available. If that time slot opens up, we can let them know through text, and they can switch their appointment by texting. They do not even have to go into our app or call us. There are many micro-interactions that we have turned into digital that make the customer experience far more enjoyable than having to pick up the phone and call us. While much of digital is focused on the sales side, I believe we have been unique with our approach.[33]

Across many companies there have been moves to embrace more self-service and automation in technology and digital divisions and beyond. One can foresee a scenario in which a service desk exists to handle complicated issues, but the tools and capabilities are intuitive enough that the need to contact a services agent minimizes over time.

FIGURE 3.7 Service desk

Role(s) responsible	Tool(s)	Metrics
• Head of service desk	• Service desk suite	• Improved speed to resolve issues • Reduced number of incidents • Improved management of incidents • Improved user satisfaction with the service desk • Increased use and satisfaction with self-help options • Improved product quality

Knowledge management

In an increasingly fast-paced and agile business environment, knowledge is the key differentiator for many businesses. What does your team know, how can it disseminate what it knows, and how quickly can it gain additional knowledge? The answers to these questions can determine the difference between leaders and laggards in an industry. It is important to hire smart, gritty, ambitious people who will not rest on the laurels of the knowledge gained long ago since what you know today may become less relevant tomorrow. However, it is equally important for knowledge generated from one person or team to be properly managed and disseminated so that others can learn it more quickly. Former HP president and CEO Lew Platt famously said in an ode to the importance of knowledge, "If only HP knew what HP knows, we would be three times more productive."[34]

The unfortunate fact is that many companies have bright, ambitious people who are forced to reproduce knowledge assets that already exist because they do not have an easy means of finding the information necessary to have a leg-up. Research shows that employees spend close to 20 percent of their day searching for information. You can imagine—there are significant productivity and ultimately cost implications to this. This problem is further augmented by pace of business and the proliferation of productivity tools that create knowledge and content silos within an organization. Despite a strong business case, many companies that I have worked with do not have defined knowledge management processes and tools, and those that do often have trouble keeping them updated. Just as companies often focus on building new products to the detriment of shutting down old, redundant products because a continued focus on the new is more exciting, likewise many people find it tedious to stop and document what they know for others to learn after-the-fact. In those organizations, most knowledge is tacit knowledge, gained through experiences, but does not turn into explicit knowledge that others can learn from.

Ultimately, a better way must be forged. A more robust knowledge and content management strategy can create a faster path to innovation and value. The key is to design a process that efficiently turns tacit knowledge into explicit knowledge. In the process, it is appropriate to also evaluate how existing explicit knowledge is documented, and how that process can be improved. This requires an explicit content management strategy and process.

Steps of the process

My colleague, Leila Dige, has defined the following steps of the process:

1 Inventory your current knowledge assets.
2 Define and understand user personas.
3 Determine management and distribution strategy.
4 Tackle tacit knowledge.
5 Drive adoption and change management.

INVENTORY YOUR CURRENT KNOWLEDGE ASSETS

Start by understanding your current knowledge and content ecosystem. What are the knowledge types that you want to uncover? Is it structured or unstructured knowledge? Where does this knowledge live today? As is true with any strategy, it's important to understand the current ecosystem before defining your parameters and establishing your vision for the future.

One common challenge that most companies face when they start down this journey is they often try to tackle everything at once. I often recommend thinking about the process of managing explicit and tacit knowledge as a gradual progression. The first phase of knowledge management maturity is to properly manage explicit knowledge. Over time, more value can be gained by surfacing tacit knowledge, providing context, and connecting experts.

No matter the approach, the overall goal is to turn tacit knowledge into explicit knowledge.

DEFINE AND UNDERSTAND USER PERSONAS

Once you have a sense of your current content ecosystem, it is important to understand knowledge users and their preferences. Identify three to five types of users of knowledge and their primary pain points and preferences in accessing knowledge. For example, in a pharmaceutical company, someone who is involved in research and development in a disease area, say, oncology, will have complex needs. Within a big company, there may be oncology researchers located in multiple countries. It is critical to ensure that each has an ability to understand advances made elsewhere so that the work each does is additive rather than redundant. By contrast, a sales leader at that same company must have information about all relevant existing and potential customers. Who has spoken with a given customer most recently, and what was the outcome? What was shared? What was learned? For each of these personas, and others that can be readily defined, what are the pain points and preferences each has, as well as the types of information each needs to access on a regular basis? Understanding the personas will help define the processes to gather knowledge, make it accessible, and to define its dissemination where appropriate.

As the personas are defined, engage multiple employees who represent those personas to draw in their preferences. How do they prefer to access information? What format is most helpful? What devices do they need to access them through? Pulling the thread on the previous example, the way a sales rep accesses knowledge is very different from the way a researcher prefers to access it. By incorporating their feedback, you aid adoption and avoid the risk of creating a knowledge repository that is neither intuitive nor useful. You want a knowledge base that is leveraged frequently.

DETERMINE MANAGEMENT AND DISTRIBUTION STRATEGY

Next, one must choose the methods and tools necessary to capture, store, organize, and manage knowledge. Start with explicit and structured knowledge. Even if you already have a method for documenting explicit knowledge, it may be necessary to rethink how it is labeled, tagged, indexed, and the like. It is also important to determine who should have access to what knowledge. Some of your most sensitive knowledge, like an analysis of acquisition targets, should not be accessible to everyone in the company.

Whereas the strategy of the company or documents that provide an overview of your culture should be accessible to everyone. Be sure to draw these distinctions as part of the process.

Next, determine the means of distribution. There are several knowledge management tools that are useful in organization and dissemination. Many companies also leverage their intranet as a means of distribution. As you evaluate a tool, also be sure that the search capabilities are baked into the choice. Employees will increasingly expect a Google-like experience to searching for information, so it's important to also consider how employees will search for knowledge management assets across multiple information sources.

Search as a mechanism to "pull" knowledge is critically important, but it's equally important not to lose sight of how you "push" knowledge or information to employees The most mature organizations can push information at key moments of trust. These knowledge "nudges" are often powered through artificial intelligence based upon employees' search and knowledge history—searches and workstreams undertaken by team members.

TACKLE TACIT KNOWLEDGE

As you are undertaking this journey, remember that not all knowledge within the company is documented or structured. Management, distribution, and search tools are often good at uncovering explicit knowledge but do not always address tacit knowledge.

Tacit knowledge lives in people's heads. It is the most at risk of loss since it is only as good as people's memories or for as long as they are employed by your company. If a person with unique tacit knowledge leaves the company, the knowledge leaves with them.

Once you have established a process for explicit knowledge, ensure you have a process in place to codify tacit knowledge into explicit knowledge where appropriate. Start by creating a taxonomy of knowledge, and then identify subject-matter experts in each of those areas. Develop a repository and a means of documenting the knowledge in a standardized fashion. The ancillary benefit of developing these networks of experts is that it can also foster new types of collaboration and may lead to insights that draw out new innovations for your company. This is another great use for AI tools to connect people of common skills, interest, and subject-matter experts.

DRIVE ADOPTION AND CHANGE MANAGEMENT

The process is only as good as its adoption. Once you have it in place, it is important to ensure you have ownership and accountability for the process and governance. Include a plan for regularly updating and refreshing knowledge across the company, including the natural points at which to do it—for instance, at the conclusion of a project or after taking training on a new topic. Remember that if the knowledge is consistently out of date, it will call into question the value of all knowledge in some people's eyes. This is a recipe for a vicious cycle toward non-use.

CarMax's Mohammad notes the connection between knowledge management and transparency:

> To me, the biggest way to share knowledge is through having a lot of transparency in the work that is going on. The company held open house sessions every few weeks where product teams could share what they knew. You have a lot of great information and knowledge, but nobody wants to go find it. So, we make it easy for people to find it and use it.

Sometimes designing the process taking into account the shortcomings of humans is the best approach.

Additional considerations

You may need to develop incentives for people to adopt the practices, both in drawing information from the system you have developed and contributing back to it. It may be a culture shift. A good thought is to set aside specific hours or even a day during a month, bring in food and drinks, and declare it a knowledge management party of sorts. You can offer a prize for the person who contributes the highest volume of information at the highest quality.

Also note that a new knowledge management strategy may significantly change the processes by which knowledge is captured, organized, shared, and distributed throughout your company. Be sure that there are appropriate ties between the processes you develop and your company's strategy overall. Good governance and frequent audits of both adherence to the process, quality of information entered, and value perceived by users are all advised. Where any of the above yield appropriate suggestions for improvement, implement those.

FIGURE 3.8 Knowledge management

Role(s) responsible

- Head of knowledge management

Tool(s)

- Intranet and extranet-enabled knowledge management
- Content management systems
- Decision support systems
- Document management systems
- Data warehousing, data mining, and OLAP
- Artificial intelligence tools related to knowledge management
- Semantic networks
- Federated search
- People management/HCM software

Metrics

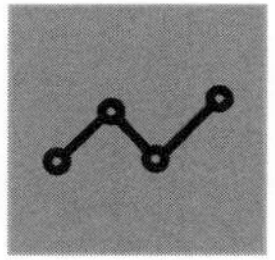

- Improved knowledge quality
  - Increase in volume and quality of information posted to knowledge management databases
  - Increased information currency
  - Increased percentage of searches noted as highly rated
- Improved knowledge engagement
  - Increased usage of knowledge management search engines
  - Percentage of knowledge harvested and stored from key employees
  - Percentage of knowledge transferred to successor employees
  - Improved employee engagement
  - Improved employee satisfaction with digital content ecosystem
- Increased employee productivity
  - Increased effectiveness of search results of knowledge management databases
  - Reduced time spent searching for information
  - Decreased in the ramp-up time for new hires based on accessibility of information through knowledge management
  - Increased productivity/time taken to submit and process common workflows

In addition to the value noted above to leveraging artificial intelligence as an aid to getting knowledge to where it is needed most, consider leveraging application programming interfaces (APIs) so that knowledge repositories, including some that may be outside of your company, are connected. (The next chapter will provide more information on APIs and their uses.)

What success looks like

- a clear process for documenting explicit and tacit knowledge
- clear governance and accountability for refreshing knowledge
- significant leadership support, particularly given the amount of change management needed
- end-user engagement, with a focus on solving user problems and delivering content that is most relevant to users
- alignment to broader business and IT practices/processes
- proper change management and incentives for end-users
- governance and content management structures, including robust QA processes to ensure knowledge remains relevant

What is implicit here is: Mature KM practitioners understand that KM is a continuous process.

In most cases, your knowledge management strategy needs to be tied to your data strategy (particularly for explicit knowledge). Make sure to coordinate these efforts. We will cover data strategy in greater detail in Chapter 6.

Chapter takeaways

If your culture defines who you are, your processes define how you do things. For too many companies, processes are inadequately mapped out, assessed, and modernized to reflect the changing times. As a result, companies do not take action to define how they do things. Initiatives are still undertaken, and work gets done, but there are inefficiencies in that work. Moreover, great technologists know great processes, even if they do not exist in your company. Technologists tend to have great networks, and given the extent to which they hear about better ways of doing things elsewhere, they may jump elsewhere to take advantage of them.

Thankfully, there has been so much progress relative to processes, and great examples to follow. Process modernization can be daunting, but it is also a great way to engage a diverse array of team members from inside your technology and digital organization, and beyond it, to define the future of work done at your company.

Notes

1 Peter High. General Stanley McChrystal (Retired), Managing Partner at McChrystal Group, Former Commander Joint Special Operations Command, *Technovation with Peter High* podcast, July 31, 2017

2 Ibid

3 Ibid

4 Mike Beedle, Arie van Benneku, Alistair Cockburn, Ward Cunningham, Martin Fowler, Jim Highsmith, et al. *The Agile Manifesto*, Agilemanifesto.org (archived at https://perma.cc/X9S6-ATJM), February, 2001

5 *State of Agile Report*, Stateofagile.com (archived at https://perma.cc/M9D3-TKVP), 2020

6 Deryl Sturdevant. (Still) learning from Toyota, *McKinsey Quarterly*, February 1, 2014

7 Peter High. How Capital One became a leading digital bank, Forbes.com (archived at https://perma.cc/Z4TW-5468), December 12, 2016

8 Ibid

9 Ibid

10 Peter High. From project to product with Mik Kersten, *Technovation* podcast, June 18, 2020

11 Michael Bertha and Chris Boyd. Crossing the project-to-product chasm, CIO.com (archived at https://perma.cc/NH8N-LE5U), May 1, 2020

12 Peter High. CIOs on project to product-focused IT, *Technovation* podcast, March 12, 2020

13 Ibid

14 Ibid

15 Michael Bertha and Chris Boyd. Creating a new funding model for product-based IT, CIO.com (archived at https://perma.cc/NH8N-LE5U), February 21, 2020

16 Michael Bertha and Chris Boyd. Crossing the project-to-product chasm, CIO.com (archived at https://perma.cc/NH8N-LE5U), May 1, 2020

17 Ibid

18 Ibid

19   Mik Kersten. Project to product: Thrive in the age of digital disruption with the flow framework, *YouTube*, July 1, 2019

20   Michael Bertha and Chris Boyd. Crossing the project-to-product chasm, CIO.com (archived at https://perma.cc/NH8N-LE5U), May 1, 2020

21   Peter High. An introduction to DevOps from one of its godfathers, Forbes.com (archived at https://perma.cc/Z4TW-5468), February 23, 2015

22   Peter High. CBRE Chief Digital & Technology Officer Chandra Dhandapani, *Technovation with Peter High* podcast, August 12, 2019

23   Ibid

24   Peter High. Google CIO Ben Fried makes change a core competency, Forbes.com (archived at https://perma.cc/Z4TW-5468), March 14, 2016

25   Blake Morgan. Companies that failed at digital transformation and what we can learn from them, Forbes.com (archived at https://perma.cc/Z4TW-5468), September 30, 2019

26   John Kotter. Leading change: Why transformation efforts fail, *Harvard Business Review*, January 2007

27   Alex Kraus. 5 change management 'moments of truth,' MetisStrategy.com (archived at https://perma.cc/2AL5-G398), September 25, 2020

28   Ibid

29   Ibid

30   ITIL 2011 edition, itilnews.com (archived at https://perma.cc/W4VT-L8YA)

31   Ibid

32   Peter High. Google CIO Ben Fried makes change a core competency, Forbes.com (archived at https://perma.cc/Z4TW-5468), March 14, 2016

33   Peter High. Comcast CIO Rick Rioboli sits at the center of an innovation ecosystem, Forbes.com (archived at https://perma.cc/Z4TW-5468), October 7, 2019

34   John Hagel and John Seely Brown. Harrah's new twist on prediction markets, Bloomberg.com (archived at https://perma.cc/D3YC-HQ5L), December 22, 2008

04

Building a more future-proof and secure technology stack

Digital transformation requires modern, digital technology. That may seem to be a truism, but it can be harder to actualize than it seems. The case of FedEx is illuminating.

Founder and CEO Fred Smith attended Yale University in the 1960s. In an economics class, he wrote a paper on the need for a reliable overnight delivery service to complement the information age. His professor responded by saying, "The concept is interesting and well-formed, but in order to earn better than a 'C,' the idea must be feasible."[1]

Smith was not deterred by this hit to his economics grade. He would go on to prove his professor he was wrong, and from the company's founding in the 1970s, technology was one of the key differentiating factors. Smith, who is now in his mid-70s, did not have a technology background in founding the company, but he has been one of the most progressive leaders when it has come to technology. He famously said, "The information about the package is as important as the package itself."[2] Being able to know where a package was in transit would be a key differentiator for the company. He was one of the first to hire a chief information officer, and everyone to hold that title has reported directly to him.

In 2000, Smith hired Rob Carter as CIO. Two decades later, Carter is still in that role. Having gotten to know Carter well, he has shared with me that several years ago, he realized that though much of the technology that was its source of competitive advantage was put in place by him at that time, it was not a modern, digital technology footprint. He told me, "It dawned on me that the technology that was the source of our success would be the source of our downfall if we did not change." That was a stunning revelation that most technology and digital leaders do not realize; first, because they do not typically have the tenure that Carter has had at FedEx, but also it can be difficult to push pride aside to note that the technology that is the source of great pride may lead to disaster if it is not changed.

Though the technology was running reliably, it was cobbled together, and some of the most critical data flowed through systems that were becoming antiquated. Carter decided he needed to create a mandate for change. He created a diagram that highlighted how the different technologies that the company employed fit together. It was such a swirling mess of a picture that the board dubbed it "Hurricane Rob." That reaction was just what he wanted, as he wanted to make the point that it was chaotic; it was complex; and it would soon be unmanageable. By contrast, he then showed the future vision, which would focus on simplicity, standardization, and a cloud-first mentality. These are hallmarks that every company should follow. And it also replaced the hurricane with a clearer picture, and even nontechnical board members could understand the value of that change.

As I have noted earlier in this book, older, tightly coupled technology architectures are still the norm of many digital immigrant companies. This means that the downstream implications of changes to technology may be more complicated than they should be. Moreover, the cost to maintain these old, cobbled-together systems, often referred to as "technical debt," can be profound. Here are a few thoughts on how to turn this around.

First, get your arms around the technology portfolio that has been assembled, warts and all. This requires enterprise architecture and will require a solid vision for the shortcomings of the current state and the pathway to an optimized state. This can then create the mandate for change that Carter created. Highlight the current status of technology, the risks of not modernizing, and then paint the future picture with relevant advantages noted.

Second, develop a cloud-first strategy. Cloud technology tends to be more flexible, scaling up and back as needed. It also tends to be more variabilized from a cost structure perspective, which means paying for the technology you use rather than buying more than you need.

Third, develop more loosely coupled technologies, so that changes to one platform can be made independent of others. This includes using microservices and application programming interfaces (APIs).

Lastly, standardize as much technology as possible, and bear in mind the security implications of all that you do. You may have multiple operating companies or business units in your enterprise, and they may be different enough to justify different technology, but remember that FedEx operates an airline, a trucking company, and an office services company, among other parts of the business. Even a business as diverse as that developed a common core technology to be used throughout, while ensuring greater levels of security.

These steps align with the four sub-themes I will cover in this chapter:

- enterprise architecture
- cloud
- APIs and microservices
- security

A starting point is to get your arms around what you have in your technology landscape or portfolio. Enterprise architecture (EA) is the means of doing so from the standpoint of business architecture, data architecture, application architecture, and technology and infrastructure architecture. EA is a foundational method to ensure that you have a solid grounding in what you own and how it fits together, and that you are cognizant of how changes to technology will impact things more broadly speaking. As the corporate and divisional strategies are developed across the company, EA and the leaders of that function should weigh in. They should highlight where technology can be reused, where standards exist, and the like.

Next is the cloud. Cloud technology is a key ingredient to ensure a company is nimble or not, as it fosters flexibility, scalability (up and down), and increasingly greater security. A convincing case can be made that the more companies go all in on cloud technology, the better positioned they will be for resilience and to be opportunistic as opportunities present themselves. There may well be reasons not to go all in, but there is no doubt that companies must embrace cloud technologies in order to remain competitive in the future.

Microservices and application program interfaces (APIs) are also critical ingredients in modernizing the technology landscape within an enterprise. In the past, technologies were developed as monoliths, and when changes were necessary to some portion of the monolith, the consequences could be profound and difficult to predict. As the name suggests, microservices are a means of breaking down technology into logical components to manage it better, update it and upgrade it with fewer unintended consequences, and improve security at the same time. Not every technology should be developed using microservices, so developing a logical strategy for microservices is important. APIs are also a building block of sorts for technology, enabling modularity in programming. They are computing interfaces which enable interactions between multiple software intermediaries. APIs define the kinds of requests that can be made of one technology versus another, how they should be made, and the technical conventions to follow. They enable better interfaces across the technology landscape within a company as well as facilitating interfaces between companies.

Finally, security is a critical aspect to be baked into all that the technology and digital teams do. It seems like every week brings news of a major company that has had a breach or a government agency that has had documents stolen. Unfortunately, as technology proliferates, so too does the threat landscape. Bad actors have many more ways into the enterprise to attempt to steal the crown jewels. Therefore, your company must have a sound methodology to evaluate and monitor security writ large. This involves both the technical and the human aspects of security. We will delve into all of the above in depth through this chapter.

In a world where companies have gone from referring to themselves as financial services, healthcare, or retail companies to referring to themselves as technology companies that are in the financial service industry or healthcare industry or retail industries, and they mean it, one would think that the technology that they use is pretty important. It is, but there is a reason why people and processes come before technology in this book. Without the first two being well equipped and nimble, developing a nimble technology landscape will be nearly impossible.

Once they are in place, or at least once the modernization of the practices associated with each are under way, it is appropriate to develop a playbook to modernize the technology landscape. Here, the practices of startups are enlightening. A fast-growing, tech-centric business has the luxury of a blank slate before it, and executives at the company can choose the latest technology to support significant growth. Startups must be nimble. These early days are periods of experimentation, trial and error, and business pivots from one opportunity to the next. Companies like these hesitate to invest in a technology portfolio that is in any way inflexible.

Larger, older organizations do not have the benefit of the blank slate that the startups have. They have invested in technology through the course of the companies' existence. Any one of them is likely to have museum-grade technology at times running important aspects of the business. Critical data may flow through mainframe computing that is decades old. The philosophy is often, "If it works, and it is fully amortized, and we have some people who know how to develop on it, why not keep it going?" There are plenty of reasons not to. The longer one waits to modernize, the more difficult it will be to pivot as opportunity presents itself or as issues present themselves. Risks increase with aged technology in the form of cybersecurity issues and the departure of those with the skills to support the old systems, to name but two risks. IT departments must make the case for modernization of the tech landscape.

Enterprise architecture

Enterprise architecture, or EA, is a commonly used framework, especially among large organizations, to monitor their technology landscape, to evaluate how new capabilities fit with existing ones, what is rendered redundant, and what should be retired.

As Schneider Electric Chief Digital Officer Herve Coureil put it to me, "From an enterprise architecture standpoint, replicability at scale is a goal, meaning [it is] your ability to efficiently replicate something that works well somewhere across the company." Having visibility into what components of your technology landscape are candidates for replicability, even before they are built or implemented, is aided mightily by EA.

There are four main components of EA (Figure 4.1):

1 Business architecture includes strategic business goals that will guide all efforts.

2 Data architecture helps organizations understand what information each business function needs.

3 Application architecture determines how to create, connect, and provide data to those functions.

4 Technology and infrastructure architecture encompasses cloud services, security, and other tools that enable business applications to run effectively.

There is a cascading logic from one to the next, and the interplay between them represents the way in which business strategy informs and drives technology strategy, while the technology strategy enables the business strategy.

Vipul Nagrath, the former Global CIO and current Senior Vice President of Product Development at ADP, said to me in a recent conversation, "Focus on the enterprise architecture, make it flexible and open, and yet adhere to the North Stars [strategy], along with security and interoperability, stability, and resilience." The "North Stars"—the strategy of the company, the division, the technology or digital unit—must be articulated, and EA should align with it and bring it to life. It should also dictate what from among the current tech landscape might already be in place to bring to life a new imperative.

FIGURE 4.1 The building blocks of enterprise architecture

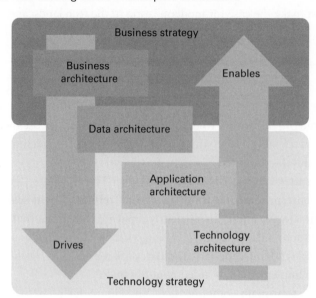

Enterprise architecture has gone back and forth between being embraced as strategically important and dismissed as too academic. As in many cases, the right balance is somewhere in between. Much like the need to identify who on your team has what skills, weighing that against the demand for those skills, EA provides a similar lens to the technology portfolio. EA is a means of understanding, managing, modernizing, and de-risking your technology portfolio. There are a few forces driving the changing state of EA as a discipline in IT departments and companies more broadly.

EA can be thought of as the prime means of controlling your landscape. On the face of it, it is remarkable that companies would allow themselves to reach a level of complexity to not understand all of the assets they have, all of the technologies they are using and for what, and all of the sources of data and what they are used for. And yet, many companies do not have that level of knowledge. A lack of knowledge of what is in your domain is a source of risk, and a lack of knowledge of the connections and interdependencies between the technologies that you own means you are bound to make decisions that have negative, unintended consequences.

The adoption of Agile as a way of working is another driving force, motivated by the demand to accelerate the speed to market and enhance digital offerings. This requires an ability to test and learn quickly rather than waiting to develop a perfect solution, and has placed growing importance on integration across systems. This has become both easier and more important to do, as teams can now easily build API integrations across multiple applications.

The growth and prevalence of software as a service (SaaS) has also affected the evolution of enterprise architecture. As organizations do less custom development or reconfiguration at the platform level, you must work with what an SaaS platform gives you. EA in a completely custom-built software world is different from EA in an SaaS-first or cloud-native world. In the latter case, there is less of a need to solve for physical infrastructure. That said, it is important to understand the growth of hybrid cloud as a paradigm or as a discipline. Whereas EA teams did not require cloud architecture skills a few years ago, now they do.

The importance of security to business continuity and brand reputation also increases the need for a solid EA strategy. EA teams may not always be the author of security architecture design, but as enterprise security plays an increasingly critical role in doing business, it has become a larger part of the broader EA conversation. Ron Ross of the National Institute of Science and Technology (NIST), and a creator of the NIST cybersecurity framework (covered later in this chapter), has told me that enterprise architecture is among the first recommendations that he offers in de-risking the organization:

> When you apply enterprise architecture, it has three critical components. You can consolidate, optimize, and standardize your information technology infrastructure. What that means is that you get leaner and meaner. You get rid of things you do not need and eliminate unnecessary redundancy. You are doing some things that are foundational to computer security.[3]

My colleague Gilberto Millares has noted the following reasons to invest in EA:

- *To provide a consistent experience, both from an employee and customer perspective: Designing an end-to-end enterprise architecture enables omnichannel integration, which can be translated into a more seamless customer journey.*

- *To enable the use of new technologies, simplifying integration: A well-defined enterprise architecture streamlines the process for introducing cloud, automation, and the use of APIs, among other technologies. It helps drive a common platform and infrastructure that development teams can use to create products and services aligned to business objectives.*

- *To enable agility and flexibility to functions that use data to inform their decision-making: By aligning the data generated by the company and the tools used to collect that data, it becomes easier to automatically join, clean, and share data sets that enable supply chain, marketing, and operations teams to make decisions aligned to business goals.*[4]

Evolution of technology and EA

Ten years ago, companies may have sought to understand a business architecture problem, then design a scalable solution that would solve the problem, integrate with systems, and finally scale up. Now, these solutions need to be not only linearly scalable, but possibly exponentially so. Those integrations will need to happen at a faster pace. Business architecture is less static than it was years ago, as companies face pressure to develop and constantly improve differentiating products, services, and customer experiences. That creates a need to balance scalability with flexibility, forces that potentially compete with one another.

The rise of a range of new technologies, from artificial intelligence and the Internet of Things, as well as the breadth of vendors providing new solutions, can lead many companies to introduce additional complexity into their organizations. New products and vendors must integrate with existing systems, and the like. This too leads to a need for a more flexible and adaptable EA, depending on the needs of the organization.

In order to wrap one's arms around one's technology landscape effectively, it requires deeper thought about integration and standardization, each of which are aided by EA. Lenovo's chief information officer Arthur Hu noted as much in saying:

> Companies should think about integration and standardization of technology. This is important especially for global, scaled organizations. Integration— applying the notion of a user journey and using that as the integrating framework—is also critical, especially in these environments.

Key roles for EA

As you build out your EA team, it is important that their skills align with the core disciplines of the architecture. Make sure teams are ahead of the curve on new and leading technologies. As changes are proposed to the different aspects of your architecture, you should have team members who can comment on the wisdom of those changes. They should be so well versed in the various facets of architecture and trends related to them to push back or to suggest alternatives, where that is appropriate. An EA team that is not seen as the expert on new technology will quickly become stale and relegated to a documentation function rather than strategic function.

As for the roles themselves, a fine-tuned EA team should consist of:

- A **chief architect**: This leader must enforce standards across the enterprise, should monitor emerging technology, and make suggestions when a new technology appears to be applicable to a need articulated by a leader in the company. They must also get involved in the projects or initiatives that the company undertakes. The chief architect needs to have the gravitas to counsel the C-suite of executives, and they must be technically and digitally savvy enough to speak with coders, as well.

- A handful (two to five) of **enterprise architects**: The enterprise architects should be tasked with optimizing business operations across the divisions and business units of the company while also fine tuning and optimizing the technology landscape. They should develop a familiarity if not an expertise in the company's processes, using that to understand where the points of leverage are for change. Key skills for enterprise architects include understanding business process and architecture and having the ability to educate and steer business decision-makers to think about how their business model designs will be brought to life through technology. They also can educate colleagues on how technology and process design will either enable or limit opportunities from a business model perspective.

- On a case-by-case basis, you may also have **solution and domain architects**: These people typically work with the chief architect on matters of strategy. Solution or domain architects are also responsible for the design of one or more applications or services within an organization. These are sometimes federated into application teams with a dotted line into EA. In other cases, they may be within the EA group and dedicated to different domains.

Additional skills needed:

- data architecture—sometimes in EA, other times in data platform or data and analytics team
- technology architecture—infrastructure (on prem and cloud), storage, network, and the like
- the EA team (sometimes this will be an enterprise architect, other times a different expert), also needs skills around integration architecture:
  o can continue to assess how tightly coupled your systems are
  o often will see dedicated focus to integration patterns within the EA team

In the world of SaaS solutions, the role of the EA team may be less about advising on detailed application architecture because, often, they come prebuilt. When choosing SaaS solutions, you want to understand the architecture of each tool. In that case, value can come through the business process design and how you connect and synchronize both custom, homegrown applications and SaaS applications.

In summary, the EA team must be filled with people operating in roles that add value. They must be advisors to the rest of the company; they must leverage their expertise as a complement to the expertise of the rest of the company. At its best, EA is a team that pushes the thinking and increases the quality of the enterprise. At its worst, EA may be seen as gatekeepers, rubber-stamping decisions without thinking of the broader consequences of those decisions. If this turns out to be the case, chances are the rest of the organization may bypass EA completely.

Operationalizing EA

EA requires a sound strategy be in place. EA is the translation of that strategy into a roadmap. There are multiple frameworks that aid the EA process. The Open Group is an industry consortium that seeks to "enable the achievement of business objectives" by developing "open, vendor-neutral technology standards and certifications."[5] The Open Group Architecture Framework (TOGAF) is an EA methodology that offers a high-level process for enterprise software development. TOGAF provides a systematic approach to development to maintain timelines, to adhere to budgets, to enhance quality, and to reduce errors. The elements of TOGAF are represented in the following steps, beginning with the preliminary phase.

The objective of the preliminary phase is to "define architecture capability desired by the organization and to establish architecture capability." According to the Open Group, "This Preliminary Phase is about defining 'where, what, why, who, and how we do architecture' in the enterprise concerned."[6] The main aspects of the approach are:

- Define the enterprise.
- Identify key drivers and elements in the organizational context.
- Define the requirements for architecture work.
- Define architecture principles that will inform any architecture work.
- Define the framework to be used.
- Define the relationships between management frameworks.
- Evaluate the enterprise architecture maturity.[7]

The Open Group references eight phases by letter. Phase A is the Architecture Vision, and it is the initial phase of the architecture development lifecycle (defining scope, stakeholders, defining vision, getting needed approvals). The objectives of this phase are to:

> develop a high-level aspirational vision of the capabilities and business value to be delivered as a result of the proposed enterprise architecture [and] obtain approval for a Statement of Architecture Work that defines a program of works to develop and deploy the architecture outlined in the Architecture Vision.[8]

At a high level, this phase includes creating the architecture project, identifying stakeholders and business requirements, confirming business goals and constraints, defining scope, assessing readiness for transformation, and identifying business transformation risks and mitigation activities, among other topics.[9]

The next phase, Phase B, centers around developing business architecture to support the vision. The objectives of this phase are to:

> develop the Target Business Architecture that describes how the enterprise needs to operate to achieve the business goals, and respond to the strategic drivers set out in the Architecture Vision in a way that addresses the Request for Architecture Work and stakeholder concerns [and to] identify candidate Architecture Roadmap components based upon gaps between the Baseline and Target Business Architectures.[10]

Business architecture is the product or service strategy as well as the different aspects of the business environment (organization, function, process, information, geography). Steps involved include developing a baseline and a target business architecture description, performing a gap analysis, conducting a formal stakeholder review, and finalizing the business architecture, among other steps.[11]

Phase C centers around building information systems architecture to support the vision. The objective of this phase is to:

> develop the Target Information Systems (Data and Application) Architecture, describing how the enterprise's Information Systems Architecture will enable the Business Architecture and the Architecture Vision, in a way that addresses the Request for Architecture Work and stakeholder concerns, [and] identify candidate Architecture Roadmap components based upon gaps between the Baseline and Target Information Systems (Data and Application) Architectures.[12]

This step involves a combination of data and application architecture. Some firms may choose to take a data-driven approach, while others may be more app-driven. Steps involved differ based on data (data management, migration, governance, etc.)[13] vs. application (develop target app architecture, identify architecture roadmap, etc.).[14]

Phase D focuses on the development of technology architecture to support the vision. The objective of this phase is to:

> develop the Target Technology Architecture that enables the logical and physical application and data components and the Architecture Vision, addressing the Request for Architecture Work and stakeholder concerns, [and] identify candidate Architecture Roadmap components based upon gaps between the Baseline and Target Technology Architectures.[15]

This step involves figuring out what relevant technology architecture resources are available, such as existing IT services, generic technology models, TOGAF reference models, etc. Steps involved include developing baseline and target technology architecture descriptions, performing gap analysis, conducting stakeholder review, and finalizing the technology architecture, among other steps.[16]

Phase E is entitled "opportunities and solutions," and the focus is on implementation planning and identifying delivery mechanisms. The objectives of this phase are to:

> generate the initial complete version of the Architecture Roadmap, based upon the gap analysis and candidate Architecture Roadmap components from Phases B, C, and D, [and] determine whether an incremental approach is required, and if so, identify Transition Architectures that will deliver continuous business value.[17]

This step focuses on delivering the architecture and is the initial step toward the creation of the implementation and migration plan. It takes into account the gaps between baseline and target architecture and is an attempt to create a roadmap based upon readiness, stakeholder requirements, business opportunities, etc. "The key is to focus on the final target while realizing incremental business value."[18] Steps involved include determining key corporate change attributes, reviewing and consolidating gap analysis results from prior phases, reconciling interoperability requirements, formulating an implementation and migration strategy, and identifying transition architectures, among other steps.

Phase F, migration planning, defines how to move from baseline to target architectures, finalizing details of implementation and migration plans. During this phase one's team should:

finalize the architecture roadmap and the supporting implementation and
migration plan, [as well as] ensure that the implementation and migration plan
is coordinated with the enterprise's approach to managing and implementing
change in the enterprise's overall change portfolio, [and] ensure that the
business value and cost of work packages and Transition Architectures is
understood by key stakeholders.[19]

The focus of this phase is to create the implementation and migration plan.
Activities include assessing dependencies and costs/benefits of the migration
projects in context of other business activities. Steps involved include
confirming management framework interactions for the implementation and
migration plans, assigning business value to each work package, estimating
resource requirements and project timelines, prioritizing migration projects,
and completing the architecture development cycle and documenting lessons.[20]

Phase G, implementation governance, focuses on "architectural oversight
of the implementation."[21] The objectives of this phase are to:

ensure conformance with the Target Architecture by implementation projects,
[and to] perform appropriate Architecture Governance functions for the
solution and any implementation-driven architecture Change Requests.[22]

This is the part where all of the information used to manage the different
implementation projects comes together. TOGAF notes that there is the
execution of an organization-specific development process that happens in
parallel with Phase G. Steps involved include confirming scope and priorities for deployment, identifying deployment resources and skills, performing
EA compliance reviews, implementing business and IT operations, and
performing post-implementation review, among other steps.[23]

The final phase, phase H, is architecture change management, and it
defines procedures for managing the change. The focus is to:

ensure that the architecture lifecycle is maintained, ensure that the Architecture
Governance Framework is executed, [and] ensure that the enterprise
Architecture Capability meets current requirements.[24]

The goal of this is to ensure the architecture achieves desired business value.
The process allows you to monitor things like governance requests, new
technology developments, and changes to the broader business environment. These processes also help the new EA be a flexible, dynamic
architecture that can evolve to changing needs. Steps involved include establishing a value realization process, deploying monitoring tools, managing

risks, managing the governance process, and providing analysis for architecture change management, among other steps.[25]

After the phases comes requirements management, which is the process of managing requirements throughout the architecture development. The objectives of this phase are to:

> ensure that the requirements management process is sustained and operates for all relevant ADM phases, [and to] manage architecture requirements identified during any execution of the ADM cycle or a phase. [It also focuses on ensuring] that relevant architecture requirements are available for use by each phase as the phase is executed.[26]

"The ADM is continuously driven by the requirements management process." This is not a static set of requirements but rather a dynamic process. Steps include determining priorities that come from the current phase of ADM, confirming stakeholder buy-in, monitoring baseline requirements, identifying changed requirements, and updating the requirements repository, among other steps.[27]

The TOGAF Architecture Development Method (ADM) is the core of TOGAF. ADM is a method to develop IT architecture leveraging the aspects of TOGAF noted above along with other architectural assets. It is specifically designed to accelerate workflow across business architecture, data architecture, applications architecture, and technology and infrastructure architecture.[28]

Introduction to evaluating enterprise architecture capabilities, health check, and team makeup

In order to evaluate the effectiveness of your EA teams, it is important to weigh the following factors:

Do teams across the organization actively seek out EA for consultation and advice on how to solve complex business problems? Engagement is a key performance indicator for EA teams. If the team's work is leveraged, pored over, and considered an important input to strategy, these are signs of EA's health and value.

Do architecture review board meetings feel like a strategic conversation or a status report and rubber stamp meeting? As noted above, the tie between EA and strategy must be underscored. Each change suggested by a strategic priority should be taken against the EA maps to understand the broader implications. How does the new technology created or implemented or refined fit with the rest of the technology landscape? Does it render anything redundant? Does it impede upon an existing standard? These are the sorts of questions necessary to contemplate before approving changes.

Do you actually see reusability of technology across the enterprise? This should be asked whenever a new technology is introduced into the company.

What is the broader value that can be derived beyond the initial use case? There are plenty of reasons to build or implement a single solution that benefits a single division or function of the company, but wherever possible, setting standards and leveraging investments more broadly make sense. This is true from a cost perspective, and it is also true from the perspective of reducing complexity.

Do you see proliferation of shadow IT, or an organic consolidation of tools because people see the value of managing architecture holistically? Shadow IT is often a sign that there is unfulfilled value from the technology or digital organizations. The extent to which shadow IT persists and proliferates often works against EA practices. There are some organizations that believe that shadow IT is something that is bound to continue and should be embraced to the extent to which the decisions made on technology outside of the IT department are known and included in the chosen EA framework. (In those cases, they might not refer to it as the pejorative "shadow IT.")

When you have complex programs, has the architecture team proactively created a point of view about the runway it can deliver to help land the plane, or is the architecture team reactive to programs, projects, or larger initiatives after they have already started? The earlier EA is involved in the process, the better. To influence decisions made on new initiatives requires that EA offers feedback before the initiative is too far along. Returning to the idea of reuse, many initiatives that prove to be redundant or even antithetical to a standard technology result from a lack of EA hygiene and leaders providing counsel on the ability to achieve the value intended by the use of existing solutions.

EA for the digital age

It is important to continue to review your EA engagement model to drive consistency with your company's overall digital and IT operating model. In the last chapter, I noted the important trend of moving from project-oriented technology and digital organizations to product-centric ones. Assuming leading organizations are adopting a product-driven operating model, companies need to define the forums in which architecture can effectively communicate standards and best practices to a federated group of empowered teams.

They also need to define the roles and responsibilities for when and how architecture engages with product teams as they build and evolve existing capabilities. In an Agile world, there are fewer natural formal stage gates for requirements gathering, tech, architecture review, etc. Anyway, they need to make sure they are plugging in to existing work and are seen as someone providing value rather than as gatekeepers.

It is important to ensure that part of EA's charter is to have a degree of accountability for execution. As noted above, for too long, EA has been seen as an ivory tower that simply dispenses advice, whereas other teams have to build and operate. Getting EA to have skin in the game for the delivery of new capabilities ensures they have a ground-level understanding of the technology landscape.

Similarly, it is important to integrate the EA function with IT and business strategy functions. As a company grows, delivering meaningful business outcomes will require increasingly complex orchestration of business capabilities. That includes harmonizing multiple business models, integrating complex systems and processes, moving at exceptional speed, consuming and leveraging vast amounts of data, and the like.

An EA team needs to influence prioritization decisions during multi-year and annual planning processes and should weigh in on resource allocation to ensure tech debt is being addressed. Therefore, if your company is large enough to have an EA function that aligns with different parts of the company, be sure that those different EA leaders coordinate efforts and communicate often. They ought to be early sources of advice when an idea is proposed in one part of the company that applies more broadly across it. Likewise, EA should weigh in when the ideas proposed might expose the company to undue risk.

Retirement of redundant or antiquated technology

Technology and digital organizations tend to be better at delivering the new than retiring the old and antiquated. It is human nature to want to go from building one new, innovative idea to the next. The problem is, if one does not stop and assess how the new fits in with the old, redundancies can creep in.

Enterprise architecture is particularly well suited to draw out these insights and eliminate redundancies while retiring old, perhaps unsupported technology. Having worked with dozens of multi-billion-dollar companies around

FIGURE 4.2 Enterprise architecture

Role(s) responsible

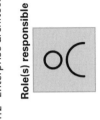

- Chief architect/head of enterprise architecture

Tool(s)

- Within enterprise architecture tools:
    - architecture framework support tools
    - analysis and decision-making tools
    - IT asset management software
    - IT portfolio planning software

Metrics

- Decreased IT total cost of ownership (TCO) as a percentage of revenue
- Increased percentage of products/projects/initiatives leveraging reused components
- Increased cost savings from
    - application rationalization
    - retiring a legacy system
    - consolidating licensing
    - introducing common shared services
    - rationalizing infrastructure investments

the world, assessing the technology and digital functions' maturity, this was regularly the least mature area assessed. It was an afterthought in many cases. This is both inefficient and unsecure. For example, maintaining a diverse array of solutions rather than picking a standard for the company's technology means that data may be created, accumulated, and disseminated from multiple places, reducing the value derived from it.

Not everything needs to be standard, of course, but a key job of the CIO is creating the mechanisms by which companies can decide what to standardize and when. In an interview I did with Lenovo Chief Information Officer Arthur Hu, he said "Though not everything should be standardized, one must regularly make judgment calls regarding the technology that is mature enough and common enough that it can and should be standardized."

When done well, EA can create the transparency that there is an issue in need of resolution. It provides a framework to pose questions and think comprehensively about the interconnectedness of technology. As a decision is made to change one part of the technology landscape, the broader impact of those changes can be better assessed.

What success looks like

The best EA teams have an ability to tell a strategic story that connects application portfolio and tech portfolio with business capabilities with financial investments. Over time, mature EA teams can quantify the value EA provides. Arthur Hu of Lenovo noted:

> How do we group things, both proactively as well as defining where the product boundaries should be, and how to evolve them over time? This has put increased weight and importance on EA. That, in addition to driving reuse, is something we have leveraged EA to do.

The effectiveness of EA can also be judged by the amount of engagement with the team. Is it magnetic? Do leaders consult with EA before making big decisions? Do they follow EA's advice when, for example, a new path or a suggestion for reuse is offered by EA leaders? For the best EA departments, they are essential sounding boards and advisors to the rest of the company.

Cloud

The notion of cloud computing is not new. Like so many concepts that feel new today or new as of the recent past, the concept is from long ago, even if the terminology has changed over time. The concept of cloud computing, though without the moniker, originated in the 1950s, when academic institutions and some corporations leveraged their large-scale mainframe computers to allow multiple users to physically access the computer from multiple terminals as well as to share central processing unit time.

Seventy years ago, a company that would become what some believe to be the first cloud company came into being: Automatic Data Processing, more commonly known as ADP. The company revolutionized payroll services, and processed payroll for many companies, growing to the point where one in six paychecks in the United States are processed by the company. Although no one knew the term "cloud" through most of ADP's history, it developed what would today be referred to as an "as a service" model of operating payroll for companies.

The concept of cloud computing really took off in the past two decades. Salesforce.com, which was founded in 1999, pioneered the idea of delivering enterprise applications via a website.[29] They ushered in the software-as-a-service model, an on-demand model for use of software in which software is licensed on a subscription basis and is centrally hosted. Cloud computing was put into another gear with the advent of Amazon Web Services. Around 2000, Amazon launched Merchant.com, an e-commerce service to help retailers build their own shopping sites on Amazon's e-commerce engine. The launch was erratic. There were several services offered, but they were woven together in a way that made it difficult for companies to use just what they needed. Amazon untangled the services into application programming interfaces, or APIs. This fostered the flexibility necessary to make these services of greater value and led to broader adoption. This was the genesis of Amazon Web Services (AWS), now a colossus within a colossus. This formed a cloud computing platform provider including a mixture of infrastructure as a service (IaaS), platform as a service (PaaS), and software as a service (SaaS) offerings. Therefore, the cloud encompasses everything from completed products (e.g., the CRM solutions that Salesforce.com became famous with) to IT infrastructure (servers, storage, and the like), and various areas in between.

AWS CEO Andy Jassy said:

> We expected all the teams internally from that point on to build in a decoupled, API-access fashion, and then all of the internal teams inside of Amazon expected to be able to consume their peer internal development team services in that way. So very quietly around 2000, we became a services company with really no fanfare.[30]

No less a business authority than Warren Buffet marveled at Jeff Bezos' ability to create two very different businesses at once:

> The remarkable thing about Jeff and everything else is he's done it in two
> industries [e-commerce and cloud computing] almost simultaneously that really
> don't have much connection. I have never seen any person develop two really
> important industries at the same time and really be the operational guy in both.[31]

Bezos himself notes that perhaps the most unusual thing was that the advantage his company had gained through AWS did not attract competition sooner. "AWS had the unusual advantage of a seven-year head start before facing like-minded competition, and the team has never slowed down," said Bezos.[32] Others would catch on eventually, most notably Microsoft and Google.

Advantages of the cloud

Today, cloud computing is an essential tool to becoming nimble. It enables companies to manage applications and infrastructure in a way that limits the necessity for on-premises infrastructure investments, which can be boat anchors, slowing the enterprise down while reducing its flexibility. Cloud computing variabilizes the cost structure to a greater extent, as well.

Other primary benefits of cloud computing include:

- a better and easier means of scaling infrastructure/capacity up or back, as necessary
- enhanced security, as most data suggests that cloud computing is easier to secure, even in a public cloud environment
- an ability to pivot quickly, giving companies the ability to seize opportunities to a greater extent without being weighed down by the fixed costs and fixed methods that on-premises computing often suggests
- increased uptime of technology
- increased application or service orchestration, integrating two or more applications and/or services together to automate a process, or synchronize data in real time
- portability of data

Notice that cost is not listed among the primary benefits. Though there are instances where cloud computing may be more cost-effective, that should not be the basis of the business case you put before your executive team or your board. Hopefully, your leadership is savvy enough to recognize that the benefits articulated above are powerful enough to make the case.

"If the goal is to adopt cloud, then you're falling in love with technology," said Andi Karaboutis, the group chief information and digital officer of National Grid. "If the goal is to provision computer power to go fast, that is a reason to pursue the cloud." Cloud is about being able to solve these problems quickly. Companies need the right focus.

CASE STUDY
FINRA

The Financial Industry Regulatory Authority, or FINRA, is a regulatory agency to the financial services industry, as its name suggests, and it analyzes up to 50 billion daily transactions looking for fraudulent activity, for example. The company's CIO Steve Randich has been a financial services industry CIO for years, including stints at Citibank, NASDAQ, and the Chicago Stock Exchange. He is a big believer in cloud technology. When describing the rationale for his commitment to the cloud, he mentioned to me in an interview, "In our approach, we built an architecture that was public cloud-enabled, which allowed us to take full advantage of all the opportunities across the software stack."[33]

Randich led FINRA's cloud journey near the outset of his tenure at the company in early 2013. First, he focused on acquiring relevant skills, in most cases hiring consultants while growing the skill base internally through a combination of training and strategic hiring. That began in early 2014:

> As we went along, we were continuously moving infrastructure into production as this was not a big bang type of implementation. Regarding the data, the databases that we previously had were small due to their commercial limitations. Because of this, we had to stage the data to make it available for our analytics users to do their queries and their surveillance.[34]

This grew to the point to where Randich's team had large-scale, big databases on the public cloud, enabling his team to keep the vast amounts of data online all the time:

> This allows all of our data to be regularly available to our users without needing IT operations intervention. Furthermore, this enables our users to complete their queries and do machine learning prototyping on the data with little IT intervention. The combination of these elements provides a self-serve approach for our users, which gives them a significant advantage.[35]

Randich contemplated the different cloud models when pursuing this path, and he opted for the public cloud option for three reasons:

- The public cloud provides a near infinite scale because you are paying on-demand. With the private cloud, you have captive hosted hardware, and you are paying even when you are not using it.

- The ability to evolve at pace with Moore's law. In our case, AWS is continuously upgrading their hardware, which would not be done at the same rate in a private data center.

- The public cloud provides immense cybersecurity benefits. This is because it is essentially impossible for a commercial firm doing it themselves to invest at the level of resources that are needed to get the cybersecurity controls of a public cloud vendor.[36]

Although Randich did not pursue a cloud strategy for cost reasons alone, as it turns out, the economics at his scale have been fortuitous:

> Our data volumes have increased significantly since we have moved additional applications to the cloud. While our usage has gone up, our cloud costs have gone down, which is something I have never seen with any technology platform or vendor in my career.[37]

Getting buy-in for cloud migration

Transforming to the cloud is not an easy proposition. It is typically high cost; it assumes more than average risk along the way as old systems are shut down and new ones are fired up; and the progress is not likely to be a straight line up. There will, inevitably, be a bumpy road.

Thankfully, this is not a bleeding-edge move for companies. Many other companies have gone before yours, and, in all likelihood, you have already made progress that proves the value, even at a small scale within your own operation.

McKinsey Quarterly noted that for companies to migrate to the cloud more judiciously and efficiently, digital leaders need to push the executive team for the following:

- *establishing a sustainable funding model to support the investments required to get business value from the cloud*

- *developing a new business-technology operating model that exploits cloud for speed, agility, and efficient scalability*

- *putting in place the HR, compensation, and location policies required to attract and retain the specialized engineering talent required to operate in the cloud*[38]

Each are important. For a large company, these transformations take years. This will be an arduous journey if you begin today. It will be even harder if you wait another year after having built and integrated technology on your existing, antiquated portfolio. Set the right expectations that this will need to be funded over years. Technology and digital executives must also set the record straight on the value that the company will derive. Ultimately, this is a nimbleness play, through and through. It is about giving you better options in the future, and an ability to pivot more readily. Lastly, the people aspects are profound. Some people on your current staff will not be able to cross the chasm to this new world. You should make an attempt with everyone, but for those who are in roles that are going away, and who do not appear to have the ability to modernize their own skillsets, finding a humane means of parting, while having them be an important part of the technology migration, is the right recipe.

Steps to implement cloud technology

There are four stages to implement cloud technology:

- Pilot/ad hoc: This is the stage when executives elect to try out cloud technology. Most companies have at least entered this stage, perhaps taking an ad hoc approach to implementing cloud technology

- Broader introduction: After cloud technology has proven its value, a broader plan is typically set to introduce cloud technology across many layers of the technology portfolio. The success factors noted during the piloting phase should be used in the business case for this broader introduction.

- Migration of data: Next is the migration of data at scale. Governance practices are defined, and lifecycles for the technologies are better articulated. Operational tools should be introduced. This is an important phase where errors can lead to systems downtime, budget overruns, and upset customers. Planning and monitoring are crucial leading up to and through this phase.

- Maturation: The biggest aspects of the cloud migration are complete. During this phase, the focus should be on improving service, and continuing to drive the value of the cloud deeper into the organization.

Steps toward cloud maturity

What are the steps to improve cloud maturity?

1 With the help of enterprise architecture, product, and development leads, determine which products are best suited for migration to the cloud.

2 Based upon these initial thoughts, develop a timeline with stage gates along the way to determine how long the migration may take, the order of the migrations, while also leaving time for learning and corrections along the way. This is an emerging cloud strategy as well as a tactical plan.

3 Communicate this plan with the executive team and all associates who will be involved in bringing it to life. Of course, the cost considerations and the potential disruptions to different parts of the business mean that this will require buy-in at the highest levels of the company.

4 Plan the process of containerization of different tiers of the technology landscape. This will require a thorough code and architecture review, as well.

5 Build cloud-appropriate processes and architecture to support the changes identified. Again, communicate progress or lack thereof, building momentum while also course-correcting along the way, including documentation of lessons learned for others to learn from as the migration continues. It will be necessary to develop forums for collaboration and a knowledge management hub to collect information for others to easily find. Ensure changes are included in product backlogs.

Private versus public cloud

There are multiple cloud options available. A private cloud is a scenario where computing services are leveraged by a single organization. The services are maintained on a private network, and resources required to administer those services are dedicated. It is private to them. It may be hosted in the company's data center. Adherents to the private cloud underscore that it is more customizable and offers greater levels of control and security. Private clouds tend to be more expensive in many cases, however.

Public clouds are scenarios where servers, storage, and the like are owned by a third-party provider, such as AWS, Microsoft, or Google. Computing infrastructure and services are shared by multiple companies and organizations. Part of the logic initially was that this was the lower-cost means of moving to the cloud. The public cloud is scalable, requires little maintenance, and has been reliable, by and large.

The public cloud was once deemed risky by those who transitioned work to the cloud in the early stages of broad adoption of cloud computing, but it is now secure and robust enough that conservative organizations like US government departments and agencies have elected to use public cloud computing to a much greater extent. Of course, strong security practices are still necessary, and nothing is foolproof.

There is also the hybrid cloud solution. This combines private and public clouds. The private cloud is used for workloads that are deemed sensitive or business-critical. In the hybrid cloud model, the public cloud is used for applications that have high variability of volume. Hybrid cloud allows for capabilities during surges in demand for certain applications. For those applications that run in the private cloud, rules can be set such that when a certain demand threshold is met, the overload volume can be run in the public cloud.

Walmart operates a private cloud in its data centers and partners with public cloud providers for edge computing for in-store uses. With the hybrid structure, Walmart can take workloads and move them seamlessly from private cloud to public cloud to make use of the flex capacity when it is needed, particularly during the December holidays. This hybrid model allows Walmart to make use of specialized compute capabilities in the public cloud, such as running "complex workloads," including machine learning models and big data.

Finally, there is multi-cloud. This is concurrent use of multiple public cloud providers. This is an approach some take when they worry about the potential risk of locking in with one provider alone. By choosing multiple providers, one can take advantage of the strengths of each, and should the relationship with one become stronger and/or should the relationship with the other become weaker, work can be transitioned from one to the other.

What should remain on premises?

Some major enterprises have set goals to be as close to completely in the cloud as is possible due to the advantages noted above. That said, some companies have elected to ring-fence some applications that will remain on premises. Examples include:

- some business-critical applications, those with particular security needs, those that are more cost-effective/efficient staying on premises
- some legacy applications, particularly ones with man dependencies, that may not be compatible with cloud. They ultimately cost more to refactor their applications and move them to cloud than to leave them on premises

- some on-premises applications that "are tuned with specific versions of their databases on certain platforms for performance and reliability reasons"[39]

- "some data can be exposed publicly, and some data cannot risk even a hint of exposure. In this second case, an air-gapped, on-premises system may provide better security"[40]

- "if you are collecting data at a high rate from local IoT devices, going directly to a public cloud may be too slow, so it makes more sense to use an on-premises database or edge cloud"[41]

It is important to note that some companies choose to migrate to the cloud for the wrong reasons ("It's primarily about cost savings," they might incorrectly note) or without thinking about the implications to people (including roles going away), processes, as well as the more obvious technology implications. The strategy you design and the pace that you choose must bear in mind these factors, or you will be destined for underwhelming results or worse.

That said, cloud computing is, in many ways, the foundational technology factor for nimbleness. It is important to note that it is rare for a company born in the past decade to build on-premises, fixed technology, as was commonplace among companies of the past. As many of those companies scale quickly, their ability to scale at dizzying paces has been aided in no small part due to their adoption of a cloud-first strategy. The number of older companies that have followed suit, such as FedEx and Capital One to name

FIGURE 4.3 Cloud

Role(s) responsible	Tool(s)	Metrics

- CIO/CDO

- By service model:
  - infrastructure as a service
  - platform as a service
  - software as a service
  - serverless computing
  - function as a service
- By deployment model:
  - public cloud
  - private cloud
  - community cloud
  - hybrid cloud

- Improved user experience
- Increased security (examining number of threats before and after)

two, is emblematic of more change to come. The change is not easy, and it is high cost and includes some risk. This should be considered an investment in your company's future. Don't be on the wrong side of this change.

APIs and microservices

Companies face an increasing need to create new products or improve upon existing products faster. They also seek to enable a wider range of seamless digital interactions. Two tools that facilitate this are application programming interfaces (APIs) and microservices. But what are they, and why are so many companies investing in them? Let me take each of them separately.

APIs

In 2002, Jeff Bezos issued a mandate (often referred to as the Bezos Mandate, in fact) to his internal development teams, highlighting how software was to be built. The mandate noted:

> Only communication allowed is via service interface calls over the network. It doesn't matter what technology they use. HTTP, Corba, Pubsub, custom protocols—doesn't matter. Bezos doesn't care. All service interfaces, without exception, must be designed from the ground up to be externalizable. That is to say, the team must plan and design to be able to expose the interface to developers in the outside world. No exceptions. Anyone who doesn't do this will be fired.[42]

This was particularly prescient, and in the nearly two decades following this mandate, Amazon did just this, empowering an ecosystem of partners, suppliers, and customers to connect in new and robust ways. In the process, Amazon's value surpassed a trillion dollars.

Key to this growth were application programming interfaces, or APIs, which specify how the different elements of an application interact and communicate with one another. A CIO friend of mine likens APIs to the waiter who takes your order from the restaurant's menu, and then relays that order to the kitchen, where the cooks cook your order. The waiter then delivers what you have ordered. APIs can be a means of sharing data or algorithms across internal systems or to external parties. They are a critical way in which data in one place can be proliferated across all systems that require that same data, avoiding data duplications or data gaps in the process. This speeds up the rate at which data gets to where it needs to be, and can hasten the pace of software delivery in the process, as plugging into an API can advance work where recreation might have been the norm in the past. For customers, employees, and external partners who need up-to-date data, APIs are a near seamless source of that data. And, powerfully, APIs can parse between the data that is appropriate to share versus that which is not. Of course, you may be an external partner to another company from whom you need comparable data.

There are private and public APIs. As the name suggests, private APIs are closed or restricted to more sensitive and secure systems. Public APIs are more transparent and accessible to others outside of the company of origin. The growth in public APIs has been much faster than private APIs as connecting with a broader ecosystem has proven to have great advantages to companies, and leveraging public APIs to do so has aided this tremendously.

The steps to implement APIs

Even though API management has become more universal, it is important for the API lifecycle to evolve. One such way to achieve this is through making the API management process agile. Those that are delivering APIs with agility should follow these phases to success.

Technologies needed for the API journey

- API design tool
- mocking and testing tool
- API testing and editing tool
- service development framework
- deployment/CI-CD platform
- API management tool

PHASE 0: IDEATION

While often the API lifecycle begins with the design phase and promotes a contract-first approach, it can be challenging to start with an API contract design from scratch. As such, it can be useful to develop a sandbox that can be used to test what future APIs should look like.

There are several approaches we can use for tooling in this phase:

- Local—utilizes a dedicated simulation tool that is used locally. These tools typically target developers and can sometimes make it difficult to share and test multiple designs.

- Team—A platform that can be used to host and share different tests. These are generally better for enterprise context.

PHASE 1: DESIGN AN API CONTRACT

This step is performed to create an API contract artifact that covers the technical and syntactic definition for a future API. Contracts are used to provide a clear description of the API methods and custom resources manipulated while serving as the foundation for a service-based architecture.

Standardization has been a focus of the last few years and has led to OpenAPI Specification becoming the standard.

Tooling can follow the same local or team designation outlined in Phase 0

PHASE 2: CREATING EXPECTATIONS AND SAMPLES

This phase does not require significant time investment but is often overlooked in the service-based architecture application build process. While technically feasible to mock from an API contract, this does not always translate the business logic as clearly as sampling can.

The sampling process should also be focused on defining business expectations that could not be defined with just a technical contract.

PHASE 3: DEVELOPING MOCK APIS AND USABLE TESTS

There are two distinct goals of this phase: (1) convert the provided samples into usable mocks, and (2) reuse the samples as a test suite for the future API implementations. Once again, there are multiple approaches that can be used for developing the mocks, both local and team approaches, each supported by multiple software options.

Important considerations during this phase for determining the best approach are how the mock will be communicated and documented as well as the lifetime of the mock. Mocks that provide the most value to organizations are those that have a long lifetime and are well understood by the customer.

PHASE 4: API DEVELOPMENT, TESTING, AND DEPLOYMENT

This is the most obvious phases in API development. Most organizations will already have a technology stack selected by this stage, but it is important to consider modern development and deployment requirements. For any new application it must be compatible with the cloud to ensure it aligns to the growing digital trend in the enterprise. The following are some general requirements for a cloud-compatible application:

- dynamic load adaptability
- flexible and centralized configuration
- dependency discovery functionality
- load-balancing mechanisms
- resilience, monitoring, and observability
- automatic log and distributed tracing

PHASE 5: CONTINUED API TESTING

Testing is a critical part of the API development process. While it is okay to launch manual testing a few times, the best practice is to have automated testing. Those with a good grasp on automated testing should consider a testing integration for APIs in conjunction with the continuous integration/ continuous delivery (CI/CD) pipeline.

Examples of companies utilizing APIs effectively

Unsurprisingly, many organizations have embraced the adoption of API development into their business. There have been numerous success stories across various industries of businesses improving their outcomes through APIs. Whether through diversified revenue streams, increasing customer value, or allowing third-party innovation, companies have found ways to boost performance.

While there are several companies whose success with APIs is well known (think digital native companies such as Stripe or Twilio), it may surprise you to learn how nontraditional technology companies have also capitalized on the need for APIs.

Rovi, formerly Macrovision—a company that started encoding metadata into physical media (video tapes, DVDs, DVRs, etc.) starting in 1985—made the pivot to offer their metadata via an API starting in 2009. As a result, their music metadata is used by companies including Apple, Facebook, Spotify, Slacker, and Pandora, all thanks to API development.[43]

McDonald's also recently entered the API game. In 2019, they acquired three tech companies to gain direct access to their APIs: Dynamic Yield, Plexure, and Apprente. These APIs allow McDonald's to modernize their customer interactions and improve the customer experience. The acquisition was part of their Velocity Growth Plan to ensure McDonald's stays innovative.[44]

Lastly there is eBay. While always an online company, they did not start out in the API game. Instead, they were forced to enter the space in response to the large amount of unlicensed third parties that relied on their ecosystem. While the rollout occurred in stages, today eBay has expanded its API territory, and over 60 percent of the company's revenues are generated from the API.[45]

The benefits of exposing assets in this way include:

• Wider reach for an organization's brand

• External sources of innovation, leading, for instance, to greater levels of open innovation

• New or enhanced sources of revenues.[46]

The speed of business is increasing, and to support that pace, applications and products often need to be able to leverage real-time data and gain easy access to both internal and external data sets. Accessing this external data can open new business opportunities with less time and cost required. The Boston-based information technology research organization, Cutter Consortium, defines the API economy as, "The economy where companies expose their (internal) business assets or services in the form of (Web) APIs to third parties with the goal of unlocking additional business value through the creation of new asset classes."[47] Think of a travel website like Booking.com, Kayak, or Expedia. We can put in our travel request to these sites, and they draw information from many airlines for the city pairs, dates, and class of service we request. We get specific time and price information for each airline. That is managed by APIs between the travel booking site and the airlines. Like the waiter, the API takes our request, goes to many sources of information, and brings back what we need.

APIs play an increasingly critical role in today's organizations. I have begun to hear from technology and digital leaders that they assess a potential acquisition target company's use of APIs in evaluating how fast an integration is possible between companies. APIs are not the last word on whether an acquisition and integration will be easy, but they can facilitate the combination of datasets or the bundling of products and services.

In his book, *Truth from the Valley*, long-time CIO, Mark Settle, notes:

An API-based approach to application architecture is a paradigm shift from the construction of monolithic applications that are wholly self-sufficient to the assembly of applications that integrate data and services from both internal and external sources. In layman's terms, it's the difference between weaving a tapestry and stitching a quilt![48]

This includes managing the flow of data between different sources or components of applications.

Cynthia Stoddard, the CIO of Adobe, agrees. She notes, "APIs drive self-service, which drives agility."[49]

API governance

Remember that APIs deal with data, and data must be governed appropriately. Therefore, a strategy for APIs must take into consideration government regulations such as the California Consumer Privacy Act (CCPA), the General Data Protection Regulation (GDPR), Sarbanes-Oxley (SOX), Health Insurance Portability and Accountability Act (HIPAA), and the Payment Card Industry Data Security Standard (PCI), to name a few. Settle notes:

> End user authentication procedures and access privileges need to be explicitly enforced at or upstream of the API interface and verifiable via system logs. A comprehensive catalog of enterprise APIs will include both internally developed and externally available APIs.[50]

Arthur Hu, the chief information officer of Lenovo, suggests the following guidelines on where to apply APIs:

> First, consider architecture diagrams. Where different data comingle and where technology intersects, this is a candidate for APIs. Second, who do you frequently contact to do something for you? Where there is a repetitive aspect to this work, an API can be effective.

Like all technology, APIs need to be managed. When they are created, they must be noted. If updates are made to those, the changes should be documented. The endpoints that APIs connect should be noted, and interface standards should be developed. Security measures must be in place given the fact that APIs can entail the sharing of critical data to third parties. Related to that, if your organization has a variety of APIs with duplicate functionality, APIs that are used by only a single API partner, and/or low traffic volume to your APIs, it can be a challenge for API cybersecurity solutions that use artificial intelligence or machine learning to detect anomalous behavior.[51]

Developing an API strategy

Prior to introducing APIs, it is important to tie their introduction to business objectives while aligning it to the broader enterprise architecture.

A *Wired* piece from 2013 entitled "Leveraging APIs as Part of Digital Strategy" suggested the following tactics to implement an API strategy:

1 Strategic fit: How does the API strategy have to be designed such that it contributes to the overarching business strategy? This is also related to the three benefits of APIs and influences on which to focus.

2 Value proposition: Which value does the API deliver to whom? How is it different than competitive offers?

3 Business model: What API business model best supports the organization's overarching business model? How does the organization create and capture value internally? How does the organization define value in this context?

4 Pricing: Do you provide APIs for free? Or charge based on usage or based on number of APIs used?

5 Technology: Which technological decisions need to be made? These include access protocols, security, the scale and scope of a developer portal, whether to build or buy the API gateway solution, and whether to host on premise or in the cloud.

6 Marketing: Who are the customers and what are their pains and potential gains? How is the APIs' value communicated? How is the product sold and delivered to the customers?

7 Operations: How are the APIs deployed, maintained, and supported? How do developers on-board?[52]

Other considerations when developing an API strategy include:

- API skills: Your technology or engineering team must have the right skills to design and build APIs. If they don't, develop a plan to recruit and/or train for the skills necessary.

- API design principles: Be sure that the APIs you wish to implement fit with the pace of change in your business. That is to say, as the business evolves, so must the APIs. They must be flexible enough to evolve while also being secure enough to keep your data assets sacred.

- API documentation: Set aside team members and steps in the process to document APIs. This is too often an afterthought in the development of APIs, and it can work against the flexibility noted in the design principles. Each code release should yield fresh documentation.

- API infrastructure: Be sure that your technology and digital infrastructure appropriately supports the scale, performance, and security needs of the APIs you will introduce.

- API quality: Be sure that you bake the quality steps into the process. There should be stage gates to mark progress or lack thereof. There should be automated and repeatable testing incorporated into the process, as well.

- Developer support: Be sure that as you migrate to APIs, especially (though not limited to) the early stages, have support in place to help consumers of your APIs if they have questions or issues.

- Marketing APIs (internally or externally): The APIs will only derive value for the company if they are used. Making internal constituents or partner or customer companies aware of their existence and the benefits of using them is essential.

- Legal considerations: Be sure your legal team weighs in on the plan to introduce APIs. There are risks and legal obligations that will be new as a result of this move, so do not proceed blindly.

Microservices

In 2017, I had a chance to sit down with Sequoia Capital Partner Matt Miller, who has an expertise in microservices. I asked him why companies use microservices. He responded by saying:

> Microservices are the easiest way to go big by going small. It is taking what may have been a large traditional application and breaking it into many smaller autonomous pieces. Those pieces are defined as services that operate uniquely across the different use cases you have. Microservices provide a lot of benefits for the startup community Sequoia works with, as well as the corporate Fortune 500, Global 2000 community we work with, since many of our companies are our startup community's vendors. Going to smaller applications makes you far more scalable because it is easier to scale smaller pieces. It is also significantly faster to iterate and make changes on small pieces. Additionally, the smaller pieces are far more resilient because the systems are designed to be completely independent. Meaning, if there is a failure in one of the pieces, the rest of the system continues to operate. The result of all of this is a better user experience. It is also significantly less expensive than maintaining the monolithic applications people have worked with for years.[53]

Microservices architectures involve breaking down monolithic applications into individual software components (services) that can be updated and deployed without the need to take down or redeploy the entire application. Individual microservices often communicate with one another through APIs. This decoupling encourages modularity and provides an ability to develop, test, troubleshoot, and deploy at scale, which can drive flexibility, agility, efficiency.

API strategy is a key part of any microservices strategy. APIs and microservices are pieces of the broader enterprise architecture discussion, as they relate to how applications communicate and how data moves throughout an organization. CarMax Chief Information Officer and Chief Technology Officer Shamim Mohammad underscored this point when he said:

> The architectural approach was so critical because if you didn't create this API-driven, microservices type of framework, we were going to have problems because we would [have needed] to move fast and we couldn't [have gone] fast. So that's probably the biggest thing that happened. [Implementing APIs and microservices] allowed us to move fast because our product teams could innovate, but they needed a platform to innovate on.

Benefits of using microservices

The advantages of using microservices include:

- agility
- efficiency
- resiliency
- revenue

Matt Miller from Sequoia noted the importance in accelerating innovation in applications and services as a means of driving greater levels of revenue from them. With monolithic technology, changes to a website take much longer than they need to, and this has revenue implications. Startups that do not have the legacy, monolithic technology are able to capitalize on their slower digital immigrant competitors.

Schneider Electric Chief Digital Officer Herve Coureil noted in reflecting upon the benefits of microservices, "Everything that can break down interdependencies, everything that allows us to remove a system change from a critical path is welcome. It means we can go faster."

Capital One CIO Rob Alexander believes that microservices are an essential element to getting the most out of Agile practices. "The way you allow Agile teams to operate with greater autonomy is to align them to microservices," he told me in a conversation we had on the topic. "In the target end state, we want Agile teams wrapped around relatively autonomous and independent microservices that can move at their own speed." This facilitates true agility.

Steps to implementing microservices

To begin a microservices implementation, start with a pilot or a small project related to this and dedicate a team to the effort. Begin simply by turning a single application, and optimally one of the less complex ones, into a microservice.

Next, be sure that the series of applications you believe to be candidates are worthy of the added complexity that microservices entail. For all of its benefits, there are more pieces to the puzzle with microservices. Not all applications are right for the change. Factors to consider are the size of the application (bigger), the frequency of changes to that application (more), as well as the need to scale the application (bigger). Lenovo CIO Arthur Hu noted in a conversation with me on the topic, "Don't forget that there is a cost to doing things in microservices. There are financial implications that must be taken into account. There's a cost of complexity." Naresh Shanker, the chief technology officer of Xerox, echoed the sentiment in a separate conversation on the topic: "There are still drawbacks. If you're designing all of these different services, they can get quite complex. You have to step back and think that through. Also you need to be very purposeful in terms of architecture."

In terms of breaking the application apart, it is important to think iteratively. Speed is also not necessarily a good thing. Better to be planful and careful when making these changes.

It is important to have sound leadership of the microservices. Sequoia's Matt Miller goes on to refer to "artisans or architects who sit on top to make sure you are not reproducing duplicate services and that there is not overlap between your services."[54] These leaders can counter service sprawl, which can happen, especially in scenarios where a technology or digital division moves too quickly. The artisan/architect model has been used extensively by companies like Amazon and Google.

It is important to map microservices to business processes. If this mapping is not done, fixes and re-architecting the microservices in the future can be difficult to undertake.

By the way, it may seem that going from monolithic applications to microservices is a retrofitting exercise only. In fact, there are advantages to developing products as monoliths first, see how they are used and by whom, and then break them into microservices based upon those insights.

As microservices are developed, tabulate all of them into a catalog or repository. This will facilitate use of the microservices in the future. The artisan/architect should be responsible for managing the catalog, ensuring it is up to date, and that there is one source of truth only.

CIO.com[55] recommends the following "eight tips for making the shift to microservices":

1 Employ domain-driven design. Using a thematic approach to app building that creates efficient development patterns and removes interdependencies between teams. In the example here, one microservice is tied to one domain, helping to delineate responsibilities.

2 Establish guidelines for code libraries. Robust processes are needed to manage the appropriate sharing and updating of code.

3 Address security concerns. Patch deployment and regular scans are important. Check often across different services.

4 Don't share databases between microservices. Development process is plug and play.

5 Avoid entanglements. Allow your enterprise architecture to help drive your microservices designs to avoid unexpected or unnecessary dependencies later on.

6 Consider building apps from scratch.

7 Measure performance when scaling. While monolithic applications can be scaled as a whole, products built of microservices may scale on a piecemeal basis, which requires continued performance monitoring across the microservices portfolio.

8 Focus on change management. Speed is great, but don't forget about governance.

To that list above, I would add that microservices increase the threat landscape for bad actors, and therefore it is important to authenticate traffic through the microservices. Determining who can work on which microservices and holding true to those designations is another important facet to this. Xerox Chief Technology Officer Naresh Shanker highlighted this point in saying, "The beauty about... microservices [is that] you isolate failures." When there are

FIGURE 4.4 Sequoia Capital's guide to microservices

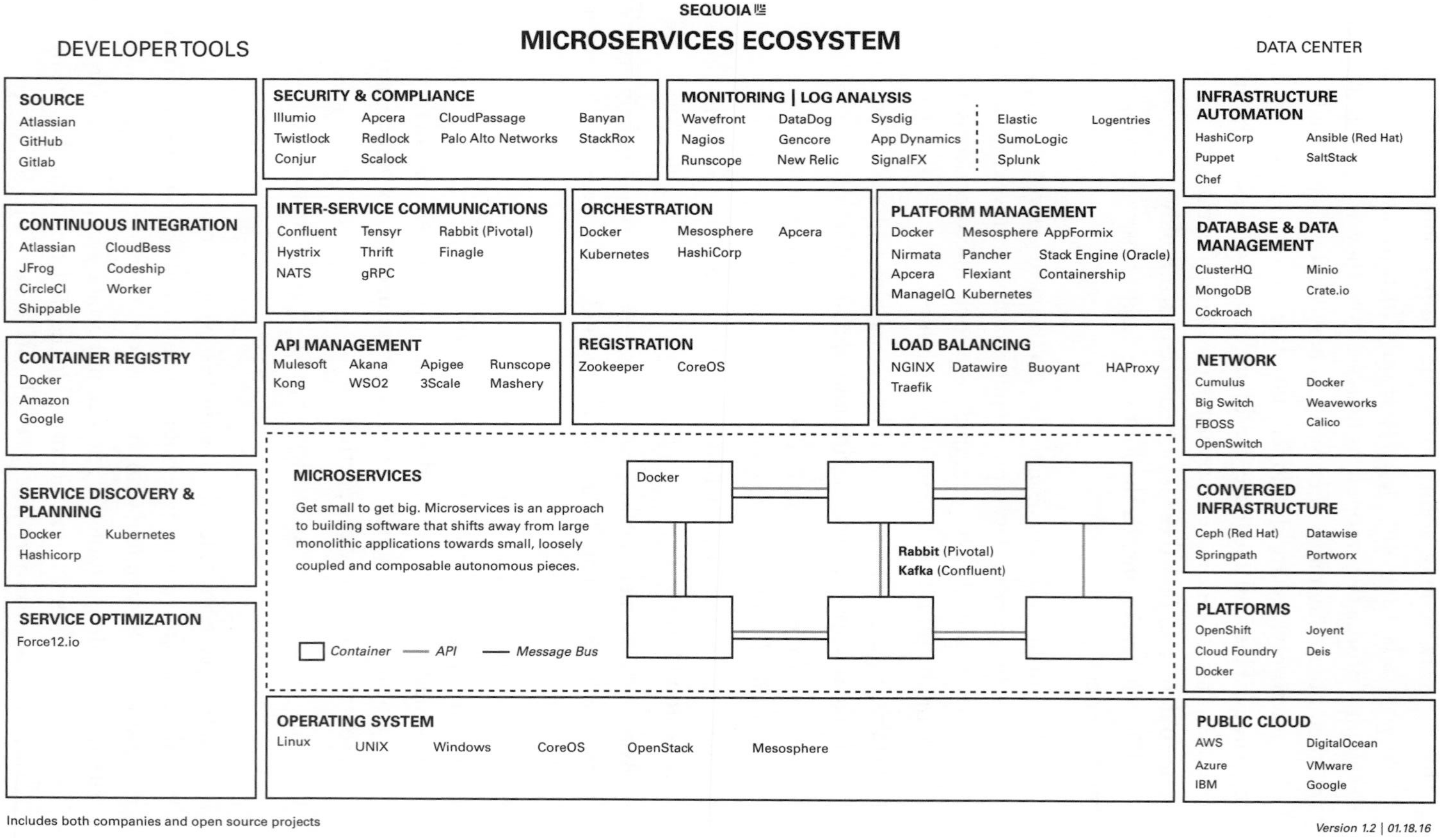

SEQUOIA 喦

MICROSERVICES ECOSYSTEM

DEVELOPER TOOLS

DATA CENTER

SOURCE
Atlassian
GitHub
Gitlab

SECURITY & COMPLIANCE
Illumio   Apcera   CloudPassage
Twistlock   Redlock   Palo Alto Networks
Conjur   Scalock

MONITORING | LOG ANALYSIS
Wavefront   DataDog   Sysdig   Elastic   Logentries
Nagios   Gencore   App Dynamics   SumoLogic
Runscope   New Relic   SignalFX   Splunk

INFRASTRUCTURE AUTOMATION
HashiCorp   Ansible (Red Hat)
Puppet   SaltStack
Chef

CONTINUOUS INTEGRATION
Atlassian   CloudBess
JFrog   Codeship
CircleCI   Worker
Shippable

INTER-SERVICE COMMUNICATIONS
Confluent   Tensyr   Rabbit (Pivotal)
Hystrix   Thrift   Finagle
NATS   gRPC

ORCHESTRATION
Docker   Mesosphere   Apcera
Kubernetes HashiCorp

PLATFORM MANAGEMENT
Docker   Mesosphere AppFormix
Nirmata   Pancher   Stack Engine (Oracle)
Apcera   Flexiant   Containership
ManageIQ   Kubernetes

DATABASE & DATA MANAGEMENT
ClusterHQ   Minio
MongoDB   Crate.io
Cockroach

CONTAINER REGISTRY
Docker
Amazon
Google

API MANAGEMENT
Mulesoft   Akana   Apigee   Runscope
Kong   WSO2   3Scale   Mashery

REGISTRATION
Zookeeper   CoreOS

LOAD BALANCING
NGINX   Datawire   Buoyant   HAProxy
Traefik

NETWORK
Cumulus   Docker
Big Switch   Weaveworks
FBOSS   Calico
OpenSwitch

SERVICE DISCOVERY & PLANNING
Docker   Kubernetes
Hashicorp

MICROSERVICES

Get small to get big. Microservices is an approach to building software that shifts away from large monolithic applications towards small, loosely coupled and composable autonomous pieces.

Docker

CONVERGED INFRASTRUCTURE
Ceph (Red Hat)   Datawise
Springpath   Portworx
Docker

SERVICE OPTIMIZATION
Force12.io

☐ *Container* —— *API* —— *Message Bus*

Rabbit (Pivotal)
Kafka (Confluent)

PLATFORMS
OpenShift   Joyent
Cloud Foundry   Deis
Docker

OPERATING SYSTEM
Linux   UNIX   Windows   CoreOS   OpenStack   Mesosphere

PUBLIC CLOUD
AWS   DigitalOcean
Azure VMware
IBM   Google

Version 1.2 | 01.18.16

Includes both companies and open source projects

SOURCE Sequoia

FIGURE 4.5 APIs and microservices

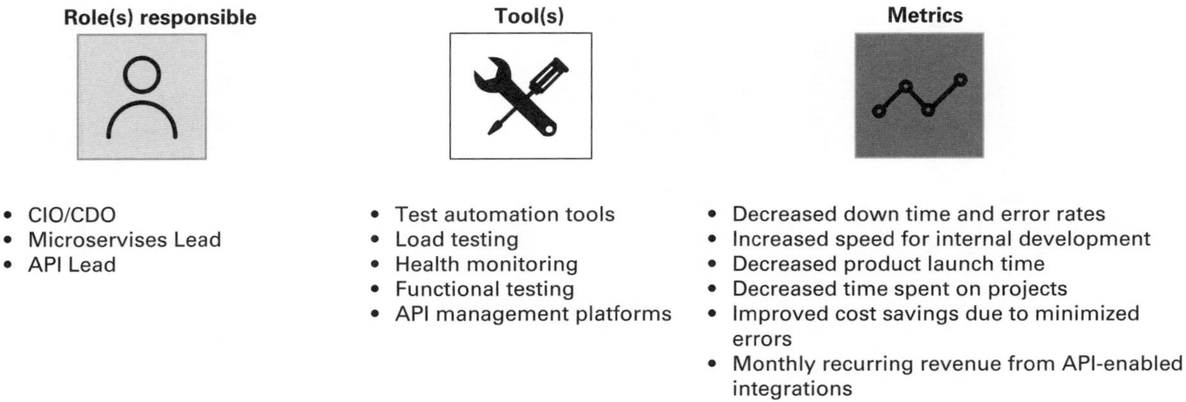

Role(s) responsible

- CIO/CDO
- Microservises Lead
- API Lead

Tool(s)

- Test automation tools
- Load testing
- Health monitoring
- Functional testing
- API management platforms

Metrics

- Decreased down time and error rates
- Increased speed for internal development
- Decreased product launch time
- Decreased time spent on projects
- Improved cost savings due to minimized errors
- Monthly recurring revenue from API-enabled integrations

issues with monolithic technology, the consequences can be more dire because the issues are much more difficult to isolate. Not so with microservices. They are designed to localize issues, minimizing the broader consequences.

Security

Security in its many forms is a topic that is, unfortunately, growing in importance. The bad actors in the world have much to gain through their actions, and many of them are well funded by governments who would wish to sow chaos in society, as well as steal intellectual capital from companies. Many hackers themselves are often very smart and innovative, to boot, and they often create tools that make it easier for their less-skilled peers to launch their own attacks, creating a kind of underground market for cybercrime and stolen data. Moreover, the job of the chief information security officer and their team is daunting. There are many pathways into the enterprise to steal the "crown jewels" of a company, and the bad actors need only be right once.

The first cyberattack is often credited to Robert Tapan Morris, a graduate student at Cornell University, in 1988. Morris claimed that he hoped to gauge the size of the budding internet. He developed what would come to be known as the Morris worm and released it through computers at MIT. The worm used weaknesses in the UNIX system Noun 1, and it slowed down computers to the point of being unusable.[56] This is believed to be the first denial of service (DoS) attack.[57] Morris was the first person to be indicted under the Computer Fraud and Abuse Act.[58] He would go on to become an entrepreneur, a tech investor and advisor, and a tenured professor at MIT.

When I started advising CIOs, it was common for them to declare a goal of having "zero cybersecurity issues." This sounded like a great goal to have, and many companies lived up to this promise at a time when these issues were relatively infrequent into the early and mid-2000s. However, this way of thinking lulled many companies and their customers to the point of complacency. I don't mean that they did not have appropriate offensive and defensive weapons in their arsenal, but if your stance is that you will have zero issues, it is possible that disaster recovery and business continuity plans may not be fully thought through. Over time, that complacency can lead to underinvestment in proper threat detection and remediation tools, which makes it that much harder to respond effectively when an inevitable attack does occur.

Jason Ruger, chief information security officer of Lenovo and head of IT (a de facto CIO) for Motorola's Mobile Business Group, remembers things in much the same way. "'Protection' is where we were 15 years ago in cyber," he recalls. "If I have a great firewall, everything is safe, do not worry." Lately, he says, the focus has shifted to detection:

> You have to have the humility that if you cannot keep the hackers out, there will be zero-days [a cyber vulnerability that is unknown to the organization upon which it has been perpetrated]. The cybercriminals are incredibly intelligent and creative. How do you detect once things happen and then lastly, how do you respond?

Ruger's experience as both a CIO and a CISO give him an insightful perspective on the healthy tension that can exist between IT and security teams, particularly as data grows in importance inside organizations. A CIO may focus on leveraging customer data to enable new products and services, for example, while a CISO will do all they can to protect that data and customer privacy. "It is an interesting mix because the exact same piece of information can be both a liability and an asset," Ruger says. As companies embrace artificial intelligence:

> the desire is to collect as much information from as many different sources as possible and build those insights, but from a CISO standpoint, it is trying to separate those data sources and not allow views across all data sources because that is a way to create lateral movement and risk.

While both of these efforts ultimately serve the customer, leaders are tasked with finding a balance between these two mandates.

I often say that it is a shame that the security issue is so white hot. In my conversations with venture capitalists, it is among the areas that receives the greatest levels of investment due to its growing complexity and a continued rise in the issues that abound. This used to be a topic that was buried in the IT department. A director or vice president of security oversaw the function, and the C-suite had little reason to know that leader. Today, cybersecurity, as well as data protection and privacy, is a board-level issue. Many boards are adding technologically savvy members at least partially to ensure that there is sufficient knowledge and representation on this critical topic. Now, security leaders are frequently members of the C-suite, and everyone in the company knows them.

One of the few benefits of the increased frequency of data breaches at prominent companies is that digital, technology, and security executives have reason to do scenario assessments, mapping out approaches and responses to potential issues. Today, as the commonly held adage goes, there are two kinds of companies: those that have been hacked and those who don't know they have been hacked. If you are in the latter camp, do not be complacent!

Another benefit to the growing prominence of cybersecurity is the growth in new approaches to prevent attacks and improve enterprise risk management. As cyberattacks grow more sophisticated, so do the researchers, startups, and others creating approaches to address them.

The breaches of Target (November 2013) vs. Home Depot (September 2014)

While not the first cyberattacks, Target's breach in November 2013 was one of the first that highlighted the various ways in which a bad actor could make its way into company systems, in this case through an HVAC vendor. It also highlighted the sheer number of customers who could be affected—roughly 70 million in this case[59]—and the formidable cost to the retailer—over $200 million.[60] It also showed how little control many companies have over disparate customer data sets, underscoring the broader data security challenges many firms face. It also hit Target's bottom line. In the fourth quarter of the company's fiscal year (the quarter in which the breach took place), profit fell 46 percent compared to the same quarter the year prior. The brand was hurt badly, and the CEO and CIO were among the executives who were shown the door.

Less than a year later, Home Depot reported a breach that by some estimates was broader, but that did not hurt the company nearly as much. One of the reasons why was because it learned from Target's example the year prior and began to prepare itself for a similar situation. That included not only internal preparations, but also thinking through how it would communicate to external stakeholders. Target's response suggested that the company did not expect to be penetrated. It did not have a well-developed communications plan, and the leadership was accused of coming across as dishonest. Home Depot, on the other hand, had a more detailed communications plan and benefited from it with much less business and stock price erosion.

Both breaches underscore the critical need for firms to have solid business continuity and disaster recovery plans related to cybersecurity and to assume that there will be issues. Conduct scenario analyses based upon this assumption. Engage companies who can attempt to hack your systems in a controlled way to draw conclusions about areas of greatest vulnerability and develop plans to plug holes that are identified.

Different kinds of cyberattacks

Cyberattacks come in many forms, but there are three that are among the most common. The aforementioned distributed denial of service (DDoS) attack denies access to websites or online services. Larger versions of these can involve thousands of compromised computers attacking the same website.

Ransomware is software that accesses and locks down vital files and systems on computers, rendering them inaccessible. Bad actors then demand fees in order to unlock the data. In 2020, a number of cities were hit with ransomware attacks, for example, and some companies have stockpiled cryptocurrency to prepare for greater levels of ransomware attacks. These were the attacks that increased the most as a result of the pandemic and quarantine in 2020.

Malware is a type of software that intrudes and infiltrates your systems. Through viruses, worms, and the like, malware often leads to the theft of personal information and can lead to the damage of files. In some more dramatic instances, malware can disrupt or even hijack technology, leading to physical damage to hardware.

Lenovo's Ruger reflected on these and offered practical advice on how to think about them:

> Hackers either want to break, steal, or control the computer. Break includes categories like DDoS and ransomware—they stop your website or server from working. Steal includes the Target and Home Depot breaches—they steal customer data, bank accounts or intellectual property. Control—they take over your computer and use it do something else, such as to launch a DDoS campaign, send emails from your account, initiate processes like receiving money and immediately sending it to another account. Malware can be used for all three, and lately hackers combine these attacks. The best ransomware not only breaks your computer, but it sends your data to the hacker so that he or she can threaten to release customer data or intellectual property if you don't pay.

As Ruger's perspectives underscore, there are many combinations and variations of attacks. With each of these increasing, many companies are turning to a zero-trust security policy. Under this framework, no one inside or outside the network or the company is trusted and identity of anyone attempting to gain access to resources on the company's network must be verified. This is an important data protection mechanism that has gained momentum due to the significant ramifications associated with breaches. In Accenture's annual *Cost of Cybercrime Study*, it estimates a total value at risk of $5.2 trillion globally over the next five years.[61]

"It is called zero-trust because you cannot trust anything, so everything has to be treated as if it is out in the world at large," Tom Leighton, CEO of Akamai Technologies, said in a podcast interview he did with me.[62]

It is worth noting that adopting a zero-trust framework and policy is not as simple as adopting a single technology, and for many companies may be a multi-year effort.[63]

A risk-based approach to cybersecurity

As security increasingly becomes a board-level issue, there is a growing need for leaders to communicate how a company's cybersecurity posture ties to its overall risk profile, thus tying it more closely to the business. Broadly, the idea is that cybersecurity is not just about protecting computers and meeting compliance requirements, but rather weighing cybersecurity as a broader element of the enterprise risk management agenda. I recall a panel Steven Norton wrote about in 2015, when the then-CISO at McDonald's said: "Any idiot can secure a computer. The trick is can you manage risk, can you help your enterprise manage risk, (can you find) that balance between risk and reward?"[64]

According to Ruger, risk can be described as the combination of likelihood and impact. Likelihood covers the layers of defenses put on an asset versus how likely it is to be attacked, while impact is largely used to describe the cost of lost data or intellectual property. A CISO may not be able to change the impact of a particular attack, but they do have an opportunity to reduce the likelihood of an attack happening, and thus lowering risk.

CIOs and CISOs who understand this tradeoff and can effectively communicate their company's security posture through an enterprise risk lens are well positioned to add value. As the National Association of Corporate Directors said in a recent report, "Cybersecurity is now a major strategic and enterprise risk matter that affects how companies operate, innovate and create value."[65]

Leverage a framework

There are a number of frameworks to potentially use for security purposes. To be candid, so long as the one that you choose is comprehensive, the specific framework you choose is less important. If you are at a crossroads, I would suggest that you reach out to your network to see what others who you respect are using.

I did just that a few years back, and the answer that came back most often was the NIST Cybersecurity Framework. The National Institute of Standards and Technology (NIST) is a physical sciences laboratory and a nonregulatory agency of the United States Department of Commerce headquartered in the Washington, DC suburb of Gaithersburg, Maryland. Its mission is to promote innovation and industrial competitiveness. One of the laboratory programs focuses on information technology.

In February 2013, Executive Order 13636, signed by President Obama, called for the development of a cybersecurity framework. The order introduced efforts to share cybersecurity threat information and to build a set of current and successful approaches for reducing critical infrastructure risk. It also laid out the following requirements that NIST used as it created its cybersecurity framework:

- Identify security standards and guidelines that apply across sectors of critical infrastructure.
- Provide a prioritized, flexible, repeatable, performance-based, cost-effective approach.
- Help operators of critical infrastructure identify, assess, and manage cyber risk.
- Enable technical innovation while accounting for organizational differences.
- Provide technology-neutral guidance that enables the critical infrastructure sectors to benefit from a competitive market for products and services.
- Add guidance for measuring the performance of implementing the cybersecurity framework.
- Identify areas for improvement to be addressed through future collaboration.[66]

NIST was chosen to develop the cybersecurity framework "because they are a nonregulatory federal agency that acts as an unbiased source of scientific data and practices, including cybersecurity practices."[67] Ruger noted that NIST's nonregulatory status "means when they build a framework, it has to be good enough that industry wants to adopt it."[68] He went on to mention, "I think why NIST was successful was because they made a framework simple enough to report to senior executives on, but also comprehensive enough to work in the public and private sector."

The first version of the framework was published in February 2014. The recency of its development and indeed of the executive order that led to its creation highlights how new these threats are in the grand scheme of things. The NIST Cybersecurity Framework (Figure 4.6) includes five primary functions that serve as its backbone:

- identify
- protect
- detect
- respond
- recover[69]

Those core components are then broken down into categories that span cybersecurity, physical security, and people security (Figure 4.7). Those categories then link to subcategories that describe specific outcomes and show how the framework ties to other frameworks.

Cloud security considerations

As a company's technology estate expands, so do its potential security risks. A broad embrace of cloud computing, for example, may inject some firms with much-needed speed, but it may also introduce new authentication or data protection challenges, not to mention pressures on IT skillsets. Lenovo's Ruger says, "With cloud services if you can't authenticate properly, then hackers can steal your credentials and then sign in as you. Due to the nature of cloud, they can then access and steal your data."

Remote work will fuel a 33.3 percent surge in cloud spending from 2019 to 2020, with reduced demand for on-premise access networking equipment (cloud security to be increasingly necessary and likely to see sustained growth over the next few years).[70] There are a variety of potential security issues that may result, including:

- Greater speed may lead to greater risk, and more pressure on skillsets in IT.
- Issues companies face: "Cloud security problems stemming from assuming the same on-premise practices apply in the cloud environment (they don't)."
- When migrating to cloud, it's important to consider if there are consistent security policies and procedures in place.

FIGURE 4.6 NIST Cybersecurity Framework categories, and examples of subcategories

Function Unique Identifier	Function	Category Unique Identifier	Category
ID	Identify	ID.AM	Asset Management
		ID.BE	Business Environment
		ID.GV	Governance
		ID.RA	Risk Assessment
		ID.RM	Risk Management Strategy
		ID.SC	Supply Chain Risk Management
PR	Protect	PR.AC	Identity Management and Access Control
		PR.AT	Awareness and Training
		PR.DS	Data Security
		PR.IP	Information Protection Processes and Procedures
		PR.MA	Maintenance
		PR.PT	Protective Technology
DE	Detect	DE.AE	Anomalies and Events
		DE.CM	Security Continuous Monitoring
		DE.DP	Detection Processes
RS	Respond	RS.RP	Response Planning
		RS.CO	Communications
		RS.AN	Analysis
		RS.MI	Mitigation
		RS.IM	Improvements
RC	Recover	RC.RP	Recovery Planning
		RC.IM	Improvements
		RC.CO	Communications

SOURCE: NIST

- "Accidental risks posed by inexperienced or inattentive users can be every bit as devastating to the enterprise as bad actors" (cybersecurity).
- Sometimes, cloud providers are not solely responsible for locking down the security of a customer's data and applications (specific terms vary)—both cloud provider and customer share the burden for data security.[71]

Another potential risk is outages at your cloud provider. This could affect both availability and security. It is important to build strong service level agreements (SLAs) into contracts to ensure uptime guarantees and that there is some recourse in the case of an outage.

FIGURE 4.7 Framework categories and subcategories

Function	Category	ID
Identify	Asset Management	ID.AM
	Business Environment	ID.BE
	Governance	ID.GV
	Risk Assessment	ID.RA
	Risk Management Strategy	ID.RM
	Supply Chain Risk Management	ID.SC
Protect	Identity Management and Access Control	PR.AC
	Awareness and Training	PR.AT
	Data Security	PR.DS
	Information Protection Processes & Procedures	PR.IP
	Maintenance	PR.MA
	Protective Technology	PR.PT
Detect	Anomalies and Events	DE.AE
	Security Continuous Monitoring	DE.CM
	Detection Processes	DE.DP
Respond	Response Planning	RS.RP
	Communications	RS.CO
	Analysis	RS.AN
	Mitigation	RS.MI
	Improvements	RS.IM
Recover	Recovery Planning	RC.RP
	Improvements	RC.IM
	Communications	RC.CO

Subcategory	Informative References
ID.BE-1: The organization's role in the supply chain is identified and communicated	COBIT 5 APO08.01, APO08.04, APO08.05, APO10.03, APO10.04, APO10.05 ISO/IEC 27001:2013 A.15.1.1, A.15.1.2, A.15.1.3, A.15.2.1, A.15.2.2 NIST SP 800-53 Rev.4 CP-2, SA-12
ID.BE-2: The organization's place in critical infrastructure and its industry sector is identified and communicated	COBIT 5 APO02.06, APO03.01 ISO/IEC 27001:2013 Clause 4.1 NIST SP 800-53 Rev.4 PM-8
ID.BE-3: Priorities for organizational mission, objectives, and activities are established and communicated	COBIT 5 APO02.01, APO02.06, APO03.01 ISA 62443-2-1:2009 4.2.2.1, 4.2.3.6 NIST SP 800-53 Rev. 4 PM-11, SA-14
ID.BE-4: Dependencies and critical functions for delivery of critical services are established	COBIT 5 APO10.01, BAI04.02, BAI09.02 ISO/IEC 27001:2013 A.11.2.2, A.11.2.3, A.12.1.3 NIST SP 800-53 Rev. 4 CP-8, PE-9, PE-11, PM-8, SA-14
ID.BE-5: Resilience requirements to support delivery of critical services are established for all operating states (e.g. under duress/attack, during recovery, normal operations)	COBIT 5 DSS04.02 ISO/IEC 27001:2013 A.11.1.4, A.17.1.1, A.171.2, A.172.1 NIST SP 800-53 Rev. 4 CP-2, CP-11, SA-14

SOURCE: NIST

Developing cybersecurity "hygiene" across the enterprise

A technology, digital, or cybersecurity executive's job is not simply to leverage technology to secure a company's information assets. Indeed, the change management involved is just as much (if not more) a cultural issue as a technological one.

All it takes is an employee clicking a malicious link in an email for a company to be potentially compromised. Given the ease with which individuals can be risk vectors, or even steal sensitive information themselves, one aspect of a CIO or a CISO's purview is to educate the organization on proper cybersecurity hygiene. Teaching people not to click on suspicious links, encouraging teams to use strong passwords, and other practices can go a long way toward protecting an organization. Driving these educational initiatives across the organization also reflects the fact that security is an enterprise-wide concern, not just something relegated to IT.

Lenovo's Ruger added:

> We also face the insider threat now—where an employee can steal "digital currency." Twenty-five years ago this was mostly a physical threat (physically steal money or other physical items (clothes from Target, computer from Best Buy)). Now employees can steal digital items that previously had no value. A list of customer emails, a list of employee bank account numbers, a list of license/ activation codes.

Chapter takeaways

As I mentioned earlier in the book, people and processes come before technology for a reason. They are more important to your ability to change and innovate. That said, technology is often the anchor that weighs down a technology and digital organization and indeed an enterprise more generally. As my team and I collaborate with executives who hope to achieve nimbleness, the path to doing so can often be assessed with some degree of accuracy by assessing the amount of technical debt the company has. The technical debt is, itself, a sign of people attributes, namely culture, and a lack of relevant processes. The more antiquated technology is used, the more it is at least a potential sign of conservatism (ironically due to the risks associated with leaning on old technology), a lack of appreciation of technology, a lack of advocacy on the part of the IT team to modernize, and the like. It also

FIGURE 4.8 Security

Role(s) responsible

- CISO

Tool(s)

- Firewall
- Antivirus software
- Anti-spyware software
- Password management software
- Penetration testing tools
- Web vulnerability scanning tools

Metrics

- Improved security ratings
- Decreased threat/breach detection time
- Decreased recovery time from incidents
- Decreased impact of attacks on productivity, operations, and business overall

often means that a process is not adequately in place to retire old systems as new ones are brought in. It also tends to mean that there are higher amounts of fixed costs in the IT department, since older technology tends to have longer amortization cycles and can mean less flexibility for the IT team.

The four areas noted in this chapter—enterprise architecture, cloud, microservices/APIs, and security—must rise to a level of prominence and should be large areas of commitment in order to create a truly nimble company.

Notes

1   Fred Smith: An overnight success, Entrepreneur.com (archived at https://perma.cc/L5RE-HR6G), October 9, 2008

2   Roberto Baldwin. Shipshape: Tracking 40 years of FedEx tech, Wired.com (archived at https://perma.cc/2QST-68Y5), April 17, 2013

3   Peter High. A conversation with the most influential cybersecurity guru to the U.S. government, Forbes.com (archived at https://perma.cc/CYV6-S49L), December 7, 2015

4   Gilberto Millares. Creating an enterprise architecture strategy for the digital age, MetisStrategy.com (archived at https://perma.cc/HC3W-W5S8), June 10, 2020 www.metisstrategy.com/creating-an-enterprise-architecture-strategy-for-the-digital-age/ (archived at https://perma.cc/56NG-8XHM)

5   Daniel Lambert. The art of measurement in enterprise and business architecture, CIO.com (archived at https://perma.cc/72R4-EMZL), July 9, 2018

6   The Open Group. *Preliminary Phase: Framework and Principles*, Pubs.opengroup.org (archived at https://perma.cc/W68W-J777)

7   Ibid

8   The Open Group. *Phase A: Architecture Vision*, Pubs.opengroup.org (archived at https://perma.cc/W68W-J777)

9   Ibid

10 The Open Group. *Phase B: Business Architecture*, Pubs.opengroup.org (archived at https://perma.cc/W68W-J777)

11 Ibid

12 The Open Group. *Phase C: Information Systems Architecture*, Pubs.opengroup.org (archived at https://perma.cc/W68W-J777)

13 Ibid

14 Ibid

15 The Open Group. *Phase D: Technology Architecture*, Pubs.opengroup.org (archived at https://perma.cc/W68W-J777)

16 Ibid

17 The Open Group. *Phase E: Opportunities & Solutions*, Pubs.opengroup.org (archived at https://perma.cc/W68W-J777)

18 Ibid

19 The Open Group. *Phase F: Migration Planning*, Pubs.opengroup.org (archived at https://perma.cc/W68W-J777)

20 Ibid

21 The Open Group. *Phase G: Implementation Governance*, Pubs.opengroup.org (archived at https://perma.cc/W68W-J777)

22 Ibid

23 Ibid

24 The Open Group. *Phase H: Architecture Change Management*, Pubs.opengroup.org (archived at https://perma.cc/W68W-J777)

25 Ibid

26 The Open Group. *Requirements Management*, Pubs.opengroup.org (archived at https://perma.cc/W68W-J777)

27 Ibid

28 The Open Group. *The TOGAF® Standard, Version 9.2*

29 Caitlin White. Cloud computing timeline illustrates cloud's past, predicts its future, *TechTarget*, December 19, 2013

30 Ron Miller. How AWS came to be, *TechCrunch*, July 2, 2016

31 Tae Kim. Warren Buffett on Amazon's cloud success: "You do not want to give Jeff Bezos a 7-year head start," cnbc.com (archived at https://perma.cc/97CE-GFW7), May 15, 2018

32 Joseph Tsidulko. Bezos: "Unusual advantage" paying off as AWS stuns Wall Street with 49 percent sales growth in Q1, *CRN*, April 26, 2018

33 Peter High. Steve Randich, CIO of FINRA, *Technovation with Peter High* podcast, October 1, 2018

34 Ibid

35 Ibid

36 Ibid

37 Ibid

38 Chhavi Arora, Tanguy Catlin, Will Forrest, James Kaplan, and Lars Vinter. Three actions CEOs can take to get value from cloud computing, *McKinsey Quarterly*, July 21, 2020

39 Joe McKendrick. 4 situations where staying on-premises may be preferable to cloud, for now, *ZDNet*, February 9, 2019

40 Ibid

41 Ibid

42 Ross Mason. Have you had your Bezos moment? What you can learn from Amazon, CIO.com (archived at https://perma.cc/NE3P-678Q), August, 25, 2017

43 Heather Weaver. 7 cases of extremely successful API adoption, *NordicAPIs* blog, July 17, 2018

44 Molly Fleming. McDonald's turns to tech to build the future of fast food, *Marketing Week*, October 30, 2019

45 Heather Weaver. 7 cases of extremely successful API adoption, *NordicAPIs* blog, July 17, 2018

46 Manfred Bortenschlager. Leveraging APIs as part of digital strategy, *Wired*, December 2013

47 Israel Gat. The API economy, Cutter.com (archived at https://perma.cc/6H36-R2G6), 2013

48 Mark Settle. *Truth from the Valley*, Productivity Press, New York, 2020

49 Peter High. Interview with Adobe CIO Cynthia Stoddard, *Technovation with Peter High* podcast, February 15, 2021

50 Mark Settle. *Truth from the Valley*, Productivity Press, New York, 2020

51 Robert Broeckelmann. API governance: A vital building block for API security, *Medium*, April 20, 2019

52 Manfred Bortenschlager. Leveraging APIs as part of digital strategy, *Wired*, December 2013

53 Peter High. What are microservices? Matt Miller, Partner at Sequoia Capital, and Jay Kreps, CoFounder and CEO of Confluent, *Technovation with Peter High* podcast, September 25, 2017

54 Ibid

55 Bob Violino. Making the shift to microservices: 8 tips, CIO.com (archived at https://perma.cc/NE3P-678Q), February 12, 2019

56 www.nato.int/docu/review/2013/Cyber/timeline/EN/index.htm (archived at https://perma.cc/M9KS-WYT2)

57 Caleb Townsend. A brief and incomplete history of cybersecurity, *United States Cybersecurity Magazine*, May 7, 2018

58 *United States v. Morris* (1991), 928 F.2d 504, 505 (2d Cir. 1991)

59 Maggie McGrath. Target data breach spilled info on as many as 70 million customers, Forbes.com (archived at https://perma.cc/CYV6-S49L), January 10, 2014

60 Reuters. Target pays millions to settle state data breach lawsuits, *Fortune*, May 23, 2017

61 Kelly Bissell, Ryan M. Lasalle, and Paolo Dal Cin. *Ninth Annual Cost of Cybercrime Study*, Accenture Research Report, March 6, 2019

62 Peter High. Akamai CEO Tom Leighton, *Technovation with Peter High* podcast, March 25, 2019

63 Samantha Ann Schwartz. Zero trust is widely praised. What's the adoption hangup?, CIODive.com (archived at https://perma.cc/N34R-LWW7), September 10, 2020

64 Steven Norton. McDonald's evolving into risk-based security organization, *Wall Street Journal*, June 25, 2015

65 *NACD Director's Handbook on Cyber-Risk Oversight*, NACD, Directors Handbook Series, February 25, 2020

66 www.nist.gov/cyberframework/online-learning/history-and-creation-framework (archived at https://perma.cc/R2YD-LCY7)

67 *History and Creation of the Framework*, www.nist.gov/cyberframework/online-learning/history-and-creation-framework (archived at https://perma.cc/R2YD-LCY7)

68 Peter High. Lenovo's CISO says cyber attacks increased 3x during COVID, *Technovation with Peter High* podcast, September 10, 2020

69 *NIST Cybersecurity Framework*, www.nist.gov/cyberframework/online-learning/five-functions (archived at https://perma.cc/A8PB-GX7L), created April 12, 2018, updated August 10, 2018

70 Samantha Ann Schwartz. Gartner shrinks infosec spending forecast for 2020, cloud security gets COVID-19 boost, CIODive.com (archived at https://perma.cc/N34R-LWW7), June 19, 2020

71 Ryan Smith. On-premise to cloud migration: Advanced strategies and pitfalls to avoid, Armor.com (archived at https://perma.cc/35P2-H76Q), October 22, 2019

05

Building and caring
for an ecosystem

Given the pace of change in business, we need to have more sources of inspiration, and a broader swath of people with whom we can test hypotheses and share war stories. Think about your LinkedIn account. I imagine you, like most, have "500+ connections." Among those are current colleagues and past colleagues, but it likely includes interesting people who you have met through your career, from the interesting person who you were seated next to on a flight to the interesting keynote speaker at a conference you attended. Have you ever thought about the value of this ecosystem of yours and how you can leverage it for greater levels of value? Most executives that I meet with do not think sufficiently about their ecosystem despite the years it has taken to build one.

Competition in business used to be about company versus company: Coke versus Pepsi, General Motors versus Ford, Nike versus Converse. When executives at companies like these plotted out their strategic and product roadmaps, the perceived roadmaps of the direct competition were never far from the mind. Today, competition is much more about ecosystem-to-ecosystem. By this, I mean most companies have a complex supply chain that they marshal to produce products. They have strategic vendor partners who provide resources and expertise that complements the expertise of the company. Not tapping into these resources for insights is foolish.

In this chapter, we will cover five categories of ecosystem partners that technology and digital leaders should network with frequently. They are:

- customers
- peers
- venture capitalists
- executive recruiters
- external (vendor) partners

Customers are a natural partner in the ecosystem to collaborate with since they buy your company's products and services. Testing new ideas with them, uncovering adjacent product or service areas to get involved in, working with them on ways of enhancing customer experience, especially digitally—these are all important ways to work with customers to draw out ideas that could be new innovations for the company.

Next is peers. Peers as technology and digital executives are important to get to know. There are enough similarities across companies of comparable size from a technology and digital perspective that these sessions can be equal parts hypothesis testing and group therapy.

Venture capitalists invest in the technology of tomorrow, and those who have significant enterprise technology portfolios have an incentive to get to know technology and digital leaders, who can help them validate assumptions behind their investment theses. Technology and digital executives can, in turn, gain insights into the entrepreneurs, companies, and technology that may be interesting to partner with or even to invest in.

Executive recruiters are important to know if you hope to change jobs, but they are also important to know to better understand the skills that are rising and falling in importance. They can offer insights into organization structures, as well as factors that lead to the success or failure of executives.

Finally, we will cover external vendor partners. Almost every company has external partners that they engage, but too often they are viewed as fulfillers of work rather than sources of insights and innovation. We will cover the reasons why they must be viewed as such.

Customers

In order to create better customer engagement as a technology and digital leader, it is necessary to comb through the metrics that your chief executive officer and your board monitor on a regular basis. There will assuredly be a revenue-centric metric among those tracked regularly by the CEO and the board. This continues to be an area of great differentiation for CIOs. Those who drive positive outcomes for the top (revenue) and bottom (efficiency/cost-cutting) lines of the profit equation will be fuller contributors to the success of the enterprise. In my career, I have had the pleasure of interviewing prominent CIOs who have become founders, presidents, and/or CEOs of companies, including Greg Carmichael at Fifth Third, Tom Nealon of Southwest Airlines, Sasan Goodarzi of Intuit, Jay Vijayan of Tekion, Mike Capone of Qlik, Chris Lofgren, formerly of Schneider National, Yvonne Wassenaar of Puppet, Tomothy Kasbe of Zoho, and Sanjay Mirchandani of Commvault. Having worked with and gotten to know well most of these executives, a key differentiator during their time as CIOs has been their contribution to revenue. If a CIO does not understand that most fundamental value, they will not have the credibility to join the ranks of board-level CIOs or to move beyond the ranks of CIO. The reason that CIOs tended to report through CFOs and COOs for decades was that they did not contribute broadly enough to the conversations that the CEO's direct reports would have together.

While historically CIO presentations have focused primarily on IT's contribution to bottom line in the form of major projects that will render the company more efficient (e.g., automating a previously analog process) or secure, today's IT leader must also focus on their contribution to as many of the key metrics as possible. These include customer satisfaction rates, perhaps in the form of a net promoter score. Why? A decade ago, most CIOs did not concern themselves with gleaning insights from customers to foster innovation.

IT should develop ideas on how to delight customers digitally, to collect data to continue to get to know them better, to introduce artificial intelligence to identify patterns in customer behavior to serve them better, and the like.

Moreover, in those cases where companies have hired a chief digital officer in addition to their chief information officer, it is often a sign that the CIO and their team have not earned the credibility to take on the customer-facing aspect of the digital agenda. This is a shame, and often means that the CDO has the sexier mandates and initiatives to follow while the CIO has the "plumbing." I am oversimplifying to be sure, but I believe that CIOs should strive to take on the broader mandate. It requires nailing the basics. It also means training and hiring for the skills necessary to develop revenue-centric ideas. This is likely a pathway to engage and retain the best of your people, as well, as this tends to be some of the most meaningful and interesting work.

It is also for that reason that I developed the Forbes CIO Innovation Award as part of the Forbes CIO Summit series that I cofounded and produced from its inception in 2014 through 2020. That award has been given to CIOs who drive revenue-centric innovation. The 18 winners developed ideas that tended to fit into five categories:

- Productize internal technology for external customers.
- Leverage third parties to develop a value-generating ecosystem.
- Organize for innovation and cross-functional collaboration across the enterprise.
- Deploy analytics at scale to boost productivity and enable data-driven decisions.
- Leverage design thinking to create superior customer experiences.

If your team has not yet engaged customers, there are a number of ways to get started. The first is to participate in customer service calls. When customers call in, what do they tend to call about? Are there digital solutions to what you are hearing? Are there opportunities to create a new offering to meet a need you elicit from that feedback? Andi Karaboutis, the chief information and digital officer of National Grid, noted that the "customer" for technology and digital leaders has changed when she said:

> I used to look internally at my company as customers who set the product development demand and pace. But what is true today is it's the true customers of the company who set the pace of change. Business has become very different. They are the ones driving the need for organizational nimbleness. Companies that ignore this will not survive.

Next, you and your team members should participate in sales calls, where appropriate. This provides invaluable insight, unvarnished, which may lead to additional thoughts on where technology or digital solutions or enhancements might aid the experience of customers. To the extent that it is appropriate, asking these customers questions about where they would have expected a digital solution (product or service) where one is not there can be effective. (You may have a more pointed question based on what you know of the offering and of customer preferences, or the early feedback in a customer session might push you in a more specific direction.) Let's remember that as the digital savviness of customers increases, as everyone is much more cognizant of digital solutions in their personal and professional lives, having a representative from IT can prove to be a boon. An ability to answer a technical question or to offer a digital insight can be invaluable. Mike Capone, the CEO of Qlik, used to be the CIO of Automatic Data Processing

(ADP). While there, he instituted a policy for IT leaders to spend a significant portion of their time with sales leaders on sales calls for the human capital management behemoth. The company found that sales leaders had a higher yield on closing business when an IT leader was with them. This was, at least in part, due to the fact that technical questions could be addressed more readily. Capone also wanted his team to be better attuned to generating ideas that would enhance digital products that the company could develop. Capone would add the chief product officer role to his CIO responsibilities due to his effectiveness.

If you are a business-to-business company, engage the CIOs of your customer companies. (There is more on other reasons to engage CIOs in the next section of this chapter regarding peer networking.) That is a great way to meet a peer, to conduct some thoughtful peer collaboration, but also to get some sound feedback from your peers on the health of the relationship along with ideas to improve it using technology or digital solutions. Granted, the CIO of your client company may need to get appropriate feedback from other executives in the company, in those cases where they are not the purchaser of your products and services. That underscores the need to build relationships with CIOs such that a request to garner unvarnished feedback for you may be easily granted.

Depending on the nature of your business, it is also good to go to where your customers are. This is all the easier if your business has stores, branches, or outlets that customers visit to purchase your products or services. If you do, you should require that members of your team spend as much as a day a month there with clients. This provides a great sign to customers that their opinions matter with the thought-provoking questions you might offer, and it also can be one of the fastest paths to insights that might drive innovation for your teams. Visiting stores, branches, or outlets in different geographies can also be helpful to understand geographic nuances, for example. Many clients of mine require that IT leaders visit a store when traveling on business. Again, what a tremendous opportunity to learn.

Another method to get to know customers is through customer events. If your company has gatherings of customers, a member of your team should be there.

Of course, digital channels also offer new opportunities for collaboration with customers. Design your website to garner just this kind of feedback. Building data science capabilities will enable you to mine the feedback for insight, which is particularly helpful if you are receiving a vast array of feedback from customers.

There is a special class of customer engagement among CIOs for companies that sell to CIOs and IT departments. In those cases, IT leaders have a great opportunity to be advocates to their peers who are also their company's customers. These same CIOs also have a great opportunity to be the first and best customers of the company's products and services. The companies often refer to these programs as "company on company," such as Workday on Workday, Oracle on Oracle, Okta on Okta, and Now on Now (referencing ServiceNow). Others like Microsoft and NetApp refer to "customer zero" programs, meaning the company is the customer even before customer number one.

At companies like these, technology and digital leaders are remarkably influential, both on the internal product as the first users of the product, but also as advocates externally to peers who buy the company's products. My colleague Chris Davis wrote about these dual perspectives. He noted that the company that implements a customer zero program fosters collaboration across product lines to be a:

- product design and innovation partner
- alpha and beta early adopter
- deployment consultant
- customer success consiglieri
- source of customer intelligence and co-innovation[1]

Outside of the company, the customer zero program will foster better sales and customer engagement by:

- designing an operating model across the company's partner/vendor ecosystem
- advising on in-production architecture and engineering
- change management and training best practices
- ongoing deployment lessons learned across new product/feature rollouts, adaptation to new regulations, or integration with other technologies
- illustrating how the company quantifies the benefit realized from its own products[2]

Even if your company does not sell enterprise technology that other digital and technology leaders would buy, you should get more involved in your company's products, especially in identifying new digital sources of revenue and digital means of engaging with customers.

Nimble aspects of customer engagement

In each of these engagement strategies and others that you might derive, it is important to find ways to close the loop with many of the customers who your team engages with. Nothing builds loyalty and satisfaction among customers more than knowing that an idea to improve a service or a new feature to a product was implemented due to their feedback. Soliciting feedback without any apparent improvement from those who you engaged can, in fact, have the opposite impact as customers may get the impression that the interactions are hollow exercises as opposed to being designed to drive action and improvement.

Ultimately, the nimbleness comes by multiplying the sources of insight from the people who provide your company's revenue, and then having a means of turning those insights into action rapidly.

Peers

A sales executive for a business-to-consumer retailer has a different skillset from a sales executive of a business-to-business or a business-to-government (such as an aerospace and defense) company. For example, many retail sales executives require a high volume of sales of lower-priced items in order to earn adequate revenue and to turn a profit compared with the latter, who can turn a profit at a lower volume given the price of the products being sold and the budgets of the companies and governments that are aerospace and defense companies' customers. Marketing executives at these two industries also use different media in order to reach their would-be customers. For those reasons, among others, you tend to see sales executives and marketing executives stay in the same industries for more of their career.

Technology and digital executives, by contrast, build a skillset that is much more fungible by comparison. Their activities and skillsets are similar to a greater extent, and therefore you see CIOs cross the chasm from industry to industry or from the private sector to the public sector and back.

Just as the CIOs' roles are somewhat fungible, so too are insights. CIOs and other digital leaders can gain as much if not more from collaborating with fellow digital leaders. Therefore, it behooves them to find opportunities to do so whenever possible. Thankfully, there are more opportunities than ever to do so.

FIGURE 5.1 Customer

Role(s) responsible	Tool(s)	Metrics
• CIO/CDO	• CRM • Social media such as LinkedIn	• Increased percentage of product or project ideas that are developed based upon customer feedback • Increased customer involvement in product or project development • Increased net promoter scores related to digital products • Increased net promoter scores related to digital customer experience

First, there are a number of virtual ways to stay connected with digital leaders. LinkedIn is a primary way to do so. Not only does it proactively provide one with news on one's network, but it also provides insights into who is writing about topics of interest that might be worth exploring more fully by reaching out to a contact. Twitter is another source of insight and a means of understanding the evolution of thinking across a vast array of contacts. I am impressed by the few digital leaders who use these media to pose questions of their networks. They use the wisdom of the crowd to develop statistically significant answers to the questions they pose. This is the human side of analytics.

One should think about categories of contacts. Who among your peers are acquaintances, and who are true friends? Who do you admire most among these two groups? For those who you admire, with whom are you also close? These are the peers to reach out to when you reach a crossroads, and need help in deciding to go left or to go right. This is invaluable advice that can be accessed fairly easily through the right channels and can help get much needed experience and data to sway you to pursue the right course of action.

There are also CIO-, CTO-, and CDO-centric groups that are convened with some frequency. These are sometimes organized by industry, other times by geography, and other times by size of company. I believe it is good to join multiples of these groups if your fellow members are people who you admire and respect. You should also ensure that the organizing body is one of strong reputation.

Conferences offer other means of both collaborating with peers, and to be exposed to thought leaders. For these, watch out for those that are vendor-led. I have had the opportunity to speak for most of the CIO conference organizers in addition to the conferences I convene, and I must say the ones I return to are the ones that keep their focus on great speakers, great attendees, and a light vendor footprint. I understand that the conference organizers have to pay the bills, so it is understandable that some vendor presence is necessary. That said, I know a couple of organizers who after multiple years of returning to the same cities annually, either find themselves recycling content, speakers, or, most often, giving the reins over to vendors to too dramatic a degree. This leads to a devolution of the conferences such that there are a few high-quality tech executives in attendance surrounded by junior IT leaders looking to get jobs from them and vendors trying to sell them their wares. Given the sea of opportunities there are to attend conferences, save your time and attention for those where you have the highest chance of gaining meaningful insights.

You should also seek advisory board opportunities with technology firms. Granted there is clearly a commercial lens that these firms have in assembling these bodies, but where they are managed well, that emphasis is not front and center, and if they convene high-quality peers, they may be worth your while.

I have been impressed by the degree to which female tech execs have created forums, both virtual and in person, where they can support each other's growth. As I write this chapter, earlier today, I spoke with a friend who a few months ago got a job as the global CIO of a major technology company. It is her third CIO role, but her prior two were with firms with hundreds of millions of dollars in revenue, and this was her first global CIO role with a firm with multiple billions of dollars in revenue. She joined this firm, which provides virtualization and collaboration technology, at the beginning of the COVID-19 pandemic, and the firm did remarkably well as their products became even more necessary with so many working outside of offices. When I asked her how she found out about the opportunity, she mentioned that she is part of one of the largest networks for female tech execs called the Tech T200. She wrote the group, letting everyone know she was seeking new opportunities, and within a few weeks, she had three meaningful opportunities available to her, including this, a dream job for her. Find ways to express your goals to your peers, and you will find that they will keep their eyes open for you. By having hundreds of eyes open for you rather than just your own, you are more likely to find the ideal opportunity when you are looking for a change.

I have another friend in the Bay Area who convenes what he refers to as a CIO group therapy dinner. He invites a big group of his CIO friends on a monthly basis, and whoever can make it shows up, and they learn, commiserate, laugh, share, and break bread. Finding ways to do the same in your geography would likely be a fast path to insight.

Nimbleness with peer networks

The bottom line is that it is important to find opportunities to spend time with smart, plugged-in peers of yours. Spend time with people who have already accomplished what you hope to, whether that be the size of the company they are part of, an industry or a geography they are in, the kind of work and the innovations they are driving; these should be taken into account. I would advise you to spend a day a month with peers at a minimum. This might be eight one-hour calls in a given month followed by a conference the next month followed by two dinners with CIOs in your city the next month, and so on.

The more you make this a regular cadence, the more you will think to leverage your network to your advantage. This book is about creating an organization that is better suited to pivot quickly toward opportunity and away from danger. Some member of your network is a month or a year ahead of you on the journey you are about to embark on. Some other member is an expert in the technology that you are newly curious about. By seeking the counsel of others, you will find the shortcuts to opportunity while avoiding pitfalls along the way. This is an ideal means of identifying ideas that might become innovations for your company, filling key roles that are currently open on your team, and ultimately finding your next role or a board opportunity that is a goal of yours.

Venture capitalists

If you are a tech leader in Silicon Valley, you probably already have an impeccable network of venture capital investors. They are in your milieu as a result of where you live. As you move from driving distance to flying distance from the San Francisco Bay Area, however, it is more likely that you may not know any venture capital investors. It also may not be obvious how symbiotic the relationships between CIOs and venture capitalists are. In fact, many of the biggest VC firms have members of their teams who have business development responsibilities who spend a reasonable amount of their time building CIO networks.

FIGURE 5.2 Peers

Role(s) responsible	Tool(s)	Metrics

- CIO/CDO

- Social media such as LinkedIn
- Peer collaboration digitally (and in person)

- Increased percentage of product or project ideas generated based upon feedback from peer executives

I regularly convene CIO dinners around the country, and I'll often bring a venture capitalist with me to those dinners. These are attempts on my part to bring Silicon Valley to the rest of the United States and beyond, while also stimulating conversation across a group of technology leaders.

The truth is that if you were to have reason to be in or near Silicon Valley and you are the CIO of a company of meaningful size, venture capitalists definitely wish to get to know you. The best of them also view these relationships as long-term relationships, just as they view their investments in companies as longer term in nature. The best of them do not view the relationship with CIOs as transactional. It is truly a meeting of the minds, with each contributing perspectives that the other can gain mightily from.

There are a few forums that I find are best for venture capitalist engagement. First are their briefings, typically done at their offices. If you contact a venture capital firm and suggest you are interested in a briefing, so long as you get a positive response from the firm, they are likely to do a prep call with you to get to know you and your operation a bit better and to understand a bit more about the topics that you are most interested in. This is a free education opportunity that will further foster learning agility on your team. As you weigh topics as diverse as the applicability of quantum computing to your business to engaging the right portfolio of security solutions to use in order to keep your enterprise safe to leveraging technology solutions to engage and motivate your employees, venture capitalists are likely to have a perspective on these topics.

The best of these firms think less about a near-term transaction and more about a long-term relationship with the technology and digital leaders who they get to know. Shardul Shah is a Partner at Index Ventures. "We don't speed date," says Shah, eschewing the practice that is common among some venture capitalists who engage with technology and digital leaders:

We don't think there's a lot to gain or that there is pleasure from short introductions and transactional-type communications…. From an Index perspective, we believe the C-level executive is our customer. We don't think of the founder actually as our customer, we want to find out what people need, what they want, and why.

Doug Pepper is a general partner at the venture capital and investment management firm ICONIQ Capital. He says that the most valuable input entrepreneurs in the enterprise technology companies that he invests in can get is from would-be customers:

There is no input that is more important and more impactful than the voice of the customer. When we talk to technology leaders, they're the ones that are feeling pain in their businesses and getting inputs from their business leadership and domain leadership internally, whether it's from engineering, from DevOps, from marketing, from sales, from their CEO… What are the business problems that they're suffering from? Where do they find themselves falling behind from a competitive perspective? What do they think will help them get ahead of the competition?

A number of technology and digital executives in my network have effectively used these meetings to create awareness and to explore a point of view with the broader executive team. A CIO, say, might bring their CEO and the rest of the executive team to visit with a venture capital firm to test hypotheses, learn about where smart money is being spent and why, and understand how this is likely to impact their firm's future. Some CIOs come away from these meetings earning a mandate for change related to a topic and extra budget to go with it.

Getting to know venture capitalists is also useful for the introductions to portfolio companies. Let me first note that just as there is risk for the venture capital firms to invest in technology companies, there is also risk engaging with them as clients. They may go belly up, and if they do, you may be left with unmet needs. That said, there are also tremendous advantages in getting involved with venture-backed companies early: Through your partnership, you can help them steer toward a path to health and longevity. You can also steer their products in directions that suit you best in many cases. You may also gain an edge on your competition for being an early adopter of a new technology. By investing in new technologies, this is interesting and motivating to your technology and digital team members.

Barry Eggers is a founding partner at Lightspeed Venture Partners. He acknowledges the symbiosis between venture investors and CIOs, especially for an early-stage investor like he is:

We're investing in markets that really don't exist yet, and so the only way for us to figure out where our market's going to go and how big it can be is to call a bunch of customers, especially those who are early-adopter customers, and ask them about the technology and how relevant it is to them and how much they would buy of it if it were available… For the CIO, it's almost like going to a car show and walking into the area where all the future cars are. They get a chance to hear from us about technologies that we're backing, companies we're backing that may not be ready for them yet, but over the next two, three, four, or five years, they will be relevant to them. So, they get a glimpse into the future. And an opportunity to preview what's coming and potentially plan their infrastructure, according to some of those emerging technologies.

Asheem Chanda is a partner at Greylock Partners, and he says that it takes a special CIO or CDO to understand the advantages of partnering with venture-backed companies:

I think there's a growing recognition at even the largest IT organizations in the world that the next innovative solution is often coming from a startup… I think the best [CIOs of large] companies are willing to take some risks and realize that in order to get the benefit, you have to be willing to try something new.

Navin Chaddha, the managing partner at Mayfield Fund, echoes this idea:

There are tech-forward companies that are looking for cutting-edge technologies to change the way they operate. They are looking to determine which technologies they should adopt that will change the way they operate and will increase their top line and bottom line and give them a competitive advantage against the people they compete with on a daily basis. The startups we have that end up doing extremely well are able to match themselves to these tech-forward and lean-forward companies.[3]

Having this long-term perspective is advantageous.

Emmet Keeffe is a former software entrepreneur turned partner in the private equity firm Insight Partners. He has built a consequential CIO and CDO network by getting to know each person's story and their plans for the future:

What we do is work with large global companies to understand, high level, what is their digital strategy? What are all the technology problems they have to solve in order to make that strategy happen? What are all the non-technology issues they are wrestling with?[4]

The more he has the answers to these questions, the better he is at suggesting companies and technologies who can help these leaders reach the goals articulated in their strategies faster.

It is also good to get to know a cadre of entrepreneurs of venture-backed companies. They are sources of insights and inspiration that can lead to interesting ideas that might guide your own leadership style, the kinds of people you might hire, the skills you might assemble, and the like. In some cases, you may even be able to invest in these companies, either personally or through your company. Also, I know a great number of technology and digital leaders of major companies who have ambitions to start entrepreneurial ventures of their own. There are good examples of CIOs who have started companies in recent years, including leading them as CEO:

- former Tesla CIO Jay Vijayan, who started the cloud-based automotive industry platform Tekion
- Stephen Gillett, who was the CIO and general manager of digital ventures at Starbucks, the president digital, marketing and operations of Best Buy, and the COO of Symantec before starting Chronicle, a cybersecurity firm born out of the moonshot factor, X, and acquired by Google in 2019. He is currently the COO of Verily Life Sciences
- former Facebook CIO Timothy Campos, who founded the calendar app, Woven
- former MetLife co-CIO Gary Hoberman, who founded the no-code software platform Unqork

It is not a coincidence that the first three reside in Silicon Valley, and each had great relationships with venture capital firms before starting their businesses. Establishing relationships with venture capital companies and the entrepreneurs they invest in can offer invaluable insights that pay dividends in the short, medium, and long term.

Several venture capital firms also have terrific conferences for CIOs. They almost always include a "dog and pony show" for some of their portfolio companies, but the sales activities tend to be fairly light-touch, and the content at the conferences tends to be remarkably thought-provoking, I have found.

Nimbleness with VCs

Again, this is about assembling a network in the venture capital community that you get along with best and who offer insights that you value most. It does not mean knowing all of them but knowing those who you mesh with best. I believe all partnerships, this one included, should be established on a win-win basis, so I would also encourage you to offer your own insights about where technology is going, how your operation is evolving, what you see in the marketplace, and the like. These are invaluable insights. The more give and take you offer with these venture capitalists, the more inclined they will be to keep you in mind and to call when interesting new ideas occur to them.

Executive recruiters

Another member of the technology ecosystem to bear in mind is the executive recruiter. As I mention them, no doubt you are thinking to yourself that this is based on the need to leverage them should you be in need of a new job. That is one of the reasons, to be sure, but bear in mind that executive recruiters have some of the biggest networks of technology and digital leaders in the world, and they have reason to speak with a lot of them frequently.

Executive recruiters also have a great network of the people who CIOs and CDOs report to—the hiring managers who would be the clients of the executive recruiters when seeking a new CIO or CDO. They understand how the expectations of this group are evolving. They understand why CIOs and CDOs succeed, and, critically, why they fail, since they are often called in due to the need to replace an executive who is judged to have failed. Tapping this group for insights while again offering the same is important.

Of course, executive recruiters are key partners when you have a role to fill on your IT or digital management team. They can also offer ideas on organization structure changes they are seeing based on past searches they have done. They understand where organization structure changes are

FIGURE 5.3 Venture capital

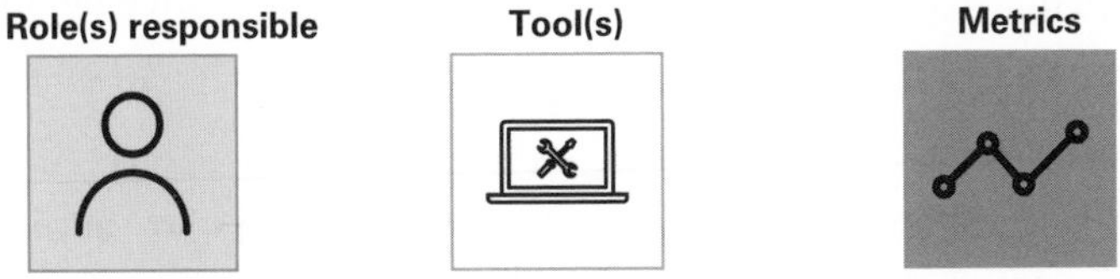

Role(s) responsible	Tool(s)	Metrics
• CIO/CDO	• Social media such as LinkedIn	• Increased percentage of vendor partnerships with venture-backed startups that achieve intended value based on SLAs

happening as they are happening since they are often called in to fill new roles that are created as a result of the changes. They also understand which roles are growing or diminishing in prominence based upon demand they see for certain searches.

If you have ambitions to join the board of a company, executive recruiters are key people to mention that to, since they can do something about that. They may need to engage a different recruiter in their firm who specializes in board searches, but the CIO search leader will be a person of influence in relevant searches. I hasten to add that it is not likely the sort of thing that an executive search executive will act on upon meeting a CIO or CDO for the first time, so this is about developing a long-term, trusting relationship.

Katie Shannon is a partner in the Digital and Technology Officers Practice at the executive recruiting firm Heidrick & Struggles. She believes in developing long-term relationships with technology and digital leaders. By getting to know their stories and their ambitions, she has more to go on as she weighs how she can be helpful to them: "I like hearing a person's story. And in that I think I hear what's important to them, what their goals are. That helps me get to know them from a personal standpoint, from a leadership standpoint."

Martha Heller, who runs the eponymously named Heller Search Associates, talks about the importance of giving to get. She especially appreciates when someone takes time out of their busy day to talk about a search even if it is not for them. The natural consequence is that the executive recruiter gets to know the candidate in greater detail and learns a bit about how they are oriented toward helping others. That person is bound to be stickier in the executive recruiter's mind when new opportunities materialize.

In one's touchpoints with executive recruiters, recommend others for roles that do not work for you. These conversations should give you reason to learn about skills on the rise, organization changes to be knowledgeable about, and the evolution of what success or failure looks like among CIOs and CDOs.

Tony Leng, who leads CIO searches at Diversified Search, indicates that he looks for people who are self-reflective and who seek to learn from many others:

> I look for people to be open about failure because that's where our biggest learning comes. And if you try and tell me you never failed anywhere in your career, you're not a whole person and I don't believe you.

Of course, executive recruiters are also the rare executives who can find you your ideal job, if you are not currently occupying it. For this reason, investing in these relationships for the long term can bear significant fruit for you. Also, you do not want to have your first call with an executive recruiter come at the point of most acute need: for instance, if you have just been relieved of your duties. Best in that scenario to have built these relationships over years.

CIOs and CDOs often misunderstand the power dynamic in the relationship with executive recruiters, at times believing that they are the clients when they are seeking a job. Rather, the client is the executive to whom the CIO candidate will report and perhaps the chief human resources officer of that company. At conferences I curate, I have seen CIOs act as though the executive recruiter is lucky to have met them, suggesting through their actions that the executive recruiter should keep them in mind on their upcoming searches. The CIO has to remember that the executive recruiter has a Rolodex of hundreds or thousands of CIOs. Your goal should be to make an impression that will have you higher in the Rolodex.

Nimbleness with executive recruiters

With executive recruiters, you want to choose both quality and quantity, in that order, as you may choose to have particularly deep conversations and relationships with recruiters who you find to be of the highest caliber, but the nature of their jobs is that only one executive recruiter works on a job at a time, so knowing many of them increases the possibility that they will keep you in mind when a new opportunity arises. Though being on the radar for as many of them as possible is also important, since they can make you aware that your dream job has just opened up.

FIGURE 5.4 Executive recruiter

Role(s) responsible	Tool(s)	Metrics
• CIO/CDO	• Social media such as LinkedIn	• Improved candidates presented for leadership openings as judged by employee ratings beginning six months after hiring • Increased number of board opportunities presented to CIO/CDO, if that is a goal of the executive

External (vendor) partners

It is important that I have put "vendor" in parentheses in the title of this section, as the thought of external partners may seem vague. After all, the other ecosystem members noted in this chapter are also "external partners" of a kind. These external partners, your key, strategic vendors, are the ones who you are likely to see the most, however. They are the ones who will have the largest role to play in determining your success or lack thereof.

I focused amply on this topic in my book *World Class IT*, but it is worth revisiting. When the book came out in late 2009, there were still many examples of IT departments that were being outsourced nearly whole hog to managed service providers. This was both due to the residual impacts of a philosophy best epitomized by the *Harvard Business Review* article by Nicholas Carr entitled, "IT Doesn't Matter."[5] Many believed it was not differentiating, and just as you would let a payroll company manage your payroll because that is not an area of strategic priority or expertise, IT was believed to be commoditized, by and large. Add to that the economic crisis of 2008, and some thought this was a fast path to efficiency.

Companies used a machete in clearing the thicket of IT resources and specialties. In reality, engaging external partners is an essential strategy for companies, but it is important to better define what is strategic and what isn't strategic, and focus mostly on the latter category for outsourcing.

Jim Fowler is the chief technology officer of Nationwide with roughly $50 billion revenue, and he was the chief information officer for GE prior to that. When asked about how attitudes about where to engage external partners have changed, Fowler reflected:

> When I joined GE, [then CIO] Gary Reiner, a long-term friend and visionary at that time was running the playbook of 70, 70, 70, which dictated that 70 percent of work would be outsourced, and 70 percent of that work would be offshored, and that 70 percent of that work would go to India. This involved how CIOs were outsourcing much of the operational side. At the time, IT was back-office, and the role was centered on keeping the lights on and running the operation as cheaply as possible. We have gone from a project-based operational mentality to a product-focused one, and we have moved from the back office to the front office.

He contrasted that with the new approach to engaging external partners:

> In the old world of outsourcing, there were many mid-level program and project managers who managed contracts. In the new world of product management,

you need more software engineers, developers, data technology specialists, and people who understand what it takes to work in the cloud and run the underlying infrastructure. You cannot completely rely on an outsourcer anymore.[6]

That said, it is important to differentiate between different kinds of external partners. There are partners who offer staff augmentation, for instance, giving an IT department an ability to scale up in certain skillsets without committing to hiring new employees. Some of these companies offer the opportunity to hire some of these staff as a sort of rent-before-you-own model.

There are external partners related to certain aspects of the technology stack. There are hardware partners and software partners. These are typically companies that have solutions that you would not attempt to develop on your own. It is important to choose these companies wisely for the quality of their products, but also for the quality of their services. Moreover, the quality of the point of contact from the partner's company can make a big difference, as well.

There are external partners who are consultants, providing strategic or tactical assistance. They are likely hired for their expertise in an area, for their breadth of experience in your industry or across industries.

Vendor segmentation

The first step in managing your vendors is to segment them. Who do you have in each of these categories? This may seem like an obvious step, but you might be surprised how often I embark on a collaboration with technology and digital executives only to discover that they do not have a comprehensive list of vendors, what they are engaged on, how much is being spent with each, and the like. You cannot manage what you do not measure. Just as with people's skills in Chapter 2 and with your enterprise architecture in Chapter 4, getting that comprehensive view is a critical first step.

Start by identifying all external partners, classifying them by how they engage with your company, as well as to note if they are hardware, software, or a services providers. You should also note if they are a strategic partner or not. You may also wish to designate particularly important partners to you as being preferred partners. It is important to understand where there are redundancies among vendor partners, offering opportunities for consolidation. Mind you, redundancy is appropriate in some cases, but overall the goal should be consolidation. You may also discover that engaging a partner across more of your portfolio will offer greater savings and greater influence over product development with the partner.

You'll need to create or purchase a central repository where all vendor information can be stored, including external ratings, performance reviews given by your team, and the like.

As you segment external partners, it is also prudent to obtain views of vendors and their products and services from industry analysts, such as Gartner and Forrester. The partner you chose 10 years ago may no longer be the top player in their field, and you may wish to adjust accordingly. Thus, it is important to develop an ongoing review cycle to ensure that the segmentation is constantly refreshed to reflect vendors who fall out of favor and new entrants that your company should consider.

I recommend establishing a body, sometimes referred to as a vendor management office (VMO), to help keep the vendor segmentation current. We will go through other responsibilities the VMO might take on when we cover vendor management more generally. As this organization continues to hone the vendor segmentation process, it should articulate rules about what should be procured globally versus what is appropriate to procure locally.

Procurement

As you reengage existing external partners, and even more importantly as you engage new external partners, it is important to have a solid procurement process in place. This is often led by a procurement department. (This might be referred to as strategic sourcing, or by other names, as well.) That group should include negotiators on behalf of the company.

As IT departments often engage specialized external partners, it is especially important that the technology or digital leadership play a role in this, as this level of knowledge and expertise will ensure the right decisions are made.

One of the most important steps in the procurement process is to establish service level agreements (SLAs). I am amazed how often I'll engage with the technology or digital teams of a company and find that SLAs are not de rigueur across all partner relationships. If you do not define success, how will you know if you have succeeded? If you do not measure performance effectively, you also will not have the necessary corrective actions defined as remedies for lack of delivery of anticipated value.

To ensure you have appropriate fee structures across the different segments of vendors you engage, it is appropriate to research pricing, competition, industry best practices, and fair market value for each segment of vendors established. Of course, it is also prudent to engage legal, finance,

FIGURE 5.5 External (vendor) partners

Role(s) responsible

- Head of vendor management or the vendor management office
- Head of procurement/strategic sourcing

Tool(s)

- Vendor management system or toolsets

Metrics

- Vendor segmentation
  - 100% documentation and management of:
    - percentage of vendors categorized
    - length of relationship by vendor
    - vendor spending level
  - Increased percentage of vendors managed based on assigned category
- Procurement
  - Reduced vendor redundancies (thus reduced costs)
  - Decreased dollars spent in hardware and software costs from initial offer from vendors to rate level of final contract
  - KPIs, OKRs, and SLAs defined for all vendor contracts
- Vendor management
  - Increased percentage of contracts yielding value anticipated
  - Increased percentage of contracts staying within budget over lifetime of contract
  - KPIs, OKRs, and SLAs managed for all vendor contracts
  - Increased percentage of breaches of service level yielding a penalty
  - Increased percentage of top vendors by contract size (cut-off TBD) who are provided formal feedback and provide formal feedback on a quarterly basis

and the ultimate users of the products or services that will be involved in an engagement with an external partner.

As for the negotiations by the procurement team in concert with the relevant technology or digital leaders, it is important that fat be trimmed from contracts while leaving muscle in them. Too often, procurement teams are incentivized to cut expenses associated with agreements. This can backfire if the contract is negotiated so low that less than optimal resources need to be used to staff the project. The adage "you get what you pay for" applies. It is important to identify other negotiating points beyond price. The quality and experience of the team is another. Also, the definition of deliverables and the timing of their delivery are important. Negotiating the timeframe may be a more effective way of reducing cost than simply asking for a rate cut. You may also find that there are superfluous deliverables included, which may offer an opportunity for reduced scope.

As a final thought related to procurement, I recommend documenting best practices and learnings from negotiations and contract development with vendors for future reference.

Vendor management

Vendor management is, admittedly, a broad topic. External partners can still be a major portion of the resources used by a technology or digital operation. Still, many companies have major shortcomings when it comes to managing external partners. Therefore, the first step is to train key members of your team, such as project managers, on practices associated with vendor management. This includes ensuring that those who manage vendors understand how success has been defined within each contract, managing the external partners toward that success, course-correcting where necessary, and enacting penalties when they are required.

Next it is important to have a standard dashboard template to evaluate vendors. There may be some differences for the templates based on the kinds of partners they are, be they service providers versus hardware versus software vendors. You need to include an evaluation of the people being used, the adherence to deadlines, the quality of the deliverables, and the value created. It may be appropriate to define service descriptions for each IT service that has defined metrics covering functionality, performance, availability, costs, and the like.

As to the timing of these reviews, just as there is a trend toward more frequent feedback of employees, I think the same should be done with external partners. A semiannual cadence strikes me as the minimal cadence, but quarterly is often better, depending on the kind of work the external partners undertake. Topics that should come up might include architecture, service descriptions, operational performance, financial management, incident review, and the like.

You should also consider having the external partners prepare a self-assessment for each of your meetings with them. It is always useful to gauge self-awareness. I believe external partners should win some points by acknowledging areas where they have fallen short before you have given them that feedback. It is important that they correct these issues, of course, but when done well, this exercise is a trust-builder that is likely to portend a healthier and more open relationship going forward.

It is important that this information be kept in a central repository where all vendor information can be stored and where ratings and performance reviews can be easily accessed. Trend data for performance should be evaluated and made available. I believe the more you share with the external partners, the more they will have incentives to improve, as well. I think greater transparency is better. I also think it is important to show them where they rank among your vendors on topics like value, efficiency, net promoter score, and the like. You may choose to anonymize the data other than for the external partner that you are engaging, but it is good to get the competitive juices flowing with external partners.

I believe that the transparency should also extend to your strategy and plans, especially as it applies to your key external partners. The more guidance you can provide as to where you foresee the business headed, the more they can tailor their work and proposals to your criteria for success.

I think a particularly good way to communicate that strategy is with all key external partners at the same time. Some companies refer to these as vendor days. A good friend who has been the CIO of several Twin Cities area companies likes to do his vendor days in the middle of winter in Minnesota. That is a particularly good test of loyalty of the external partners. By sharing your plans with all relevant external partners at once, it saves you time, ensures they are hearing the same message, and in seeing that there are others who will be aligning their work to the plans that have been communicated, again, this introduces some positive competition among those partners.

I have also seen several companies encourage the external partners to break into groups and brainstorm together how the technology or digital team can accomplish its strategy more readily. These are scenarios where no external partner will wish to be seen as providing less insight or less creative ideas than others present, perhaps for fear of not being invited to the vendor day next year, for instance. Truly creative ideas can be derived from these sessions, when managed well.

That speaks more generally to the need for technology and digital teams to see external partners as sources of insight capable of coming up with innovative new ideas. The more clarity you provide them, the more the onus should be upon them to deliver their best ideas back to you, aligned with your strategy. Consider developing a vendor performance incentive program that rewards vendors for efficiency, cost savings, enhanced capabilities, and customer experience. And ensure that the right people are running these contracts.

As noted, I use the term external partners because these should truly be partners. As such, I think great partners should be provided incentives to deliver beyond the agreement, or to add more value than anticipated, possibly taking home additional fees when they do so. Mind you, it is important that this not lead to sand-bagging projections of value, but if managed well, this can be a major incentive. It is smart to provide contractual incentives to invest in innovation on behalf of your company.

External partners should also be pushed to provide training on areas in which they are expert. During the procurement process, you should try to negotiate these in as part of the general agreement. You are hiring your partners for what they know. The extent to which you can leverage those relationships as opportunities to learn to fish rather than to be given fish, so much the better.

Finally, the best partnerships are mutually beneficial. There is often a cynical view taken regarding external partners, and at times that cynicism is warranted. That said, when engaging an external partner for the first time, give them the benefit of the doubt, support them where you can, be a reference for them where that is applicable, speak at their customer events, if that is helpful to them and to you, and show that you are willing to invest in them. It is true that the squeaky wheel gets the oil, and sometimes the squeaks come in the form of critical feedback. That said, when the squeaks come in the form of praise when warranted, that can have the better impact.

Chapter takeaways

Investing in and growing your ecosystem is of critical importance to foster nimbleness. First you must invest in the ecosystem, as this is a scenario where the more you give, the more you get. Therefore, offer to be of assistance to

FIGURE 5.6 Procurement

Role(s) responsible

- Head of vendor management or the vendor management office
- Head of procurement/strategic sourcing

Tool(s)

- Vendor management system or toolsets

Metrics

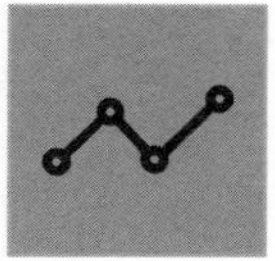

- Increased percentage of vendors categorized
- Length of relationship by vendor
- Vendor spending level
- Scope and real-time business impact of vendor services
- Vendor spending level, adjusted for contracts that span over multiple-year contracts
- Increased percentage of vendors managed based on assigned category

members of your ecosystem with words of advice, endorsements, perspectives, and the like. You do not want the first contact with people in the various categories of the ecosystem mentioned herein to be one where you are making the request.

Make sure to maintain a regular cadence to your correspondences with the various members of your ecosystem, scheduling quarterly or semiannual reminders to find time if the reason to be in touch does not present itself. Prepare for those meetings with insights to share from your company, from other parts of your ecosystem, from what you are reading, and the like. This creates a magnetism to these conversations which will keep you front of mind with the most important members of your network.

Finally, recognize when it is right to tap your ecosystem for insights or for advice. Most err on the side of not doing it enough or not doing it at all. When you are at a crossroads, seek the counsel of your ecosystem to make better decisions.

Notes

1 Chris Davis. 5 lessons when creating a "customer zero" program, CIO.com (archived at https://perma.cc/NE3P-678Q), September 24, 2020

2 Ibid

3 Peter High. Mayfield Fund Managing Director Navin Chaddha, *Technovation with Peter High* podcast, January 20, 2020

4 Peter High. Unlocking digital change with Emmet B. Keeffe III of Insight Partners, *Technovation with Peter High* podcast, September 17, 2020

5 Nicholas Carr. IT doesn't matter, *Harvard Business Review*, May 2003

6 Peter High. Nationwide CIO Jim Fowler, *Technovation with Peter High* podcast, April 15, 2019

06

Strategic nimbleness

Does strategy matter in an age when the pace of change is so dynamic? This is a fair question, as change happens so frequently that as soon as you put the strategy to paper, some portion of your strategy is likely to need to be altered to accommodate a change in the marketplace. That said, constant change does not render an entire strategy irrelevant. Strategy helps your team know where to focus and where not to focus. It also plays a critical role in ensuring that everyone is pushing in the same direction. If a company is driving forward without a unifying plan, they may find themselves inadvertently pushing against each other, wasting time in the process. There is an African proverb that says, "If you want to go fast, go alone. If you want to go far, go together." To these meaningful words I would add that if you want to go far, take a map, and be sure everyone has read it. That map is the strategy. And if you want to gain a competitive edge, you will need to innovate. Innovation is also best done with the guidance of strategy.

With that in mind, the topics to be covered in this chapter are:

- communications
- strategic creation and alignment
- IT/digital strategy
- data strategy
- business capabilities
- innovation

Here is the rationale for each:

Communications   Solid communications are the lifeblood of an organization. Those companies that provide timely and relevant information to the right constituents with frequency are often the ones who succeed. Those conversations need to be from top to bottom, but they should also be from the bottom to the top. They should reflect the many modern means of communicating.

Strategy creation and alignment   Technology and digital leaders need to engage the rest of the executives at the divisional, functional, and business unit levels to ensure that strategies are well articulated, and that they are at the same level of clarity and granularity. Since technology breathes life into most parts of a company, technology and digital leaders must be engaged to help formulate plans as early as possible.

IT strategy   Based upon IT's involvement in the formulation of the enterprise and business unit and divisional plans, it must create its own plan, reflecting the unique areas that IT must drive in order to create capabilities for the rest of the company and its customers.

Establish data strategy   As the enterprise, business unit and divisional, IT, and digital strategies will be driven forward with data solutions, data products, and simply by reading the tea leaves of what data tells executives, a sound data strategy is more important than ever. Data are everywhere, but if it is not harnessed to create better insights to make better decisions more efficiently, it is of little use.

Business capabilities   The best way for technology and digital leaders to engage the rest of the company is by working with them to define the business capabilities across the company, and then to determine the people, process, and technology components to each. By defining these together, there will be a better grounding into the areas to focus on to drive the greatest value for the company.

Communications

What is the number one differentiator between those companies that have great cultures, that are great at strategic planning, those that execute at a higher level than others, those who get the most out of their external partners? There are many answers you might offer which play a factor: better people, better compensation, better means of evaluating productivity and taking corrective action, more efficient processes, more resilient infrastructure—each of these is a logical answer to the question. I would argue that among the most important factors is effective communication.

One needs to communicate with colleagues, customers, peers, strategic partners, and others in order to draw out the insights necessary to inform strategy. Without holding regular meetings and documenting the substance of those conversations, strategy will be suboptimal.

Communication is taken for granted as important when a company is in startup mode. Whether the startup is in a garage, a la Hewlett-Packard, Apple, or Google, or it is in a small, shared office space, in the earliest stages of a startup, everyone is likely in the same room. Communications are seamless. One cannot help but hear all else that is going on, hearing in real time the victories and defeats of daily goings-on at the business. It is when those victories far outpace the defeats and the company takes off when communications become more complicated. When employees operate in different office spaces on the same floor, then on different floors, then in different buildings, then in different geographies, communications must evolve, or the company will suffer. As Jonathan Swift noted, "Falsehood flies, and truth comes limping after it, so that when men come to be undeceived, it is too late."[1] Negative rumors can start and become assumed wisdom if there is not a good communications process in place to ensure that the truth wins out. Moreover, best practices cannot easily spread, and the wheel must be reinvented over and over. Lastly, and perhaps most importantly, strategy, once concluded, cannot be understood and processed such that all members of the team push in the same direction to ensure it is achieved. There is wasted effort when there is confusion about the path forward. In fact, in the absence of a well-articulated path, your team will figuratively get out machetes and hew their own paths.

The truth's partner in this endeavor is transparency. Communication is aided and culture sustained by erring on the side of more transparency. Bridgewater Capital is legendary for its transparency. Meetings, including one-on-one meetings discussing performance or a manager disciplining a subordinate, are videotaped for anyone to review and learn from after the fact. Performance rankings of all staff are shown with full attribution for everyone to see.[2] Without this being part of the culture from a company's founding, as it was at Bridgewater, it is hard to implement radical transparency to the same degree.

That said, most companies operate at the opposite extreme and could stand to adopt a lighter version of what has worked well for Bridgewater. There are a cadre of senior leaders who plot and plan the way forward for a company, and few people, even at fairly senior levels, understand the plans. Again, when people are left to their own devices, and they can only guess at the path forward, by definition, they are likely to draw incorrect conclusions, which can slow progress and have even more deleterious effects. Transparency can seem scary. What if I'm proven wrong? What if I'm asked questions that make me uncomfortable? The benefits of increasing the level of transparency outweigh the risks, generally, even if it is appropriate to have some limitations. It is important to be comfortable with more transparency, to let some respectful disagreements be known, and to encourage subordinates to ask tough questions of senior team members. Those are factors that can be layered into a culture without it having been a founding set of factors like they have been at Bridgewater.

Communications in crisis

In the early stages of the outbreak of the COVID-19 pandemic in March 2020, Marriott, the world's largest hospitality company, was acutely hit by the economic fallout of the need for people to remain quarantined at home. By definition, most of society was not traveling for business or pleasure, and they were not staying in hotels. Arne Sorenson, the first CEO of the company not to be part of the Marriott family, noted in a video to Marriott associates that the economic impact of the pandemic was greater than the fallout of the September 11, 2001, terrorist attacks and the Great Recession of 2008 *combined*! Those crises led to a 25 percent decline in business, whereas the pandemic had led to a 75 percent decrease.

The video was Sorenson's first to all associates where he appeared without hair, the consequence of a treatment regimen he was in the throes of due to pancreatic cancer. He called the message the most difficult video message we have ever pulled together," not because of his health, but because of the impact to Marriott's business. In the video, he announced that the executive team had agreed to accept a 50 percent decrease in salary, and that the company's chairman Bill Marriott and Sorenson would forgo compensation for the remainder of 2020. With his voice breaking as his emotion rose, he noted, "There is simply nothing worse than telling highly valued associates, people who are the very heart of this company that their roles are being impacted by events completely outside of their control." They would need to close many hotels and operate others with reduced staff. Many employees were furloughed, and others were let go. He ended his remarks with a note of optimism, saying, "Together, we can and we will overcome this, and we'll thrive once again."[3] As an additional step suggesting selfless goodwill, Sorenson and the company reached out to many of its suppliers asking that, if they had the capacity to bring former Marriott associates into their folds, they do so. They would rather the employees impacted find new, more secure jobs in the near term than to ask them to wait.

Sorenson, rightly, received praise for his genuine, realistic, and transparent comments. There is a natural human instinct to avoid pain, to avoid confrontation with staff who have done wrong or who are in need of improvement, to avoid being open about one's own vulnerabilities. The better path is always in being truthful and almost always in being transparent.

I say almost always because there are some matters that should remain private. If a colleague confides in a manager or human resources that they are ill, for instance. Most companies treat as confidential salary information and performance records, as well. There are rightly some topics that are suitable for the board or the executive team only. That said, the more the rest of the team knows about what the future holds, the more likely they will be to wish to be a part of it. Moreover, employees are more likely to tune their personal radars toward ideas that will have the biggest impact on the vision implied when they understand and buy into that vision.

The organization structure and the silos of the company can create communication challenges. Silos either need to come down or at least to become more permeable to collaboration. In order to overcome these challenges, make sure you are meeting, both formally and informally, frequently with employees across the organization so that you can gather as many useful insights to inform your strategy as possible. Let's cover some methods to do each.

Informal communications

Informal communications are facilitated as appropriate collaboration tools. In the former camp, many companies have experimented with different office formats. There was a trend from dedicated offices to cubicles to open spaces to hoteling and back to offices as companies gathered more data on what makes people productive.

There is also more thought being put into making the office format malleable such that those people who need to collaborate more closely can have reason to be in the same space. Rather than have IT in the IT department, marketing in the marketing department, product people in the product department, and so on, it is better to create spaces that bring them together, reflecting how work will be managed in the future. Thus, as more cross-disciplinary teams become commonplace, space should match the need. It should foster regular communication and collaboration. If questions or ideas arise, it is best to have the people who need to be in conversation co-located. In essence, this is recapturing the magic of the startup scenario, where everyone, no matter the skillset they bring to the company, was in the same room, collaborating throughout the day.

In larger, multinational businesses, virtual versions of what I've described are important. We also saw this same need during the COVID-19 pandemic when everyone was forced to work remotely from their homes. This requires virtual chat rooms, videoconferencing, as well as tools like Zoom, Slack, or Microsoft Teams, which enable moment-to-moment collaboration, replicating what I have noted above.

As virtual meetings become more the norm, there are some factors to bear in mind to make them more impactful:

- Only invite those who are necessary for the questions that are to be asked.

- Determine who among those not invited need to be informed about the results or resolutions from the meeting.

- Ensure someone is ultimately the leader of each meeting and push that person to facilitate the meetings to reach necessary conclusions. Meetings that require follow-up meetings to reach answers should not be the norm.

- Shorten meeting times. Steven Rogelberg, a University of North Carolina Charlotte professor and an expert in meetings, has written a book called *The Surprising Science of Meetings*. In an interview I did with him, he noted that people naturally fit their dialogue to the meeting time set.[4] Constraint can be your friend in this case, so shortening meeting times while keeping enough time between meetings to reflect on actions, send emails to those who were not in attendance, and the like can be helpful.

- Rogelberg also notes that framing the agenda as a series of questions helps drive the conversation more efficiently, and it helps determine whether the meeting has been a success. Were the questions answered or were they not?[5]

- Use video by default, but during periods of frequent videoconferencing (like during the period of quarantine during the COVID-19 pandemic), give teammates the option to occasionally dial in or turn their video off rather than always being on video.

- Engage the introverts on your team. Susan Cain wrote a terrific book on this topic called *Quiet*, in which she describes how best to engage and ensure equal participation of introverts, letting them speak first, pushing them to prepare talking points ahead of time, and the like. These ideas are even more important with virtual meetings, where it can be easier for one or a couple of people to dominate a meeting to the exclusion of others.

- At the conclusion of the meeting, review the takeaways, conclusions, next steps, and people responsible for each, ensuring that there is clarity as to who will do what after the meeting concludes.

- Create more frequent touchpoints across the company, especially from senior to junior levels, even skipping levels of seniority at times. It is important to have a regular read on how the team is doing when operating virtually, since the normal visual cues will not be readily apparent.

Who do you meet with and how often?

YOUR OWN TECH/DIGITAL TEAM
This is your core group, so I'd advise standing meetings with different constituents. These should be both time-based (e.g., every Friday this group meets) and event-driven (e.g., there is an emergency that needs to be addressed pronto). In these meetings, you should share strategic collateral and draw from this group reactions, feedback, suggested edits and additions, as well as begin to do some of the thinking of where the technology and digital division can best aid the rest of the organization.

BOARD MEETINGS
Tech and digital leaders are invited to participate in board meetings with increased frequency, and that is for good reason. This began in earnest after major security breaches to companies like Target and Home Depot happened in 2013 and 2014, respectively, as described in more detail in Chapter 4. Companies realized that great companies with strong reputations were being

hacked, and they needed a plan for this. In recent years, tech and digital leaders have been asked to participate for reasons of opportunity as well, as digital innovation is a defining area of opportunity for this age. As more companies refer to themselves as digital businesses, getting the tech and digital leader involved in board-level discussions becomes an imperative.

Board-level communications should be higher level, not necessarily getting into the weeds of the most technical details, but should also be substantial enough to go into the costs and the value anticipated for the investments made. They should involve honest exchanges about risk management, gaining buy-in from the board about the appropriate level of risk tolerance given the innovation levels demanded by the board and ultimately by customers. The board-level discussions are opportunities to get the influential opinions of leaders who spend time in multiple settings, as often board members are, themselves, leaders of other companies. This is an opportunity to share your IT/digital strategy, but also to glean insights that might impact your plans. The cadence of these meetings tend to be quarterly and potentially more often if there are urgent matters that arise.

EXECUTIVE TEAM MEETINGS (CEO AND THEIR DIRECT REPORTS)

Optimally, the CIO or CDO reports directly to the CEO and, as such, is involved in all executive committee meetings rather than receiving the wisdom and orders from that group through a surrogate such as the CFO or the COO. Thankfully, the number one reporting relationship for CIOs is the CEO, so more companies recognize this.

These should provide the same sort of substance as the board presentations with more detail associated with them. Of course, unlike in board meetings, the products and projects that technology and digital teams will be working on often will be developed in concert with these very constituents with connection points back to the parts of the strategy driven by each. You might think that the details of what is being developed with or for each should be reserved for conversations with them and their teams, but it is important to use the executive team meetings to foster understanding across the executives regarding the products and projects pursued. This level of transparency will help identify new opportunities for the group to partner together in interesting ways, or may uncover new uses for a project that was intended for a single business unit, expanding the value and use of that project to other parts of the company. These meetings should provide thoughts about the enterprise strategy, divisional and business unit strategies, progress made against each, and issues arising relative to each. These meetings are ways to continue to test ideas, communicate progress on IT/digital strategy, and to ensure that everyone is informed of the others' progress or lack thereof. The cadence of these meetings is typically at least monthly if not weekly.

MEETINGS WITH PEERS AND THEIR TEAMS

These meetings provide opportunities to delve into greater depth into the work that the technology and digital teams are undertaking for these leadership teams at the business unit or functional levels. They should be focused as much on discussing existing initiatives (products and projects) as on future opportunities and issues that will allow the technology and digital leadership team to diagnose where best to be involved.

These conversations should have a cadence such that technology and digital leaders are influencing the strategies of those parts of the company.

WITHIN THE TECH AND DIGITAL TEAMS

All-hands meetings   It is important to have a natural rhythm to all-hands meetings—meetings that include the entire team for the technology and digital functions. All-hands are opportunities to explain and reiterate strategy, and to provide updates on progress or lack thereof in areas of significance. They are opportunities to highlight good work done by an individual or by a team. It is also an opportunity to highlight recent anecdotes, research, conversations, and other topics of consequence. These might be based on conversations with executives across the company, peers at other companies, external partners, or thought leaders. As an executive, you should think about bringing your network back to your team, and thus when you are out of the department, you should collect details that would be of interest to your team. Remember, you are coach to your team, you have a lot of experience, a big network, and insights that can benefit them. Communicating these lessons offers invaluable learning opportunities, and keeping your radar up for these anecdotes and lessons also primes your mind to learn and catalog in a way you might not otherwise do. These might be macroeconomic insights, technology trend insights, competitive landscape details, vendor partner-centric, or the like. Think of your all-hands meetings in the same manner that your CEO probably thinks of their all-company meetings. Needless to say, the insights you glean from peers in your network should lead to interesting ideas that can inform your strategy. There is enough that rhymes from IT department to IT department and digital division to digital division that, so long as you are not speaking with a competitor, you can glean great strategic collateral in these sessions.

The cadence of these meetings ought to be monthly, though these might become more frequent during times of great change or great turbulence.

TECHNOLOGY OR DIGITAL LEADERSHIP TEAM MEETINGS

This is the team with whom you should review people, from team performance to individual performance to succession plans. You should review all product and project initiatives, gauging what is going well and what is not. The broader health of the operation should be evaluated. All themes described in this book ought to be covered with this team, and they should be divvied up between the leaders so that someone is in charge of each, helping each mature and driving improvements.

You should push this team to become experts in your current strategy but be awake to inputs from across the company and from across each leader's network that inform strategy. These meetings should take place as often as weekly and should at least take place every couple of weeks in order to maintain a regular flow of communications.

CASCADING MEETINGS FROM MANAGERS TO THEIR REPORTS

This is one of the primary ways in which information should be disseminated, both from top to bottom but also from bottom to top. The former is better understood, as managers provide updates on strategic plans, provide strategic collateral, and the like. The dissemination of information from managed to managers is equally important, as this is often where new ideas can be generated, where issues with the team can be uncovered, and where thoughts on rising stars on the team might be discussed. Oftentimes the people with the most profound inputs to strategy are those who are deeper in the organization. Mine these conversations for insights and to test hypotheses.

There should also be a regular cadence for these meetings, again optimally multiple times per month.

Who is responsible for communications?

If you are a leader of a medium to large-sized technology or digital team, you should consider hiring a communications professional dedicated to your team. This may be a member of your communications team who is a rising star and is interested in greater access to leaders of an important division. It is not necessary that the person have technology or digital experience;

it is important that they have interest in the topics, and they should take training programs in order to understand the topics such as the ones covered in this book.

The role of business information officer, a role that is a liaison between the technology and digital organizations and the business units and functional areas, should be considered. By creating roles that have a foot in technology and a foot in another business discipline, this ensures that technology and digital are in the conversations early and often, positively influencing them, proposing new strategies to pursue, learning from other business information officers about strategies or initiatives that might be right for one's business unit or functional area, ensuring that there is appropriate reuse of technology and, where necessary, adherence to standards.

The person should have a purview both inside and outside your company, communicating your strategy to the broader organization, wherever you may have teams, and working with others to translate the strategy into other relevant languages, where necessary. As you articulate cultural attributes, your communications teams should also identify creative ways to publicize those. Likewise for high-priority initiatives.

There are several creative means of communicating; whether it is through print, video, or audio communications, each should be employed. I have been impressed by technology and digital leaders who develop their own web programs or podcasts for internal consumption. These can be effective ways to keep teams informed, and they work well with the natural way in which employees consume information on their own. These are also effective ways in which to keep disparate teams informed, since one can hear news, priorities, progress, or lack thereof from the leader in their own voice.

It is also appropriate to inject levity into these communications. The example I often cite when counseling executives on effective communications are the comedic safety videos that airlines have used in recent years. First, the airlines leveraged the personal technology provided to customers (television screens at the seat) in order to record a safety message once for everyone to see the same way to free up flight attendants to focus on more important matters as a flight goes through final preparation for takeoff. Second, many airlines have used the combination of humor in the videos along with having them change seasonally or even monthly to keep frequent flyers engaged. This is a great way to produce something once (or perhaps different versions of that thing) to convey an important message and ensure that (a) it is watched, and (b) it is learned.

A few other principles of communication

When it comes to communication, remember these principles:

- simplicity
- repetition
- cross-media
- bidirectional (senior to junior and back)

SIMPLICITY

It is important that messages are simple. Simplicity is harder than it sounds because simple does not mean mundane. It means conveying messages clearly using as few words as possible. The simpler it is, the more memorable it is. The extent to which you can use acronyms to further make messages stick, so much the better.

REPETITION

Repeating important messages, like those regarding strategy, safety, products, customers, and the like, helps ensure that the messaging is sticky. You may find different and creative ways to repeat the messages, but if you want the message to stick, identify multiple opportunities to convey the message.

CROSS-MEDIA

It is important to leverage multiple methods for communications, from in-person to videoconference to phone to recorded video to podcast. It is important to reach employees through the methods they are most comfortable with, and there are ample opportunities to innovate as new means of communication emerge. Record a video and make it available as a podcast. This long-form content can be divided up and repurposed in a variety of ways, as well.

BIDIRECTIONAL

It is important that communications flow down, which is the more traditional way that communications is thought of. The plans of the CEO are translated through the organization from managers to the managed. It is important that communications also flow up, as often the junior members of the team are best suited to identify opportunities and issues.

FIGURE 6.1 Communication

Role(s) responsible

- CIO/CDO
- IT leadership team
- Head of IT communications
- Business information officer

Tool(s)

- Chat and messaging platforms
- Video conferencing tools
- Discussion forum tools
- Tracking and case software

Metrics

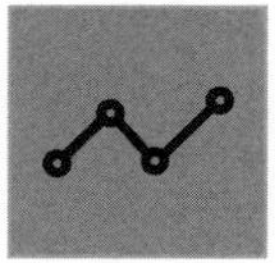

- Improved internal communication based on survey results related to:
  - culture
  - vision/mission
  - enterprise strategy
  - IT/digital strategy
  - company products and services
  - customers

Strategic creation and alignment

It may seem strange to think of a technology or digital leader being responsible for aligning strategy across the enterprise. Since the inception of the CIO role, for example, strategies were created and then brought to them. They were not engaged in the strategic planning processes of the rest of the organization. Rather, they had to bring to life the outcomes of those strategies.

If you think about it, though, aside from the chief executive officer, only the chief financial officer and chief human resources officers have the breadth of purviews comparable to a CIO or CDO, and the technology and digital executives are increasingly involved in customer-facing activities in a way that the CFO and CHRO roles have not been historically.

Technology and digital leaders must recognize that they engage with the rest of the enterprise and the company's customers, and that is rare if not unique. As such, they must leverage this advantage to a greater extent in fostering strategic alignment. By strategic alignment, I mean ensuring there is alignment from enterprise strategy to divisional/business unit/functional strategy. It is often this alignment that is misunderstood or lacking in companies, and that disconnect means wasted effort and money for the enterprise. For technology and digital leaders, if there are not well-articulated plans at the divisional level, the path to bringing those plans to life will be murky at best. Thus, for reasons of self-preservation and value-creation, technology and digital leaders must push for better.

The translation of strategy from the enterprise level to the divisional level is important because that is where the work is done. Enterprise strategy typically calls out objectives related to revenue growth, cost-efficiency, customer satisfaction, geographic expansion, product innovation, and the like. It is the divisions of the company that determine how each of those will happen. Let's take revenue growth as an example. Growing revenue is vital to the health of a company, but the role marketing plays versus the sales organization versus product or service areas versus a function that is evaluating an acquisition of another business all contribute in different but important ways. The specifics of what each will do needs to be formulated clearly to have teams go and find the new revenue through the various mechanisms available across the company.

If you find that the rest of the organization does not have clear strategic plans, engage them to better articulate plans. Begin with a strengths, weaknesses, opportunities, and threats, or SWOT, analysis. It is simple, easy to understand, and will ensure that you gather information quickly, easily, and likely at the right level of granularity:

- Strengths are a firm's resources and capabilities that can be used as a basis for developing a competitive advantage. They tend to be current and internally focused.

- Weaknesses are areas where the company has traditionally not done well or in which it has gaps in its business capabilities (more on those later in this chapter). They also tend to be current and internally focused.

- Opportunities are areas where the company can improve or innovate, exploit a gap in the marketplace, or create or improve a business capability. These can be characteristics that provide a competitive advantage for the company. They tend to be future state and externally focused.

- Threats are anticipated conditions (internal, market, competitive) that do not bode well for the company. They also tend to be future state and externally focused.

As you gather feedback from these SWOTs, it is important to categorize the feedback into topics like people, processes, product, brand, geography or market, financial, customers, organization or culture, competition, technology, vendors or partners, and the like. These form the vestigial versions of objectives for the enterprise or division.

Optimally, you should gather that feedback into a common framework. The one my team and I use is called objectives, goals, tactics, and measures (see Figure 6.2).

The **objectives** are the enterprise's or division's overarching pursuits for the mid to long term. The **goals** are the quantifiable metrics that determine the degree to which an objective is successfully pursued or reached. The **tactics** are the various actions available to the company that will help it reach the goal. Finally, the **measures** are the quantifiable metrics that determine the degree to which a tactic is being successfully pursued. In using a common framework, your IT leadership team can "read the tea leaves" from the enterprise and the various divisions of the company at a common level of clarity and granularity. This is especially useful where there are common themes that emerge from across multiple parts of the company.

Each objective should have a goal associated with it. This is a success metric that helps chart the path to success. Using the same rather generic enterprise strategies, the goals might be defined as:

- Revenue growth: grow revenue by 15 percent in the next year.

- Cost-efficiency: grow costs at a rate 5 percent under revenue growth in the next year.

FIGURE 6.2 Objectives, goals, tactics, and measures (OGTM) framework

Objectives The organization's overarching pursuits for the mid to long term.	**Goals** (Objective KPIs)	• *the quantifiable metric(s) that determines the degree to which an objective (theme) is successfully pursued or reached* • *Goal 1... n*
Tactics	**Measures** (Tactic KPIs)	
The various **actions** available to the company that will help it reach the goal.	The **quantifiable metric** that determines the degree to which a **tactic** is being successfully pursued: • Measure (...) for Tactic 1	
• Tactic i • Tactic ii • Tactic *n*	• Measure i for Tactic i • Measure ii for Tactic ii • Measure n for Tactic *n*	

- Customer satisfaction: improve customer satisfaction with our products from 70 percent satisfied to 80 percent satisfied in two years.

- Geographic expansion: open 10 new offices in the coming year.

- Product innovation: introduce two $50 million revenue products in the next year.

Try to limit the number of goals to two, as if you go for more than that, the strategy is less of a filter and is permeable to too many ideas.

Next, the digital and technology leader can work with members of the enterprise or divisional team who are expert in the area noted by a given objective to brainstorm tactics. As noted above, these are the various actions available to the company (or division) that help it reach the goal(s) articulated. It is important to note that tactics should never have solution language in them. The extent to which a project name or a vendor product is noted in a strategic plan renders it more important than it is. The action is one thing; the means of delivering the action are another. You may believe that Salesforce is the solution you wish to use for customer relationship management, but better to articulate the need for CRM than to note the solution. The solution should be debated.

The tactics can be more plentiful, and during the brainstorming phase, definitely err on the side of more rather than fewer tactics. After the list is finalized, the tactics should be prioritized. The prioritization should be undertaken based on the perception of which ones are being pursued today, which ones are likely to be pursued in the near term, which will be undertaken in the medium term, which will be undertaken later, and which ones may or may not be undertaken.

Finally, a measure or measures should be defined for each tactic. For the same reason noted for the goals, try to limit them to two. For the goals and measures, remember the acronym SMART. Figure 6.3 provides an overview of the concept of SMART.

The technology or digital leader's role in strategic alignment

It may seem presumptuous for the technology or digital leader to push the other divisional heads to define their strategies more clearly. Who is the CIO or CDO to question the plans for the CMO or the SVP of sales? The approach the technology or digital leader should undertake is to compel them by saying that in developing clearer plans, the technology and digital division will be able to drive higher value and prove that by highlighting ideas that will bring these plans to life.

FIGURE 6.3 The SMART metrics framework[6]

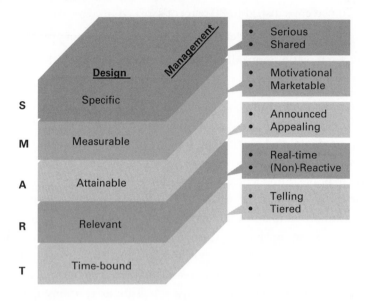

Another advantage the technology or digital leader can claim is that they will be better equipped to understand where there are converging or diverging views of the future that should lead to greater collaboration across the enterprise in the former case and a reconciliation of the paradox in the latter. The technology or digital leader can ensure that teams are effectively pushing in the same direction by playing this strategic facilitation role. Furthermore, the technology or digital leader can be a source of strategic insight and ensure, where there is strategic overlap, the solutions and initiatives to bring those to life can be overlapping, as well. The technology or digital leader should foster efficiency by identifying where overlapping needs can be met with a single solution, where possible. Minimizing effort, spend, and complexity should be a goal of the enterprise in general (the latter factor being a proxy for de-risking the enterprise, as well), and the technology or digital leader is well positioned to play this role.

As Figure 6.4 highlights, common needs represent areas where IT can suggest one solution to meet a need across divisions. In many cases, divisions will have needs that are truly unique, and it is justifiable to pursue unique solutions. Contradictory areas indicate where there are plans for different functions to pursue unique solutions where a single solution across both would suffice. If this is the case, IT should chair a series of conversations with relevant leaders to determine where reconciliation is in order to ensure there are no redundant investments. For example, if the marketing function were to pursue mobile capabilities for external-facing customers,

FIGURE 6.4 Assessing the overlap across OGTMs

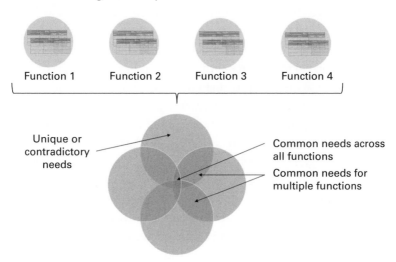

and human resources were pursuing mobile capabilities internally, this could be an area where IT could facilitate conversations between the two areas to pursue a joint solution.

It should be noted that a number of chief information officers who have acted in this way have been asked to take over the strategy functions of their enterprises. This has been the case at companies as diverse as Union Pacific, Dunkin Brands, Qantas Airways, CHS, Pacific Life, Olin, AARP, and Red Robin Gourmet Burgers. In a variety of ways, CIOs at these companies filled a gap that existed in the strategy function, and they made the case while in the CIO role. I don't mean to suggest that every CIO or CDO should aspire to become a chief strategy officer. The CIO and CDO roles are now so strategic and important to the future of businesses that they are worthy destinations at the apotheosis of a career. That said, it is good to know that there are a variety of examples of CIOs asking difficult questions of their peers about their plans for the future, and far from being admonished for so doing, they were rewarded with a new a set of responsibilities. (I grant that for some, adding responsibilities to the complexity of the CIO role may not seem like a reward but a punishment, but I hope the point is made, nevertheless.)

The role of the business information officer

The larger your organization, the more ideas the technology and digital division must generate in the form of new initiatives. This issue is exacerbated if your company has a plethora of business units or multiple operating companies.

Often the leaders of different divisions, business units, or operating companies do not know what the other divisions of the company have as priorities for the technology or digital team to work on. As a result, they have the false perception that the priorities they have articulated are the ultimate priorities for the technology or digital team. What if the top five projects from one division are all less beneficial to the enterprise than five from another division?

It is true that there was a point years ago when the tactics defined by a division of a company may not have required technology or digital initiatives to fulfill them. Now the reverse is true, and the reason is that technology is an essential ingredient for innovation in most business disciplines today, and customers are increasingly technologically savvy, even if they do not have technology backgrounds due to the consumerization of IT. Now everyone has a more powerful computer in their pocket than those that were used to launch and monitor the Apollo 11 mission to the moon. This is an opportunity for the technology and digital division.

The aforementioned business information officer, or BIO, is a role that can help. For larger organizations these would be members of the IT team who are embedded in a single division, business unit, or operating company of the enterprise. Within mid-sized companies, a single BIO might align with multiple divisions of the company. They typically report to the CIO while having a dotted-line relationship to the leaders of the divisions that are their counterparts.

The profile of the BIO should include a chameleon-like ability to think as a technologist but also to represent and think in the terms and with the strategy and success metrics of the other division or divisions in mind. It should also include an ability to network inside and outside of the company, since this needs to be a position that draws insight from across the enterprise and beyond, but also can influence the discussions happening within the company. The BIO should focus on speed-to-market, as this is a key performance indicator for the role. Your BIO should be at the strategy-setting meetings happening within the division or divisions that they are aligned with, and should help provide insights that will allow the division to reach its objectives more readily. They should provide advocacy in both directions, as the BIO needs to represent the interests of the division or divisions they are aligned to back to IT, but also act as an advocate on behalf of IT when dealing with the divisions.

The BIO should be chosen based on their empathy and an ability to listen, as these leaders need to have deep discussions with leaders in IT and in the divisions to understand how the relationship can improve, as well as understand when a need or opportunity that is being articulated could be addressed by an

FIGURE 6.5 Strategic creation and alignment

Role(s) responsible	Tool(s)	Metrics

- CIO/CDO
- Business information officers (BIOs)

- Strategic planning software
- Road mapping tools

- Increased percentage of the company's priorities met by technology and digital solutions
- Increased shared priorities across the company
- Increased percentage of technology and digital division's activities focused on the highest priorities of the rest of the enterprise
- Increased revenue derived by technology and digital division products and initiatives

IT solution of some sort. The BIO should have a bias toward reusing technology wherever possible, as you have probably experienced that many divisional, business unit, or operating company leaders tend to think that each of their IT needs are unique, when they rarely are. The BIO role should help your IT team understand where there are new needs in one part of the company that can be addressed with solutions other parts of the company are already using.

The characteristics and process necessary to use in identifying candidates to be BIOs are, first, to identify particularly business-savvy technologists on your team, especially those who are your best performers who might be interested in a new, strategic assignment like this. Second, identify technology-centric members of other divisions who can join your team in this way, as they will already have the depth of knowledge in the division that they would then align back to. Third, look for people who have great internal networks, and are especially good at influencing your colleagues. Lastly, find people who are autodidacts, and are willing to do the homework necessary to remain abreast of progress and innovation happening both in IT and in the disciplines that are the domains of the division or divisions that they are aligned to.

Develop IT/digital strategy

The IT department is one of the few divisions of the company that touches every part of the company. The IT team is ideally suited to work with the leaders of all other divisions on their plans, with a special focus on advising them on how best to bring to life those plans through better use of information and technology. Just as important, members of the IT team are positioned well to see strategic priorities that are in common or that diverge from multiple parts of the company that may not even occur to the divisional leaders who propose them. As such, the IT team can help ensure that common strategic priorities are addressed commonly and diverging or antithetical needs are reconciled, where that is necessary.

In reviewing all other divisional plans, the IT leadership team will be ideally suited to understand where emerging demands for technology may not yet have a supply of resources, processes, or tools to support them. That opportunity or disconnect may well lead to a strategic priority within the IT strategy.

Let me give you an example. The IT team may identify that multiple parts of the company wish to invest in artificial intelligence. The engineering team wants to use it to help write code, the product areas want to do it to synthesize the data gathered on the company's products to make better decisions or to highlight opportunities for the creation of new products, and the human resources team may wish to use it to analyze data on employee performance, on hiring practices, and to assess who is leaving the company and why, which could impact everything from compensation to incentives to work environment to culture. If the technology and digital division does not yet have any people who possess AI skills, nor processes to take advantage of AI, nor AI technology in its portfolio, the technology and digital division should formulate its own AI strategy to fill this gap. With the strategy declared and shared, the technology and digital team can take the necessary actions to ensure that the supply of AI meets the demand for it by the rest of the organization.

This give and take between the other divisions and IT must be free flowing. The conversations should be regular, and IT should strive to be a part of the conversations at the point at which demand is first articulated. Too often, by not having a regular cadence or even the forums for these conversations, the technology and digital division finds out about new strategic priorities only after they are fully formulated. That is the point when the plans are less malleable. If IT leaders can get involved earlier in the process, they can advise colleagues on the "art of the possible." As the technology and digital team's ability to do this improves, they will increasingly be invited to weigh in on more strategic imperatives, creating a virtuous cycle of sorts.

Therefore, the technology and digital leaders need to get more actively involved in the strategic planning processes of each division of the company and use those conversations to inform IT or digital's own strategic plan. I recommend the same SWOT analysis and objective, goals, tactics, and measures (OGTM) framework described in the previous section. The advantage of using the same method ensures there is appropriate alignment across the plans. In fact, the tactics at the enterprise level ought to align to the objectives at the divisional level. Likewise, the tactics at the divisional level should align with the objectives at the technology/digital strategy level.

CASE STUDY
Dow

Dow has been around for nearly 125 years, and Melanie Kalmar has been with the company since 1987. Kalmar became the company's CIO in 2016. Soon thereafter, the company merged with DuPont, and began the process of creating three new companies: the new Dow, the new DuPont, focused on specialty materials, and Corteva, an agriculture-centric company.

This was a time of extraordinary change and challenge, but she used the opportunity to modernize IT for what she refers to as "the new Dow."[7] She added the chief digital officer title to her CIO title to more fully announce her leadership in the realm of digital.

An area of great investment was in the IT and digital strategy that she and the company drove. She hoped to identify the areas of greatest leverage and value creation from the technology and digital organization to the company and its customers. She developed three pillars to her strategy:

- working and being closer with our customers
- making work easier for our employees
- improving the speed and how we work

An overarching goal was to make the new company a "real-time Dow," according to Kalmar.[8]

She believed there was power in the simplicity of having three main objectives in the fact that the language was plain and lacking any techno-speak. "There are three simple themes that we can check everything we are doing against in the company," said Kalmar. "Everybody can relate to what we are trying to work on, both internal and external to the company."[9]

This plan linked to broader objectives of the enterprise, ensuring that the work that individual contributors that the technology and digital division of the company focused on could be connected to the objectives of the company at large.

(Please note that IT strategy is the topic of my book, *Implementing World Class IT Strategy*, and so if you wish to go deeper on this topic, please consider reading that book.)

Data strategy

Data is the key ingredient for insight in today's organizations, the fuel that can turn a seemingly incomprehensible series of facts into information and knowledge. It is often referred to as the new oil given the growing role technology plays in powering the global economy. The analogy is apt because, just as the oil out of the ground is not useful until it is refined, data alone will not provide knowledge or insights. A strategy must be developed to address how to access data, how to pool it, how to synthesize it, and how to

FIGURE 6.6 IT/digital strategy

Role(s) responsible

- CIO/CDO
- Head of IT/digital strategy
- Business information officers (BIOs)

Tool(s)

- Strategic planning software
- Road mapping tools
- Digital marketing tools for IT

Metrics

- Increased revenue based on technology and digital team's initiatives driven by its strategy
- Decreased costs based on technology and digital team's initiatives driven by its strategy

get it into the hands of those who can interpret it and make decisions regarding the company's employees, operations, suppliers, and customers. Note that this goes beyond simply processing "big data" and encompasses an intentional discussion about how data can be applied to deliver business value while taking into account considerations such as privacy, security, and other forms of governance.

It is important that organizations develop a data strategy that incorporates their business strategy and IT strategy.

Data is pervasive enough at this point that it may already be a part of your organization's enterprise strategy, and in some cases divisional strategies as well. To drive efficient, secure, scalable, and cost-effective data operations, it is critical that any data strategy cascades from the enterprise strategy and is developed in concert with the IT strategy.

A well-articulated data strategy allows an organization to identify data, use data, manage data, and control data. It also should:

- minimize redundancy
- remove inconsistencies in data
- enhance data-sharing and reuse across departments
- increase communication and collaboration on data methods and projects and systems
- create new business development opportunities

Data is the fuel that powers the engines of digital-forward companies by turning raw individual facts and measurements into information, knowledge, and ultimately wisdom:

- **Information:** structured data with context of a snapshot in time
- **Knowledge:** understanding of patterns, cause and effect, and significance of what has happened
- **Wisdom:** insight into how to apply knowledge to improve outcomes for the future

An expensive and time-consuming mistake that many organizations have made in the last decade is to focus solely on collecting and processing "big data," without an intentional design of a holistic data strategy. A data strategy is an integrated approach of how structured data management enables the application of data to deliver business value. My colleague Chris Davis suggests that data strategy should comprise three interlocking components (Figure 6.7) that address the six Vs of data (volume, velocity, variety, veracity, variability, and value):

- **Business strategy:** Clearly defined experiences and outcomes that will be improved by the transformation of data into information, knowledge, and wisdom. The development of the use cases create purpose, drive prioritization, and provide the rationale for investment into data capabilities. The experiences and outcomes will most commonly benefit one or several of five categories: customer experience, products and services, partner and go-to-market experiences, employee experiences, or operational capabilities.

- **Data application:** This is the way in which an organization harnesses data for information, knowledge, and wisdom, as well as action at scale. Data is most commonly applied through synthesized informational documents, visualizations, statistical models, and human or automated decision systems. A data strategy will define how, across various formats, tools, and interfaces, data can be used for descriptive analytics and reporting, diagnostic analytics, predictive analytics, prescriptive analytics, and cognitive analytics.

- **Data management:** This fosters preparation of high-quality, scalable, secure, and trusted data to be used for general data application. Managing data first means defining your overall approach to data strategy with intentionality, clearly specifying how the people and organization, policies, processes, technology, systems of measurement, and performance improvement will establish a sustainable operating model. This operating model will be required to define and manage data architecture and data platform, data governance, data operations, data privacy, and data security. A critical discipline for complex organizations is to establish a master data management (MDM) capability that ensures *trusted* data can scale by integrated data governance into data operations.

More than the volume of data that can be processed, the data strategy's effectiveness can be assessed by the degree to which:

A people in an organization can make better decisions, faster, than competitors

B automation enables a product/service, customer experience, or business process to be delivered at a faster speed, with greater precision, accuracy, security, and scalability

C A and B improve at an accelerated pace as the variety and volume of data increases

As was noted in the section of Chapter 3 on knowledge management, knowledge and access to it is a source of competitive advantage. A well-formulated data strategy is essential in fostering and building new sources of knowledge.

FIGURE 6.7 Three interlocking components of data strategy

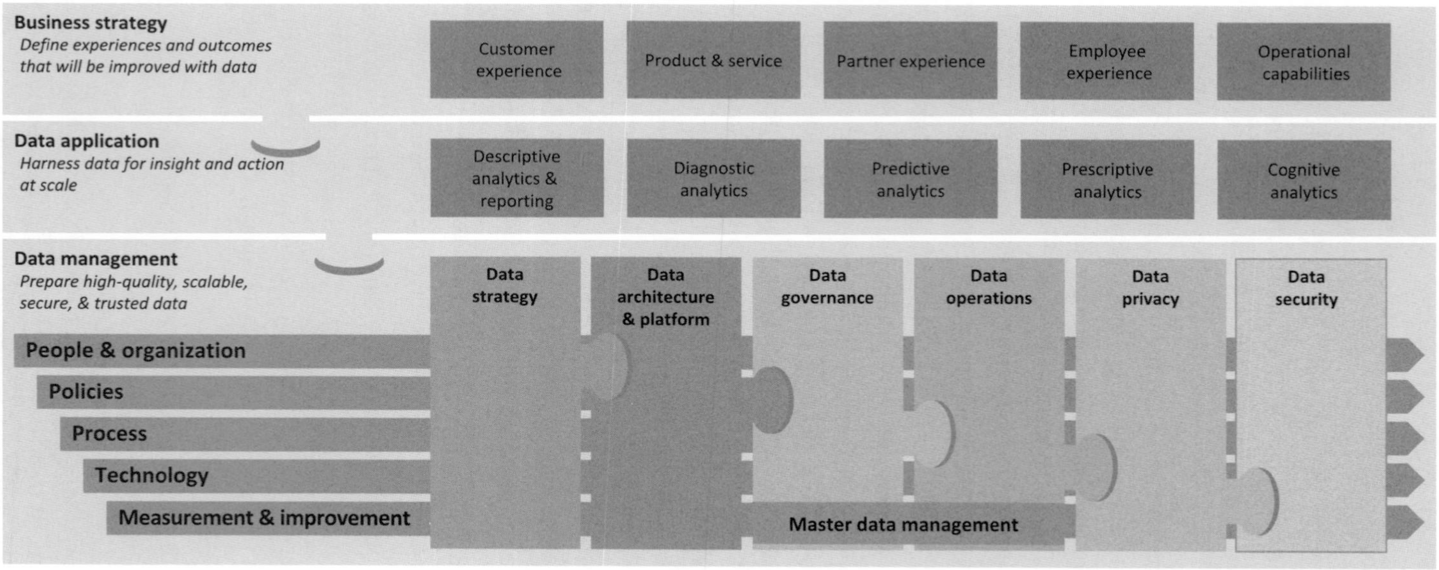

Business strategy
Define experiences and outcomes that will be improved with data

| Customer experience | Product & service | Partner experience | Employee experience | Operational capabilities |

Data application
Harness data for insight and action at scale

| Descriptive analytics & reporting | Diagnostic analytics | Predictive analytics | Prescriptive analytics | Cognitive analytics |

Data management
Prepare high-quality, scalable, secure, & trusted data

| Data strategy | Data architecture & platform | Data governance | Data operations | Data privacy | Data security |

Master data management

People & organization
Policies
Process
Technology
Measurement & improvement

Business strategy cascading to IT and data strategy

A data strategy cannot be designed independent of a business or IT strategy. A business strategy should identify the *why* and the *what*, and a data strategy is a subset of the IT strategy in bringing the *what* to life through the *how* (Figure 6.8).

A data strategy will provide more specificity into particular domains of an IT strategy. While an IT strategy may outline an overarching approach to people, process, technology, and metrics, there will be nuanced use cases for which the data strategy will be unique. A data and analytics department within a technology and digital division may commonly adopt an Agile product management and software development approach, or share the cloud-based infrastructure that other departments use, but it will also be responsible for unique and shared data management and data application capabilities to meet the business strategy needs. A leading data and analytics department will be responsible both for the data architecture of its own data platform, visualization, and analytical tools, and the data architecture that is a component of the organization's overall enterprise architecture.

It is critical to develop the data strategy in concert with the IT/digital strategy. Chris Davis notes that organizations that establish a data strategy independently often:

- have less efficient, scalable, and cost-effective infrastructure
- struggle to drive adherence to data governance, regulatory, and compliance standards at the source of data creation
- have less recourse to establish and maintain a "single source of truth" for enterprise data assets

FIGURE 6.8 Relationship between business strategy, IT/digital strategy, and data strategy

FIGURE 6.9 Cascade from enterprise strategy to data strategy

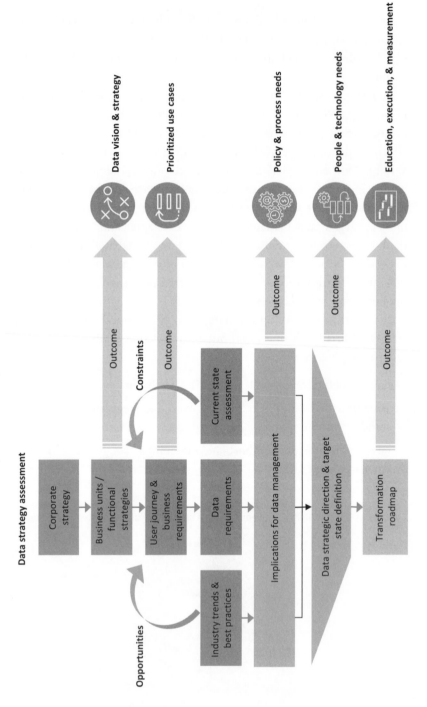

FIGURE 6.10 Aspects of business strategy that drive the direction of data strategy

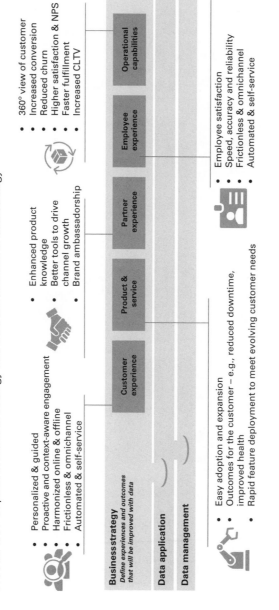

FIGURE 6.11 Cascade from enterprise strategy to IT/digital strategy to data strategy

Three-Year Strategy (Enterprise-Level Objectives, Goals, Tactics & Measures (OGTM)

| Product Design and Development Obj. & Goals | Sourcing and Manufacturing Obj. & Goals | Marketing Obj. & Goals | International Obj. & Goals | Customer Obj. & Goals | Other BUs Obj. & Goals | eCommerce Obj. & Goals | IT Objectives & Goals |

IT/digital Objectives, Goals, Tactics & Measures (OGTM)

Align IT strategic priorities and initiatives to the overall company goals and the priorities and initiatives of the other functional areas

Establish and implement governance practices and Enterprise Architecture across the IT organization

Simplify, consolidate and optimize the IT portfolio (encompasses project, infrastructure and application)

Improve and enhance communications and collaboration across the IT organization and the between IT and the other functional areas

Simplify, consolidate, and optimize the External/vendor portfolio

Data Strategy
Objectives, Goals, Tactics, and Measures (OGTM)

Objective:
Advance Analytics & Reporting Capabilities in Line with Business Drivers to Provide a Seamless Customer Experience

Tactics	Measures (Tactic KPIs)	Goals (Objective KPIs)	Initiatives

Objective:
Streamline and Cross-Leverage Tools and Vendors

Tactics	Measures (Tactic KPIs)	Goals (Objective KPIs)	Initiatives

Objective:
Optimize the Integration of Data Sources across the Ecosystem

Tactics	Measures (Tactic KPIs)	Goals (Objective KPIs)	Initiatives

Objective:
Enhance Efficiency and Impact of Data Analysis

Tactics	Measures (Tactic KPIs)	Goals (Objective KPIs)	Initiatives

Objective:
Establish Enterprise Data Governance to Support Growth & Scalability

Tactics	Measures (Tactic KPIs)	Goals (Objective KPIs)	Initiatives

Objective:
Empower Users and Business Contributors of Data

Tactics	Measures (Tactic KPIs)	Goals (Objective KPIs)	Initiatives

- face limitations in the ability to integrate real-time advanced analytics, automation, and machine learning into other core business applications
- introduce security concerns by nonstandard identity and access controls

The process to ensure this cascade is well coordinated is shown in Figure 6.9.

Figure 6.10 shows examples of business strategy needs that can be used to set the direction of the data strategy. A data strategy will translate these multiple use cases and identify the common capabilities needed to enable the highest priority needs.

Once these needs and data capabilities are clearly understood, the data strategy should be defined in context of the IT strategy so that the data and analytics teams can conceptualize and prioritize the initiatives it must undertake in service of the broader strategic plan (Figure 6.11).

An example of a company that clearly maps its business strategy to its data strategy is Adobe, enabling the application of data at speed and scale to drive business outcomes.

CASE STUDY
Adobe's data-driven operating model drives scale and revenue

A leading example of data management maturity driving business value is Adobe, an $11 billion revenue software as a service company, which established what it calls a "data-driven operating model (DDOM)." Adobe's CIO Cynthia Stoddard recognized that for the company to continue its breakneck pace of scaling the business, key business decisions needed to be founded in reliable, commonly defined, real-time data. To put this into context, the company expanded its Creative Cloud franchise by 45 percent by 2019, with 11.5 billion annual visits, 61 sites, 31 languages, and 30 percent enterprise traffic from mobile. One can imagine that the sheer volume of this information could overwhelm one person, and, if unmanaged, could lead to significant complexities and misalignment on the single source of truth. In partnership with several key functional and business unit leaders, IT set out to help the company define a common framework that would drive the improvement of customer experiences, and thereby influence daily business decisions. See Figure 6.12.

The objective was to align all departments and leaders to meet weekly to discuss performance with a unifying plan on how to operate cross-functionally. With the framework defined, IT then enabled the data management capabilities with a clear priority both on information timeliness and accuracy. Stoddard explains that, "Some of the cornerstones of bringing the data together include consistency of measurement, having a governance process in place, and having the technology framework put together." The company has gone on to say:

FIGURE 6.12 Adobe's customer improvement framework

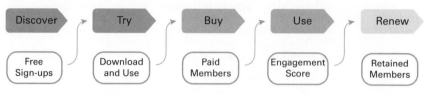

SOURCE www.adobe.com/customer-success-stories/adobe-experience-cloud-case-study.html

---

With a digital customer journey, we bring in a lot of data. But by focusing the model on specific and well-defined customer-centric KPIs, we are able to decide which data we really need. But this means the ability to stitch data across the entire customer journey is mission critical. Being able to gather data, segment it, build audiences, and act on those segments is the backbone of personalization. The model helps us make sense of the data around us. Otherwise, there's no point collecting it in the first place—we're just swimming in it.[10]

Applying data for business value

Applying data to deliver business value is often the "missing middle" for many organizations. Most companies can develop grand plans for how data can improve their competitiveness. Many are also able to establish robust volumes and a variety of data and organize it into information. But not all are able to harness data and turn it into knowledge to understand cause and effect and the insightful wisdom of how to chart the course for the future. Another challenge is that the hype around artificial intelligence and machine learning has led to a substantial amount of confusion between both what is possible given an organization's current maturity level, and what would be valuable given its needs. Business leaders who are less data-literate tend to jump right to "how do we uncover a game-changing insight through AI?" when their companies do not even have basic regression analysis to understand the correlation of past events. Further still, there are other statistical concepts that are less understood, such as the difference between correlation and causation.

A well-designed data strategy will chart a roadmap for the capabilities needed to apply data and realize business value that is proportional to the current maturity of the organization and aggressive enough to meet its business needs and investment tolerance. Data leaders are often required to walk the tightrope of conveying the art of the possible, without overpromising and underdelivering. My colleague, Chris Davis, notes that the data strategy

FIGURE 6.13 Data strategy's influence on five facets of analytics

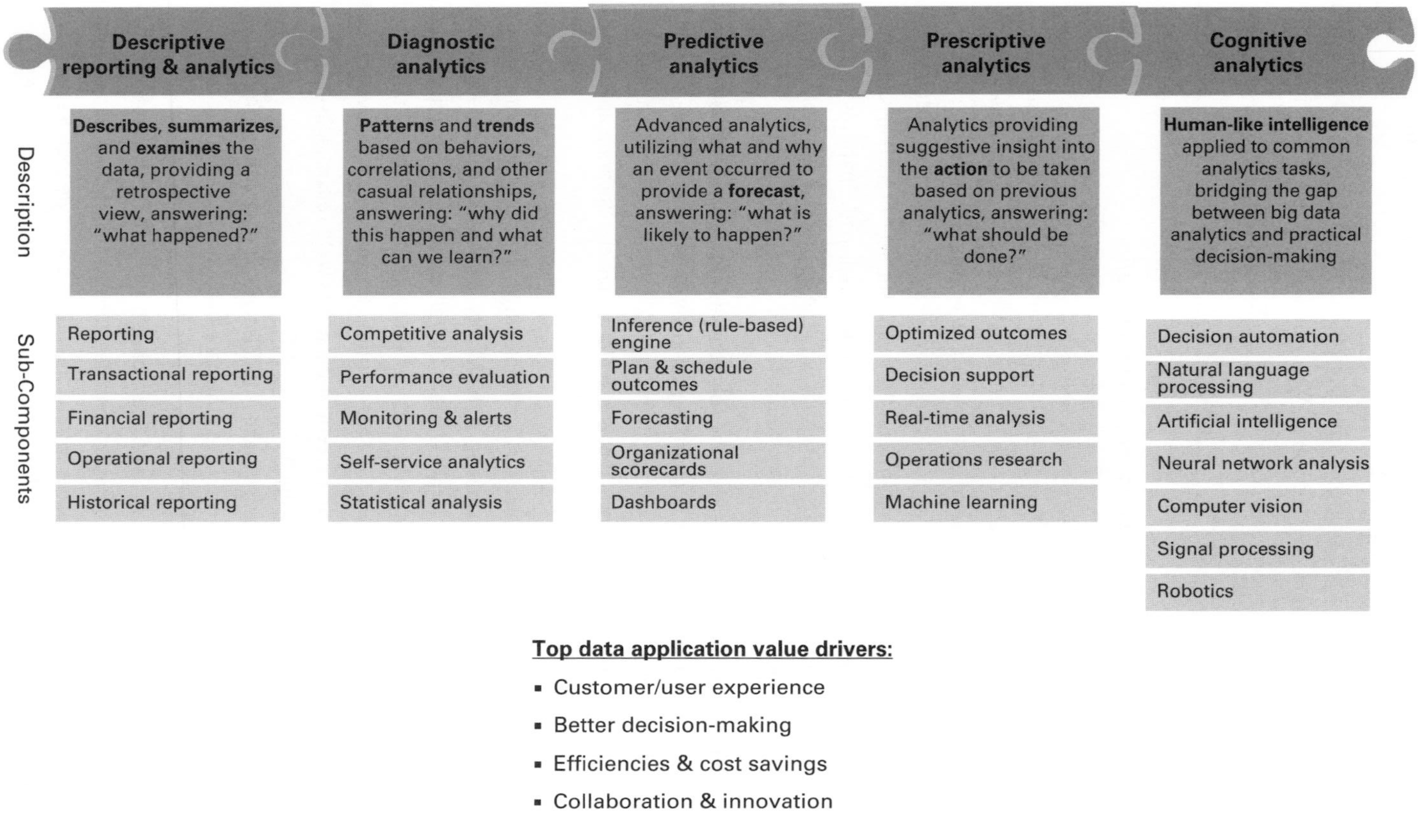

	Descriptive reporting & analytics	Diagnostic analytics	Predictive analytics	Prescriptive analytics	Cognitive analytics
Description	**Describes, summarizes,** and **examines** the data, providing a retrospective view, answering: "what happened?"	**Patterns** and **trends** based on behaviors, correlations, and other casual relationships, answering: "why did this happen and what can we learn?"	Advanced analytics, utilizing what and why an event occurred to provide a **forecast,** answering: "what is likely to happen?"	Analytics providing suggestive insight into the **action** to be taken based on previous analytics, answering: "what should be done?"	**Human-like intelligence** applied to common analytics tasks, bridging the gap between big data analytics and practical decision-making
Sub-Components	Reporting	Competitive analysis	Inference (rule-based) engine	Optimized outcomes	Decision automation
	Transactional reporting	Performance evaluation	Plan & schedule outcomes	Decision support	Natural language processing
	Financial reporting	Monitoring & alerts	Forecasting	Real-time analysis	Artificial intelligence
	Operational reporting	Self-service analytics	Organizational scorecards	Operations research	Neural network analysis
	Historical reporting	Statistical analysis	Dashboards	Machine learning	Computer vision
					Signal processing
					Robotics

Top data application value drivers:

- Customer/user experience
- Better decision-making
- Efficiencies & cost savings
- Collaboration & innovation

should articulate the company's approach in how it will achieve maturity in the areas shown in Figure 6.13.

A leading example of how data management enables the application of data to drive insight and action is Western Digital, a $20 billion high-tech manufacturer.

CASE STUDY
Western Digital delivers major operational benefits

Western Digital's former CIO Steve Phillpott also headed the company's Digital Analytics Office. Upon taking on these new responsibilities, he hoped to build momentum by developing a list of hundreds of data sources, working with his team to prioritize use cases that were both solvable as well as accretive.

An example of this is a machine learning application called DefectNet, which was designed to detect test/fail patterns on the media surfaces of hard disk drives. Process engineers could take the images that detected spatial patterns on the media surface and could trace this back to issues with the upstream equipment in the manufacturing facility. As Chris Davis noted in his CIO.com column:

> From the initial idea prototype, the solution was grown incrementally to scale, expanding into use cases in metrology anomaly detection. Now every media surface in production goes through the application for classification, and the solution serves as a platform that is used for image classification applications across multiple factories.[11]

A comparable approach was pursued in developing a digital twin to simulate material movement and dispatching in the factory. The idea at the outset was to mimic material moves from within Western Digital's wafer manufacturing operations. This smart dispatching approach proved a level of incremental value that created momentum to broaden the scope of the solution. The eventual value was that when new factories were created, 80 percent of the assets were reused, leaving only 20 percent site-specific customization.[12]

The mistake many companies make is to falsely craft data strategy based on technology, which is backwards. Given the pace of change, committing to a technology too early can take away one's nimbleness, and may mean over-engineered solutions that may be obsolete once they make it to the market. By contrast, Phillpott recognized this risk and developed a technology architecture that provided the core building blocks without locking into a single tool. As Davis noted, "This fit-for-purpose approach allows Western Digital to future-proof its data and analytics capabilities with a flexible platform."[13] The three core building blocks of this architecture are:

1 collecting data with big data platforms

2 processing data with analytics platform and governing data

3 accelerated value realization with data embedded in business capabilities[14]

Managing data for application

Data management, if done well, can be a source of competitive advantage, but it must be actively tended like a garden. Data management is essential to deliver value by addressing the five Vs of data noted earlier: preparing for volume, enabling velocity, differentiating variety, ensuring veracity, and adapting to variability. A well-designed data strategy will define how the data-driven operating model will address each of the data capabilities (Figure 6.14) in order to prepare high-quality, scalable, secure, and trusted data to be used for general data application.

A complicating factor of the strategy for data management is that it must apply across a wide variety of data types (Table 6.1). These types will be dictated by the business strategy and means of applying data. Not all organizations will emphasize each data type in the same way. For example, a pharmaceutical company may place greater emphasis on scientific research papers (unstructured data), whereas other industries may be less critically dependent on robust unstructured data management capabilities.

A well-designed data architecture will establish the standard for each of these types of data, which in turn should be adhered to by all designers and creators of systems and processes that manage data.

Do not underestimate the importance of data governance

The only way to ensure that data can be translated into information, knowledge, and wisdom is to ensure that it is trusted. The saying "garbage in, garbage out" applies to the use of data as much as anything else. While some practitioners scoff at the importance of data governance as an academic exercise, there are countless examples of how, when left unaddressed, an organization's data can be changed from an asset into a liability.

One example is a multi-billion-dollar technology company that had, over time, added whatever data attribute was requested by a sales team to its CRM

FIGURE 6.14 Data-driven operating model

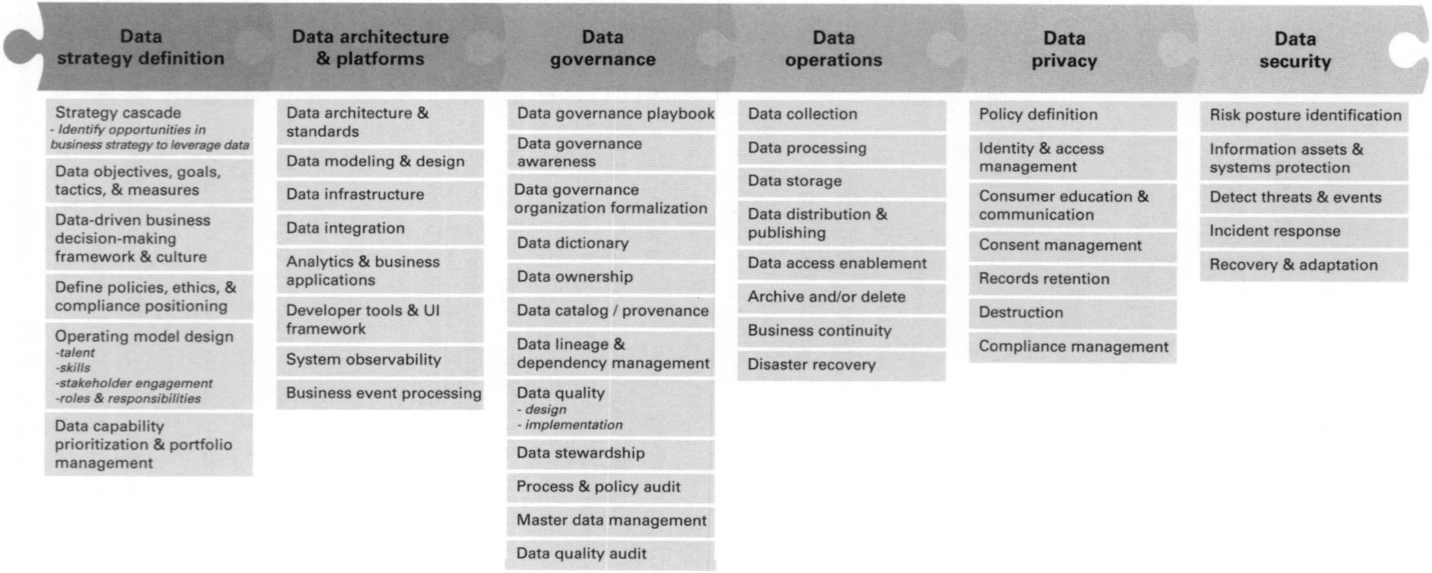

Data strategy definition	Data architecture & platforms	Data governance	Data operations	Data privacy	Data security
Strategy cascade - *Identify opportunities in business strategy to leverage data*	Data architecture & standards	Data governance playbook	Data collection	Policy definition	Risk posture identification
Data objectives, goals, tactics, & measures	Data modeling & design	Data governance awareness	Data processing	Identity & access management	Information assets & systems protection
Data-driven business decision-making framework & culture	Data infrastructure	Data governance organization formalization	Data storage	Consumer education & communication	Detect threats & events
Define policies, ethics, & compliance positioning	Data integration	Data dictionary	Data distribution & publishing	Consent management	Incident response
Operating model design -*talent* -*skills*	Analytics & business applications	Data ownership	Data access enablement	Records retention	Recovery & adaptation
-*stakeholder engagement* -*roles & responsibilities*	Developer tools & UI framework	Data catalog / provenance	Archive and/or delete	Destruction	
Data capability prioritization & portfolio management	System observability	Data lineage & dependency management	Business continuity	Compliance management	
	Business event processing	Data quality - *design* - *implementation*	Disaster recovery		
		Data stewardship			
		Process & policy audit			
		Master data management			
		Data quality audit			

TABLE 6.1 Six types of data

Unstructured data	Data found in email, white papers, magazine articles, corporate intranet portals, product specifications, marketing collateral, PDF files, and through voice and video channels.
Transactional data	Data about business events (often related to system transactions, such as sales, deliveries, invoices, claims, etc.) that have historical significance or are needed for analysis by other systems.
Metadata	Data about other data. It may reside in a formal repository or in various other forms, such as XML documents, report definitions, column descriptions in a database, log files, connections and configuration files.
Hierarchical data	Data that stores the relationships between other data. Sometimes considered a super master data management domain because it is critical to understanding and sometimes discovering the relationships between master data.
Reference data	A special type of master data used to categorize other data or used to relate data to information beyond the boundaries of the enterprise (e.g., countries, currencies, time zones, etc.).
Master data	The core data within the enterprise that describes objects around which business is conducted. Master data is not transactional in nature, but it does describe transactions.

system. While this company had optimized for speed, implementing requests to get answers quickly, it led to over 1,000 different data elements for a single set of activities, multiple different, hard-coded definitions for the same information, and countless incomplete or duplicative records. The consequence was that the sales teams and finance team would show up to the same meeting with different accounting for sales orders, booked revenue, and recognized revenue. The lost time and frustration that followed each of these misaligned meetings finally led the organization to address the untenable situation by completely re-architecting its customer and sales data models. The lack of data governance not only cost millions to fix in new work, but uninformed decisions and misalignment created an unknowable amount of opportunity cost.

The benefits of good data governance are:

- alignment of business and data-related activities, prioritizing and protecting stakeholder needs
- standardization of data systems, policies and procedures, reducing operational friction
- greater transparency, monitoring, and tracking for data-related activities
- increased quality and value of data, leading to better decision-making

- reduced costs, compliance complexity, security risks
- increased data literacy through training and education

ROLES RESPONSIBLE FOR DATA GOVERNANCE

The best way to optimize your data governance practices, without allowing them to become overly bureaucratic or neglected, is to define clear roles and responsibilities of the parties involved. The key roles will typically comprise the data governance program manager, the data steward, the data owner, the data architect, and the data user.

The **data governance program manager** is accountable for defining and facilitating the data governance operating model. The data governance program manager:

- defines roles and responsibilities across teams
- facilitates prioritization of use cases of focus for the data governance team
- communicates progress to cross-functional stakeholders and drives data literacy across the organization
- defines and evaluates data quality metrics
- manages data governance meetings for key strategic and operational decision-making

The **data steward** is accountable and responsible for data and processes that ensure effective control and use of data assets. The data steward:

- defines policies and advises on the implementation of policies
- plans information requirements
- ensures control of information
- coordinates delivery efforts with data, application, and infrastructure engineering
- creates and manages core metadata
- executes operational data governance activities
- usually resides in a business discipline

The benefit of utilizing a data steward is that a more consistent set of policies and processes will be in place to manage data use, sharing, and collection internally and externally.

The **data owner** is responsible for ensuring that information is defined, governed, and used across systems and lines of business. The data owner:

- defines data requirements
- ensures data quality and availability
- usually resides in a business discipline rather than technical team
- defines access management for data
- in some organizations, is a senior stakeholder, collaborating with multiple data stewards
- in many cases will empower or delegate operational responsibilities for data quality to a team member, who may also be a data steward (e.g., examining match/merge/link rules for a master data set)

The benefit of instituting the data owner role is that a clear point of contact will be set up to own and manage a data set as a strategic asset.

The **data architect** is responsible for designing and managing an organization's standard and scalable approach for data management. The person in this role:

- defines the data model, schema, hierarchies, and standards for all teams to use when structuring data sets
- defines data ingress and egress approaches for standard data collection and publishing
- defines data storage and computing standards in conjunction with enterprise technical infrastructure (on-premise, cloud-only, and/or hybrid-cloud)
- ensures security of information
- resides in technology or digital division

This role provides a holistic view of how data is modeled, collected, processed, and distributed in a standard, secure, and scalable fashion for the benefit of the enterprise.

Finally, the **data user** is a consumer and user of data for analytics, reporting, or regulatory needs. The person in this role:

- selects the best data source and application(s) to meet their needs
- understands and utilizes the information accessed
- complies with data management policies
- creates data extracts to meet specific needs
- articulates needs for new data onboarding to the respective data owner or data governance program manager

The benefit of this role is that the appropriate data will be used by the right people to comply with regulations and perform analytics.

CASE STUDY
The chief data officer

The chief data officer is a relatively new role. In 2012, only 12 percent of Fortune 1000 companies had a chief data officer according to a survey from NewVantage Partners. By 2018, that had grown to 63 percent, and it is expected to be 75 percent in 2021.[15]

Fawad Butt has been a data leader at Northern Trust, Kaiser Permanente, and was the chief data officer of United Healthcare and Optum, one of the largest healthcare companies in the world. He has been involved with data strategy long enough to understand its evolution. "In the beginning, we were really data janitors, and we didn't even have our own brooms to sweep up the data when we found it," said Butt.[16]

The role has advanced in some circles to be one of influence, attempting to have leaders from across the enterprise do the right things with their data but lacking an ability to mandate it. The further evolution, which is still the domain of the best of the chief data officers, is to the point of having authority and delivery responsibilities. It might seem obvious that a company would want a true data leader with full authority to make change happen, but the issue is that the discipline is new enough that there are few people like Butt who have had such depth of experience to have the credibility to drive change. Butt offered me five lessons to establish and maintain strong data organizations.

Not so surprisingly, the first step is to **establish a clear data strategy**. The strategy provides the "why" of data. What are you solving for? Butt says that with each role he has taken on, he has asked, "Why are you pursing a data strategy now, and what is the purpose?"[17] He wants to know if the company is under cost pressure, or are consumer behaviors changing, or is the company in the throes of a digital transformation? Is there a competitive threat of some sort? Each are reasons to establish a new data strategy, but the methods one will use will be quite different in each case. Butt notes that once you establish the "why," it is important to focus one's attention on the business capabilities for opportunities relative to data strategy. This will help establish a sequence to the roadmap.

Second, Butt notes one needs to **develop the data organization**. Even without an existing data team within the company, there are likely a number of data-centric roles on the team from database administrators, extract transform load (ETL) developers, security engineers who focus on data assets, and enterprise architecture teammates who focus on data, as well.[18]

Butt notes that it is important to develop lifecycles for data. In organizing a team, Butt recommends starting with data management to develop and refine core data capabilities. This is the stage to stand up to the team and to develop a budget and some quick wins with data.[19]

Second, Butt recommends establishing what he refers to as the **city planning view of data**. "You don't just build a city, you plan," he says. "There should be residential areas, commercial areas, industrial areas. This breakdown will help one determine where schools and hospitals should be, where highways are needed, and where skyscrapers are most likely to be built."[20] One must continue to review data platforms and capabilities during this phase to demarcate the flows of data. The city planning view should establish the current and the future state of data, along with the migration path between them.

The fourth phase is about using the data. "This is when you need reporting, business intelligence, advanced analytics, machine learning, protocols to manage data, governance models, and other tools," said Butt.[21]

After those four, Butt suggests that over the next 18 months, one must focus on three other areas, in the fifth phase:

> The first is to **focus on the foundation**. What do we need? The second is **enablement**. What do we need to do to extract value in the near term? Third is **modernization**. How do we modernize our practices and our technology so that it will be sustained for the foreseeable future?[22]

The next broader recommendation is to **remember that people are sources of data just like systems**. There is a tribal knowledge within organizations, and people know who to turn to for certain kinds of insights. That tribal knowledge must be tabulated and documented to become repeatable, as well as to ensure that it is not stuck in any one person's mind. It should be rendered into data catalogs. This facilitates an understanding of when data is produced and the metadata requirements, and it also provides insights into data privacy, which must be baked into the process early.[23]

Next, Butt argues for **a balance between a centralized versus a federated approach to data**. Butt says that rather than determining one approach or another, go for both:

> You need centralized data and federated data. It is more a question of degree. Are you 30 percent centralized and 70 percent federated? Are you the reverse? Innovation tends not to happen in the board room or at headquarters. It happens at the last mile, closest to customers. That is where sustainable innovation happens in great organizations.

This argues for a degree of federation even as there may be a need to do more centrally.

Lastly, Butt suggests one must **avoid the pitfalls that can trip up chief data officers**. The average tenure for a CDO is less than two years. Butt diagnosed three primary reasons for failure:

1   Poor change management. Change management is especially important when the CDO role is new, and there may be a perception of a loss of autonomy by business unit leaders, for example, who once had a tight grip on their data. Explaining why the changes are coming, when, and to what value is critical, and communicating often is critical.

2   Less than steadfast support from the leadership team. "It should not be the CDO's boss, but really the boss's boss," championing the importance of data, noted Butt. "Optimally, that is the CEO. They can influence the blockers, and they can express ongoing support when mistakes or missteps happen."

3   A lack of data literacy. "The CDO has to expose the problem and explain the complexity," said Butt. Thus, they must be an educator throughout the process.[24]

A great data strategy ties together in a clear view how business strategy can be enhanced through more insightful human or automated decision-making. An innovative customer experience cannot scale and maintain differentiation if there is not instrumentation and telemetry to prioritize improvement opportunities; a beautiful dashboard provides no value if the data cannot be trusted; and the largest, highest processing power data lake's cost will outweigh its value if there is no operating model to harness data for decision-making. Lastly, the data strategy will inevitably face challenges in organizational change management, security, and scalability if defined disconnected from the IT strategy. Data can be a source of competitive advantage for an organization, and though your company may be among the many who choose to bring in a chief data officer, the technology and digital leader (the CIO or the chief digital officer) are still likely to be the best executives to navigate the balance between business strategy, data application, and data management.

Business capabilities

Not long ago, the strategies developed at the enterprise level or at the business unit or divisional levels might be addressed by and large without technology. Today, the majority of those strategies are likely to have a major technology component associated with them. The technology and digital leaders of the company have to increasingly play a role in helping bridge the gap between what those plans suggest and the means of accomplishing the objectives articulated. Arthur Hu, the chief information officer of Lenovo, has said:

FIGURE 6.15 Data strategy

Role(s) responsible

- CIO/CDO
- Chief data officer

Tool(s)

- Data collection
- Data processing infrastructure and applications
- Data storage infrastructure and applications
- Data integration, distribution, and publishing
- Data discovery, catalog, and governance workflow management
- Master data management
- Data privacy, access, and compliance
- Data security monitoring, alerting, and controls
- Reporting, dashboarding, and data visualization
- Analytical and diagnostic tools
- Data science and algorithm engineering toolkits
- Financial visibility and cost controls

Metrics

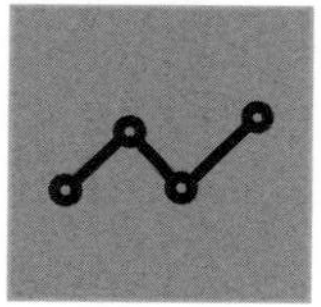

- Business strategy
  - Increased revenue from data-driven insights
  - Increased cost savings from data-driven insights
  - Improved business process efficiency and effectiveness for customer experience, product and services, or internal operational capabilities
  - Increased number of data-driven A/B or multi-variate tests run within a year
- Data application
  - Increased user adoption of analytical reports and self-service tool sets
  - Increased completeness of customer 360 profile and connected modeling variables
- Data management
  - Increased completeness of training for data literacy education
  - Increased scalability of data team operating model relative to company and user growth
  - Increased data platform uptime
  - Decreased data latency for time-sensitive workloads
  - Increased percentage of data assets with lineage and observability
  - Increased percentage of reused data assets
  - Increased data quality index or "trust" score for prioritized data assets

Technology will only continue to accelerate as it moves from backstage to center stage, and I believe this evolution puts a premium on the technology leader's ability to act as a bridge and translator between the technology and the business world… technology leaders must speak in a language that is concise, compelling, and easy to understand.[25]

As a technology or digital executive, it is important not to communicate with the leadership team in strictly technical terms. Lowe's CIO Seemantini Godbole noted:

When speaking with business partners and aligning IT strategy with the broader company strategy, it is important to speak the language of the business and to be outcome oriented. Business capabilities are a great way of accomplishing this as they target the "what" without diving into the technical details and connect strategy to near-term actions.[26]

Defining business capabilities

As Godbole notes, a means of ensuring the appropriate linkage can be made is to use business capabilities. In a white paper that my firm produced in 2018, we defined business capabilities as:

an integrated set of processes, technologies, and deep expertise that are manifested as a functional capacity to capture or deliver value to the organization. They outline "what" a business must do to succeed, as opposed to "how" a business operates.[27]

The key is to span the entire enterprise in defining business capabilities. It is at this holistic level that the best ideas can be generated and the highest value can be achieved.

As an example of a business capability, take "generate sales," a version of which will be a business capability for most for-profit businesses. As Figure 6.16 notes, there are people who are responsible for generating sales (e.g., salespeople and account executives) who use a process to do so (e.g., forecasting sales and leveraging sales enablement) while also leveraging technology (e.g., a CRM system) to help undertake this.

To take another example, consider the recruiting process. There are a number of steps that make up this process:

- identifying a need for a new resource
- developing a requisition for the role to be filled

FIGURE 6.16 Components of a business capability[28]

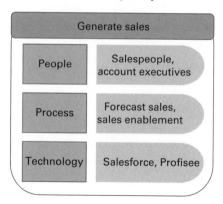

- engaging executive recruiters
- leveraging online tools such as LinkedIn to identify other candidates
- screening candidates for relevant experience and academic credentials
- interviewing candidates by phone or videoconference
- conducting in-person interviews
- ranking the candidates based on pre-set criteria
- extending an offer to the most qualified candidate

There are people, process, and technology facets to the steps described. For recruits, they should be as seamless and efficient as possible. The human resources department, the technology or digital division of the company, and external partners are likely to have roles in the process. If the hand-offs are efficient and well managed, it will make for better outcomes for everyone. In some companies, these different parts of the recruiting ecosystem operate like silos, and the inefficiency may mean frustration for the candidates and for the managers who badly need the roles to be filled by a capable new employee. Business capabilities foster greater understanding and collaboration.

Steps to implement business capabilities

Metis Strategy's white paper on business capabilities defines five steps to implement business capabilities:

- define the capabilities
- segment and prioritize

- evaluate maturity
- define capability roadmaps
- continuously improve

Let us cover each in order.

DEFINE THE CAPABILITIES

Enterprise architects or business information officers are roles that have a foot in the technology or digital division of the company, but who also have relationships and insights into the processes used throughout the company. Have these leaders work with leaders from the various business units or divisions of the company to identify business capabilities. The conversation should identify pain points to be solved, and the technology or digital representatives should provide insights regarding technology enablement to match the business unit or divisional leaders' insights into business process improvement.

SEGMENT AND PRIORITIZE

When the capabilities are defined, they need to be prioritized. Focus on those that are associated with the highest value to the operation or to customers or that are key to the company remaining competitive. By focusing on the highest value areas first, greater progress will be gained in terms of value to the company and in value derived from leveraging business capabilities.

EVALUATE MATURITY

Each capability should be assessed for its maturity in the current state. The target future state maturity should also be evaluated. It may seem strange that each would not be fully optimized or operating at a world-class level in the future state, but it is not feasible that each business capability will operate at that standard. Define those areas that will be focal for the greatest level of performance and maturity gain, and others where industry average levels of maturity may be appropriate. Those capabilities that are sources of competitive advantage should be emphasized for improvements to the highest levels of maturity. For some others, achieving parity may be sufficient because they are capabilities that are not differentiating, and you will not gain or lose enthusiasm from employees or customers in not shooting for world-class maturity in these areas. Across the business capabilities, understanding which will be focal in the first 12 months, the 12–24-month time horizon, and beyond that will also be helpful so that there is a means of tracking progress across all business capabilities. It also sets appropriate expectations that the company will not attempt to improve all areas at once.

DEFINE CAPABILITY ROADMAPS

Once the capabilities are defined and prioritized and assessed for current and future state maturity, business stakeholders and the technology and digital representatives can collaborate to define what is being done currently in support of each capability. Perhaps no people are currently responsible for the capability, there is no process that guides it, and there is no technology that has automated the process. This represents a greenfield opportunity to define new means of driving maturity and progress relative to a given business capability. In other cases, those same collaborators may determine that there are several applications supporting a given capability. This is an opportunity to choose the winner among the redundant applications.

CONTINUOUS IMPROVEMENT

This should not be viewed as a "one-and-done" exercise. This should be a living process that is updated as time marches on, and as progress (or lack thereof) is charted. As the business matures, the business capabilities should mature, as well. Over time, some business capabilities may be consolidated or may go away, and new business capabilities may be defined.

MEASURING THE EFFECTIVENESS OF BUSINESS CAPABILITIES

- Completeness of the business capability roadmap is judged by technology and digital resources and business unit and divisional resources.
- Maturity plan is set for all business capabilities together with means of improving each:
  - plans on which business capabilities will be candidates for highest level of maturity versus those that are appropriate to grow or keep at average levels.
- Over a three-to-five-year time horizon, the company should achieve the levels of business capability maturity targeted.
- As time passes, the dynamism of the business capability roadmaps should be assessed to ensure that it is being refreshed, with some consolidation, some elimination, and some additions. It is difficult to predetermine the percentage in each category, but track each to ensure that refreshment is focal.

FIGURE 6.17 Business capabilities

Role(s) responsible

Tool(s)

Metrics

- CIO/CDO
- Business and functional leaders for their respective areas of responsibility (e.g., capability owners, stewards, and SMEs)

- Business capability mapping and modeling software

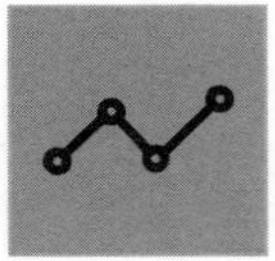

- Improved business capability maturity assessment scores (e.g., Metis Strategy uses a 0–5 scale for current and future state, similar to the CMMI)
- Increased speed for risk assessments
- Decreased overlap of business capabilities across the enterprise

Driving innovation

Ultimately, the reason you would assess the maturity of the topics raised throughout this book, and then do something about raising your team's performance relative to each, is to build the capability and the capacity to innovate on behalf of your company. This is the lifeblood of the company that ensures that new product offerings are developed, that improvements and efficiencies are identified to impact the internal operation. Innovation is a source of pride for a company, and can be a cultural touchstone for employees. It can also foster brand strength, and make the company a talent magnet.

First, you should develop a definition of innovation. I believe innovation is the introduction of novel concepts, ideas, and methods that create new value for the enterprise and/or its customers. It may come in the form of cost or risk avoidance. It may also lead to augmented revenues for your company. There are "small i" innovations, which may be innovative add-ons to existing products or services. There are also "Big I" innovations that introduce completely new products or services. The pursuit of the latter is understandable, as they can lead to major growth for the firm, but they should not be pursued to the exclusion of the former, which can offer meaningful if lower levels of value.

Who is responsible for innovation?

There is an interesting philosophical argument about whether innovation should be the domain of a small, elite team within a company versus being the responsibility of everyone. There is something compelling to thinking of it being everyone's responsibility, but without a shepherd guiding innovation and taking responsibility for the ultimate success or failure of the pursuit of innovation, you may have the situation where you ask everyone to be responsible, and yet no one is. It is easy to think about new, creative ideas for a time in the pursuit of innovation only to retreat to one's day job.

That said, I do think that innovation should be pursued by everyone. There simply needs to be guidance as to where they should focus their attention, and someone who is ultimately responsible for seeing that innovation happens. It should begin with a well-articulated strategy. Strategy should be the guide to innovation. It is not to say that an innovative idea cannot lead to a rethink of a strategy, but that is the outlier case. Rather, as the organization determines where it will focus its attention, and, due to exclusion, where it will not, that should help the entire team focus on where innovation should be focused.

Regarding the "small i" innovation I referred to earlier, you should also focus on existing products and services as areas for incremental innovation.

This is aided by having product teams who focus on shaping, improving, and, indeed, innovating around existing products.

It is important to ensure that innovation has its own bucket of funds. The amount should have inputs that are both top–down (an amount based on historic spend on innovation) and bottom–up (based on the actual innovative ideas that are presented throughout a given year).

Innovation is aided through the greater degree of collaboration that has been covered in various parts of this book. As I have mentioned before, innovation increasingly happens at the intersection of disciplines rather than within traditional organizational silos. Therefore, where groups within your organization are tasked with pursuing innovation, ensure that they are staffed with people from across different disciplines. You want product people collaborating with marketers collaborating with technologists collaborating with data scientists collaborating with designers. Each brings their own view of the world and adds necessary and creative lenses to the innovation process.

It is important to note that each of the members of the ecosystem highlighted in this chapter is a potential source of inspiration, and each should be called upon in ways formal and informal to help drive ideas. Customers may offer the best ideas inasmuch as the ideas they dream up presumably align with needs they have that are unmet and that they will pay for. Identify the most creative as well as the most trusted of customers to play intellectual tennis with. If you are a business-to-consumer company, find diverse arrays of customers to bring together, and ensure they represent your customer base well, with the appropriate representation based on gender, race, ethnicity, nationality, and the like.

Finding the best and most creative of your peers to get together with in order to have creative brainstorming sessions should yield ideas that you can each take back to your offices. You may even identify creative partnerships or joint ventures between your firms to pursue the ideas that are developed. I would suggest having a regular cadence, say, a monthly dinner, and introduce a topic that everyone will brainstorm on. Perhaps a different executive will choose the topic each month. As aforementioned, also engage your peer group through forums like LinkedIn to ask questions and get quick but often statistically significant feedback.

Innovation labs

The venture capital community can be good judges for innovation, since it is a topic they often judge. The way in which they work can also be an inspiration to change how you think about your innovation activities. John Marcante, the chief information officer of Vanguard, the world's largest mutual fund company, was involved in the development of the company's Innovation Studio. The inspiration for the Studio was based on a trip he led with the executive team to Silicon Valley. He described to me what happened when that team met with venture capitalists and academics from Stanford, talking about how people work, and the nuances of business in Silicon Valley:

> Specifically, the speed at which they were working was different, which caused us to stop and think about speed. Having that speed was one of the main motivations around building the Innovation Studio. We wanted to work in a different way. Specifically, we wanted to work in co-located, full-stack, and collaborative teams so we could move along in a faster way.[29]

The three main reasons for pursuing the Innovation Studio were finding new ways to work, looking to disrupt the market, and attracting more talent.

The Vanguard Innovation Studio also has a board to oversee and weigh in on its activities. Half of the board is made up of executives within the company, and the other half includes people from academia and people with venture capital experience. They offer perspectives on innovation with a much broader context. This is an innovative approach to bring the ecosystem into a company to offer deeper insights and perspectives.

Executive recruiters can weigh in on the people component of innovation, including the skills to bring it to life. If yours is a burgeoning innovation function, for example, you may need new leaders who understand the nuances of establishing a team and marshaling resources down a path that yields results from innovation.

Finally, external partners have a breadth of experience that they bring. They may well have insights into what good looks like across your industry, as an example. Also, in pushing them to include their best resources to collaborate with your team, and by exposing them to your strategy, as noted in the prior chapter, they will have a better sense of the context into which innovative ideas are likely to drive the best results. You should push them to develop innovative ideas and provide them rewards for doing so.

As the example of the Vanguard Innovation Studio highlights, some companies have fostered innovation best through the development of innovation labs. In CIO.com, my colleagues Chris Davis and Brandon Metzger offered "7 considerations when creating a corporate innovation lab." The seven factors are:

1   Defining the charter. This is crucial to ensure that the lab has focus.

2   Identifying innovation metrics. As I noted at the top of this section, it is important to define and measure success relative to innovation to know whether you have been successful, and if you are not, to course-correct accordingly.

3   Employing a process for innovation. Davis and Metzger note that companies should:

   a) *embrace customer centricity*

   b) *experiment relentlessly, with the desire to learn from failures*

   c) *leverage new technologies and business models*

   d) *accelerate the build/measure/learn cycles; and*

   e) *utilize the customer development method and lean methodologies.*[30]

They highlight the example of the Lowe's Innovation Lab (LIL), noting:

> [LIL] uses a narrative-driven approach to identify and articulate opportunities. First, LIL conducts market research, compiles trend data, and collects customer feedback on unmet needs and pain points. Next, LIL shares this information with science fiction writers who create strategic documents in the form of comic books, which follow characters through a narrative arc that illustrates a new solution to the character's problem. Then Lowe's executives use the comic books to make prioritization decisions, and, finally, LIL works with its partners to create the solutions introduced in the comics.

4   Determining who and how to recruit. Davis and Metzger note, "It is essential that they recruit for passion and cognitive diversity, rather than just skill. Labs often include a wide range of technical and non-technical roles, from data scientists and designers to experts in anthropology and psychology."[31] An appetite for risk and an aptitude for operating in environments with uncertain pathways to success are crucial.

5   Establishing a funding source and budget. The lab must be paid for, initially with seed funds, and ultimately it should be self-sustaining.

6   Determining where to locate the lab. Vanguard's headquarters are in suburban Philadelphia. They intentionally placed their Innovation Studio in Center City Philadelphia, the city's downtown, to attract younger staff who prefer to live in the city and walk to work. The location was close enough to headquarters for cross-pollination between the Studio and headquarters, but far enough apart so that it could operate as a separate entity.

7 Developing a strategy to successfully integrate innovation. Davis and Metzger note, "From Kodak's invention of the digital camera to Xerox pioneering the GUI, there is no shortage of companies that failed to capitalize on their innovations." It is important the ideas see the light of day, weave themselves into the product and services of the company, and that they scale. Innovation labs fail when they essentially amount to being labs where clever people tinker with ideas and develop a series of prototypes. If a company already has many billions in revenues, then ideas that yield $1 million in new revenue are not moving the needle adequately.[32]

An innovation lab that I have been particularly impressed with is the Capital One innovation lab. I have on several occasions brought groups of CIOs to see the lab the company maintains in Arlington, Virginia. I spoke with one IT leader who had responsibilities with the lab, who indicated that a key to the lab's success has been using a wide array of technolology. If you are going to hire innovative staff, they expect to use the latest and greatest technology available, so you may need different technologies than those used at headquarters, as an example.

A different risk tolerance may be required in an innovation lab. Not unlike a startup, the odds of succeeding in the lab are small. Not every piece of technology will be successful, but in the Capital One lab there were numerous examples of things that started in the labs that either were moved into a line of business or the concept was adopted and then picked up by other parts of the organization.

Innovation is brought to life when the power of the company's ecosystem helps bring the art-of-the-possible to the enterprise. Ultimately, by taking great care to build a world-class ecosystem to complement a world-class team inside of your company, the pathway to greater levels of value will be within sight.

Chapter takeaways

In many ways, the substance of Chapters 2–5 and the work required to optimize people, processes, technology, and one's ecosystem, should yield value through the strategy sub-themes noted here. That said, these sub-themes are also key to ensure that the insights, improvements, efficiencies, and opportunities are realized through the sub-themes covered in other chapters. Technology and digital teams are not likely to optimize performance in these areas without strength in the other sub-theme areas. If people are not operating well and great people are leaving, it will be difficult to

FIGURE 6.18 Innovation

Role(s) responsible

- CIO/CDO
- Chief innovation officer or head of innovation

Tool(s)

- Mind mapping tools
- Collaboration software
- Modeling software
- Knowledge and idea management systems
- Innovation management tools

Metrics

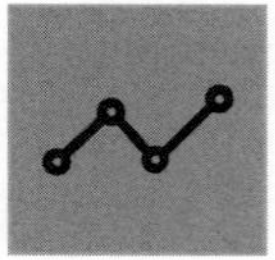

- Increased percentage of revenue derived from innovative ideas generated by the technology and digital team
- Decreased costs derived from innovative ideas generated by the technology and digital team
- Increased quantity of ideas to pursue
- Increased idea development speed
- Decreased time to market
- Decreased costs for innovation – "bad" ideas die faster

focus on higher-level strategic priorities and to drive innovation. With broken and suboptimal processes, the great ideas noted in the plans will not be realized to derive the value intended. With antiquated technology, one's data strategy will not be worth the pages it is printed on, figuratively speaking. And without the collective wisdom of one's ecosystem, the quantity and quality of new ideas to communicate, plan, and drive to fruition will be lacking. Thus, the symbiosis across the sub-themes.

Each of the sub-theme areas are worthy of people dedicated to driving them to higher levels of maturity and value. A technology and digital communications officer can aid internal and external communications, and for particularly complex organizations make sure that those are standardized across offices, regions, and languages nimbly. A head of IT and digital strategy together with the business information officers can ensure a nimbleness to strategic planning in all areas. Finally, a head of innovation, perhaps given the title of chief innovation officer, can help ensure that innovation has a shepherd despite the fact that new ideas can come from anyone inside the company or in the broader ecosystem.

Notes

1 Jonathan Swift. *The Examiner No. XIV*, November 9, 1710
2 R. Dalio (2017) *Principles: Life and work*, Simon & Schuster, New York
3 Arne Sorenson. Earlier today, I shared with Marriott International associates an update on the impact of Coronavirus (COVID-19) on our business and the steps we're taking to respond to it, LinkedIn post, March 20, 2020
4 Peter High. Half of all meetings are a waste of time—here's how to improve them, Forbes.com (archived at https://perma.cc/CYV6-S49L), November 25, 2019
5 Ibid
6 Chris Davis. *Managing through Metrics: The other sides of SMART*, Metis Strategy white paper, March 2013
7 Peter High. CIO and CDO Melanie Kalmar has the new Dow on a path to innovate. Forbes.com (archived at https://perma.cc/CYV6-S49L), April 21, 2020
8 Ibid
9 Ibid
10 Customer success stories, Adobe.com (archived at https://perma.cc/PZ23-RYB4)
11 Chris Davis. Analytics drives competitive advantage at Western Digital, CIO.com (archived at https://perma.cc/NE3P-678Q), December 23, 2019

12 Ibid

13 Ibid

14 Ibid

15 Stephanie Overby. Chief data officer: The CIO's new best friend?, *The Enterprisers Project*, December 11, 2019

16 Peter High. UnitedHealth Group's CDO on the key success factors for chief data officers, Forbes.com (archived at https://perma.cc/CYV6-S49L), August 25, 2020

17 Ibid

18 Ibid

19 Ibid

20 Ibid

21 Ibid

22 Ibid

23 Ibid

24 Ibid

25 Peter High. Art Hu, CIO of Lenovo, *Technovation with Peter High* podcast, October 29, 2018

26 Peter High. Business capabilities with Lowe's CIO & Novant Health CDO/ CTO, *Technovation with Peter High* podcast, February 27, 2020

27 *Leveraging Capabilities for Planning Strategic Business*, Metis Strategy white paper, October 19, 2018

28 Ibid

29 Peter High. Best practices from Vanguard's Innovation Studio, Forbes.com (archived at https://perma.cc/CYV6-S49L), May 20, 2019

30 Chris Davis and Brandon Metzger. 7 considerations when creating a corporate innovation lab, CIO.com (archived at https://perma.cc/NE3P-678Q), December 5, 2017

31 Ibid

32 Ibid

Conclusion

When I began writing this book, the United States economy was in the throes of the longest bull market in its history and companies had been competing to recruit the best and brightest talent for many years. That same period brought on the demise of many once great companies. Even though I knew that the bull market would not last forever and we were bound to have a correction, I believed the lessons I outlined in the book would apply in good times and bad. Little did I know that we were on the cusp of what would become a drastic upsetting and upheaval of business as we know it. I was halfway through writing the first draft of the book when the COVID-19 pandemic struck, and a little further when the economic consequences became clearer.

The good news is that all things being equal, those companies that have proven to be most resilient were those who had taken the steps outlined in this book earliest. They were nimble in their response to disruption, as a result. As investment theses and macroeconomic factors changed profoundly, their ability to change strategy and to use what little wind there was to plot a course to where the wind turned out to be more plentiful was important. Having planned for more challenging times, these companies created cultures that fostered nimbleness. They invested in their people. They instituted nimble processes that incorporated user feedback. Through adoption of cloud and as-a-service technology, they changed the fixed cost structure of technology investments to a more variable cost structure. They fostered scalability of the technology (up and down) to better handle spikes and dips in usage, while remaining mindful of the security implications. They took great care in building an ecosystem of thought partners outside of the company to be able to better test hypotheses. And finally, they were able to nimbly change their strategies as remarkable and unprecedented (in our lifetime, at least) inputs to those plans conflicted with the reality in which the plans were originally drafted.

As I write these concluding pages, the social and economic consequences of the pandemic are not fully known. However, I believe that the current disruption as well as the continuing exponential pace of change and innovation underscore the importance of the ability to be nimble both in good times and bad. Being nimble starts with your organization's culture. It requires a culture that makes smart, big bets, while ensuring that the bets do not over-leverage the company. It is important during good times that the organization takes steps to remain competitive during those inevitable rainy days. Over-leveraging the company is as much a mistake as not taking some risk to drive innovation in the first place.

It is critical to keep innovating during a downturn. The complexion and depth of innovation will be different, as funds will be harder to come by, but you must never put your company in a position where the muscle of innovation is unused for a prolonged period of time. This can lead to atrophy of the muscle, and the company may have difficulty reestablishing itself as an innovator.

While leaders of the companies profiled in this book have laid the path for resilience in advance of this crisis, one might argue that it is easier to make change happen during a crisis, so long as you do not go out of business in the process. As Winston Churchill once noted, "Never let a good crisis go to waste." Take the opportunity now to focus on what is most important to foster resilience.

When budgets for innovative activities are higher, nimbleness provides the best opportunity to try many different shots on the goal. You will miss the mark quite often, but the key is to learn each time. Just as a great athlete cannot expect to make every shot, to innovate is to make mistakes and missteps with a degree of frequency. Great athletes will take notes about what they did wrong, or how a goalie reacted to a shot to help on the next attempt. Likewise, your team must do the same. If an innovative initiative is unsuccessful, a diagnosis of why that is the case should be undertaken, and the learnings should be documented. With the next set of activities, those learnings should be applied, and the chance for future success should increase. This is the essence of nimbleness.

If I were to ask you to generate a list of the most innovative companies in the world, most readers would include Amazon on the list. If you ask Jeff Bezos, he will say that the company makes more mistakes than most. "Amazon will be experimenting at the right scale for a company of our size if we occasionally have multibillion-dollar failures," Bezos wrote in the company's annual letter to shareholders in April 2019.[1] When I mention

Amazon, you probably do not first think of the Fire Phone, Amazon Destinations, Amazon Local, or Amazon Wallet. Each of these were unsuccessful and were major investments for the company. For Amazon to fund multi-billion-dollar business ideas like Amazon Web Services, the Kindle, or the Amazon Echo, the company must pursue a portfolio of ideas, much as a venture capitalist does. By fostering cultural nimbleness, Bezos has created an idea factory that is almost unmatched. Bezos is fond of saying, Amazon is "the best place in the world to fail"[2] because failure is tolerated so long as there is learning from each failure, and the failure is not repeated.

From companies to countries

In addition to companies, it is also imperative for countries to develop nimbleness in order to survive. Estonia is one country that has taken the opportunity to push for change.

Creating a mandate for change

From an early age as an Estonian refugee in the United States, Toomas Hendrik Ilves understood the transformative power of technology. He learned to code in BASIC in the 1970s as a ninth grader from a teacher who was pursuing her PhD in Math Education. He studied psychology at Columbia University and at the University of Pennsylvania, but returned to Estonia once it gained independence after the Soviet Union collapsed. He was the first Estonian Ambassador to the United States and became Foreign Minister before becoming President of the country in 2006—a post he held for a decade.

President Ilves has told me a bit about Estonia's emergence from the Soviet bloc, making the point that postcommunist countries in Eastern Europe chose several paths forward from harsh authoritarianism to more open societies. "Our government focused on economic reforms, privatization, and liberalization of the economy," said Ilves. "We created a currency board system that allowed convertibility of our currency at the time."[3]

Though Ilves had pursued a path from psychology to government, technology remained an interest of his, and he recognized the potential transformative power that technology could have on Estonia, a country with a fresh start in the 1990s. It was not his passion alone. The lessons of the Finnish economy were illuminating:

As a point of reference, in 1938, the last full year before World War II, Finland and Estonia had the same GDP per capita. When we emerged in 1991 from the Soviet period, Finland had a GDP per capita 13 times that the GDP per capita of Estonia. Then, we had this direct contrast between them. One of the things associated with that was the enormous success of tech in Finland, such as Nokia.[4]

The emergence of the first web browser, Mosaic, led Ilves to a powerful conclusion. "I realized that in all other areas we were way behind, but when it came to digital, we were on a level playing field. No one had a leg up."[5] As he presciently foresaw the transformative power of this technology, Ilves became convinced that Estonia had to push for a radical digitization of the country:

The first step was a program that was implemented in '95 which was to put all Estonian schools online. That was completed by '97 or '98. All Estonian schools had computer labs which were open to the public after-hours to encourage other people to use them. That was the first big step in digitization.[6]

By 2001, Ilves and his team had introduced a core platform that would foster greater degrees of innovation in the form of additional digital services. The two main components which Ilves believes are critical for digital transformation are:

- strong digital identity online that includes end-to-end encryption and two-factor authentication
- distributed architecture

Adoption was slow by the country's citizens, but it grew. As it did, it created an interaction between the government and its citizens that was the envy of many others. American readers would hardly recognize the user-centricity of the Estonian government's processes:

We are at the point where there are only three interactions that citizens or residents must do in person. The first one is getting married. The second is transferring property, which is becoming increasingly relevant in countries like the UK and the United States. We do not want to allow any shell companies, and this is a concern that largely comes out of our geography. Finally, you must show up to get divorced.[7]

The guiding principle for Ilves was to offer services that citizens liked. One service he introduced was a digital tax filing system that takes an average of three-to-five minutes, taking many steps out of the process. Another was digital prescriptions. Ilves highlights that in Estonia:

There are never issues with doctors writing prescriptions in bad handwriting, which can lead to all sorts of problems. This means that once you have gotten an initial prescription from a doctor, if you ever need a renewal, you just call up your doctor or send them an email. He will update your prescription and you can go to any pharmacy in the country and get your prescription.[8]

During Ilves' presidency, he worked to make this system interoperable with Finland.

Ilves has also established an e-residency program to attract new talent. The program to establish e-residency is rigorous, as everyone must be vetted. "We take your fingerprints, your picture, and we investigate your background to ensure you do not have a criminal history," said Ilves.[9]

Companies and entrepreneurs have chosen to take advantage of Estonian e-residency because:

If you run a business in a country that does not have PayPal, which is a major form of payment in the world, and you do international business, you probably want to be in the European Union to take advantage of being established there as a business so that EU rules apply and you do not have to pay tariffs.[10]

Brexit has also increased enthusiasm for establishing businesses within the European Union. By establishing e-residency, a company can take advantage of some of the services that Estonia provides its citizens, and it can establish a beachhead in continental Europe.

In 2007, Russia embarked on the first ever recorded nation-state cyberattack on another nation.[11] The attack involved a distributed denial of service (DDoS) attack, which consists of bombarding servers with so many messages that they are overloaded and stop functioning. Upon reflecting on this period during his presidency, Ilves noted:

We were the first to experience anything like this in real time. We immediately started devoting a huge amount of attention to making our system resilient to those and other kinds of attacks. We focused on the security of our digitally run infrastructure, which remains an issue around the world today and remains an issue in my own country. As we see newer forms of cyberattacks, we must constantly be on our toes to stay ahead of those things. We are probably more sensitized since 2007 than most other countries to the damage that can be wreaked upon your country or your society through digital means.[12]

The nimble strategies taken by Estonia provide some valuable lessons for business leaders. Estonia did not feel constrained by its past; nor was it constrained by what other Eastern European countries were doing (or not doing) digitally. By focusing on its citizen-customers and making their digital experience sacrosanct, the country improved the lives of its citizen-customers, which attracted new talent and business to the country through their e-residency program.

Today, among the activities that Ilves undertakes during his post-presidency is advising other countries on how to follow suit.

So, I ask you: If a government was able to usher these sorts of changes, why can't you?

The road ahead

The road ahead will not be paved evenly or be free of potholes. Thankfully, there are maps and guides for this journey. You are not the first to travel these routes. Think of this book as your guidebook along the way. If you have great people on your team to help you, great processes to guide you, flexible, secure, and scalable technology to react to the starts and stops on the journey, a great ecosystem to draw insight and inspiration from, and a great strategy, the world is your oyster. What are you waiting for? Get going, and good luck!

Notes

1 Jeff Bezos. Amazon letter to shareholders, April 2019

2 Ibid

3 Peter High. An interview with the architect of the most digitally savvy country on earth, Forbes.com (archived at https://perma.cc/CYV6-S49L), April 23, 2018

4 Ibid

5 Ibid

6 Ibid

7 Ibid

8 Ibid

9 Ibid

10 Ibid

11 Elizabeth Schulze. When this country faced a suspected Russian cyberattack – it took some big steps to stop another, CNBC.com (archived at https://perma.cc/97CE-GFW7), September 21, 2018

12 Peter High. An interview with the architect of the most digitally savvy country on earth, Forbes.com (archived at https://perma.cc/CYV6-S49L), April 23, 2018

INDEX